ETERNAL CHALICE

'*Eternal Chalice* is an authoritative, informed and highly readable account of the Grail and the traditions which accompany it, ranging from early Celtic legend to *The Da Vinci Code*. Juliette Wood debunks, explains and brings to vivid life the extraordinary true history of the Holy Grail.'
– **Carolyne Larrington, St John's College, Oxford, and author of *King Arthur's Enchantresses***

'There are many valuable and exciting aspects to this book. First, it is wonderful to have the Grail legend treated by somebody who is equally at home in the fields of history, folklore, literary criticism and conspiracy theory. Second, it breaks new and important ground to have the legend investigated by a scholar who is just as conversant with its modern developments as with the medieval originals, and can place both in a proper cultural context. The author's careful analysis of the modern aspects is particularly helpful. A great deal has now been published by proponents and debunkers of one particular contemporary Grail tradition or another, but this is the first book written by somebody who knows about the lot. In one sense *Eternal Chalice* is a work about one of the world's great mythical traditions; in another, about what it meant to be medieval and means to be modern; and, in still another, about the nature of myth itself. All aspects are handled equally well by Juliette Wood, and with no little aplomb.'
– **Ronald Hutton, Professor of History, University of Bristol and author of *Witches, Druids and King Arthur***

'The Grail is by definition the most mysterious of objects, and Juliette Wood is a wise and well-informed guide to the numerous legends it has spawned. She tells something of a wonder tale, not about the Grail itself, but about the unslakeable thirst to identify it, explain it, and produce conspiracy theories about it, wherever evidence is lacking. She explores the various beliefs about its origins in Christianity or Celtic paganism; she discusses the earliest texts in which it appears and the many later adaptations and inventions to which they gave rise. Glastonbury, Shugborough Hall, Rosslyn and Rennes-le-Château are all here, as are the Cathars, the Templars, the Freemasons, the Priory of Sion and all the eccentric personalities who promoted their links with the Grail. The assorted objects that claim to be the thing itself are discussed and illustrated. The book offers interesting insights into the various anthropological movements, psychological needs, wishful thinking and gullibility that have combined to generate our present-day obsessions.'
– **Helen Cooper, Professor of Medieval and Renaissance English, University of Cambridge**

Marrying scholarly rigour with a lively, approachable style, Juliette Wood reveals how – and why – the Grail theme has lent itself to reinterpretation for every age under the influence of contemporary legends and concerns. *Eternal Chalice* bridges the usual gulf between academic and popular writing and will become essential reading for everyone fascinated by the Grail, from medievalists to the most enthusiastic fans of *The Da Vinci Code*.'
– *Ceridwen Lloyd-Morgan, formerly Head of Manuscripts and Visual Images, National Library of Wales*

'Juliette Wood's *Eternal Chalice* is a fascinating interdisciplinary study that attempts to answer the question "What is the Holy Grail?" In exploring ways in which the Grail weaves in and out of medieval and modern culture, Wood discusses crucial aspects of the legend that have been overlooked or understudied by previous literary and cultural scholars. Her research is comprehensive: in the course of her wide-ranging investigation, she examines literary works, folklore and mythology, religion and philosophy, medieval and modern history, and esoteric beliefs. And she incorporates texts from Chrétien's Perceval to Dan Brown's *The Da Vinci Code*, places from Glastonbury to Rosslyn Chapel, groups from the Templars to the Priory of Sion. Drawing on folklorists and literary scholars – including such central figures as James Frazer, Alfred Nutt, Jessie Weston, and R. S. Loomis – Wood analyses theories of the Grail from the Christian to the pagan to the New Age. One of the strengths of Wood's book is that it brings this diverse material together convincingly, thus revealing the interconnectedness of the seemingly diverse strands of Grail lore. For anyone interested in the Grail, either as a subject of literature and folklore or as a key theme in modern conspiracy theories, *Eternal Chalice* is essential reading.'

– **Alan Lupack, Director of the Robbins Library and Adjunct Professor of English, University of Rochester; author of *The Oxford Guide to Arthurian Literature and Legend***

'The origins of the legend of the Holy Grail are as various as they are obscure. The legend itself has fascinated western man for more than a thousand years. It has been the subject of intense and often fanciful research. It has inspired devotion and spawned conspiracy theories, and there is no sign of interest slackening. Indeed in our age, which has lost any unifying coherent belief, the Grail myths are the subject of ever more extravagant fantasies. Juliette Wood punctures many of them in this comprehensive study of the subject. She brings true and thorough scholarship and common sense to a subject which has often been devoid of both. This is the best survey of all that pertains to the Grail legend that I have ever read. Written with an admirable freedom from academic jargon, it shines light where there was previously darkness.'

– **Allan Massie, author of *Arthur the King***

'Juliette Wood's *Eternal Chalice* takes the reader through the sources, origins and developments of the Grail myth, covering its formulation in the medieval romances, with extensive treatment of variants and later developments as a myth. But she does something no one so far has done, in that she treats in detail its manifold appearances in the modern secret societies, occult orders, mystical revivals and in the adventure myths of *The Holy Blood and the Holy Grail*, as well as *The Da Vinci Code*. Alone of all Grail historians, she takes as much care and attention with these modern narratives as she does with their older inspirations. With the respectful care of a scholar, but with the passion of a debunker, she demonstrates in case after case how legend, myth, fabrication and spiritual aspirations have interwoven – and she leads us through the Freemasons, the Glastonbury Christians, the earth mysteries adventurers, the modern pagans and more. Wood's attention to the particularities of the claims makes her book an essential resource in the scholarship of western esotericism, Celtic identities, as well as The Grail itself.'

– **Christina Oakley Harrington, Treadwell's Bookshop, London**

Juliette Wood is one of Britain's leading experts on myth and folklore, as well as Associate Lecturer in the School of Welsh at Cardiff University and former President of the Folklore Society, London. A regular contributor to TV and radio, she is the author of several books on Celtic myth and legend.

ETERNAL CHALICE

The Enduring Legend of the Holy Grail

JULIETTE WOOD

To Olympia Aurelia,
scholar, inspiration and much loved godmother

Paperback edition published in 2016 by
I.B.Tauris & Co. Ltd
London • New York
www.ibtauris.com

Hardback edition first published in 2008 by
I.B.Tauris & Co. Ltd

ISBN: 978 1 78453 520 9
eISBN: 978 0 85773 090 9
ePDF: 978 0 85771 243 1

A full CIP record for this book is available from the British Library
A full CIP record is available from the Library of Congress

Library of Congress Catalog Card Number: available

Typeset in Sabon by Ellipsis Books Limited, Glasgow
Printed and bound by CPI Group (UK) Ltd, Croydon, CR0 4YY

MIX
Paper from
responsible sources
FSC
www.fsc.org   FSC® C013604

Contents

Acknowledgements

I would like to express my thanks to the many friends, students and colleagues who have listened to my thoughts and theories about the Grail legends over the years. Special thanks go to Gerald Morgan in Aberystwyth, who first invited me to speak about the Nanteos cup. The School of Welsh and the Centre for Lifelong Learning at Cardiff University and the Folklore Society have given me many opportunities to present various aspects of the Grail legend. Both Professor Sioned Davies and Dr Clive Wood have encouraged me throughout this project.

Alex Wright has been a patient and encouraging editor and I would like to express my gratitude to him and to all the I.B.Tauris team. In particular I would like to thank those of my friends and colleagues who so generously allowed me to use their photographs and illustrations for this book: Jennifer Westwood, Helen Nicholson, Robert Cooper, Carlos Sanz Mingo and Nancy Hollinrake. Peter Keelan, Head of Special Collections and Archives, Mark Barrett of Cardiff University Library Services, and Andrew McVay helped so much with the images.

Every effort has been made to trace all copyright owners for illustrations reproduced, but in some cases this has not proved possible. The cooperation of everyone who has agreed to the reproduction of illustrations is gratefully acknowledged.

List of Illustrations

Introduction

A YOUNG KNIGHT ACCEPTS an invitation to dinner from a lame old man. After a sumptuous meal, he witnesses a procession in which a maiden carries a jewelled object which is called a 'graal'. Thus Chrétien de Troyes introduces one of medieval literature's most enduring themes, the quest for the Holy Grail. Chrétien's romance recounts the adventures of Perceval, a naive young man whose quest teaches him how to be a knight. The romance was unfinished when Chrétien died, but other writers completed the story. Some are known by name, some are anonymous. The narratives they wrote transformed this mysterious object into one of the relics of the central event of Christianity. The Grail became the very cup from which Jesus Christ drank at the Last Supper when he instituted the Holy Eucharist, the sacrament by which, according to medieval Christianity, ordinary bread and wine changed into the body and blood of Christ. In the romances, it was the means for certain knights in Arthur's court to aspire to the supreme achievement of the chivalric code, physical prowess combined with the perfect Christian ideals of spiritual love and sacrifice.

This alone would have made it a story worth remembering, but continued interest in these tales encouraged new readers to ask questions about the meaning of these romances. Readers who did not have the same attitude to religious history and the world of medieval chivalry wanted to identify with the Grail quest and to understand the sources for the stories. As a result, critics in the nineteenth century began to look for the meaning of the Grail before it became identified with the Last Supper vessel. They looked for it in Celtic tradition, in primitive ritual, and in esoteric philosophy. In the twentieth century, the Grail story entered popular culture as a theme for fantasy epics, detective novels and films. New readers looked to history for a key to the secret of the Grail, and the quest for meaning became the stuff of codes and secret documents, the central nub of a vast conspiracy stretching back to the dawn of civilization. This is how it has come down to us at the beginning of the twenty-first century. It is no longer just a theme in romances aimed at a Christian audience of medieval courtiers. It now weaves in and out of modern culture and popular consciousness.

Modern editions of the medieval Grail romances appeared in the nineteenth century and with them the sense that these texts belonged to another age. Renewed interest sparked discussions about how to interpret the mysterious object and encouraged speculation about the ultimate sources of the 'Grail story'. Many suggestions have been put forward over the years, including Celtic myth, the eucharistic rites of the Eastern Orthodox Church, ancient mystery religions, Jungian archetypal journeys, dualist heresies, alchemy, Templar treasure, and a divine bloodline. In addition several objects are venerated as the Grail, and any of these suggestions combine into even more possibilities. The permutations create a dizzying kaleidoscope for the modern reader, but the thread running through it all is the assumption that the Grail story is special, and its meaning needs to be explained.

The audiences for the Grail romances were men and women of the feudal courts of Europe. The narratives expressed their concerns with personal honour, duty and a new ideal of courtly love between men and women. They also reflect growing lay piety which resulted in greater participation in Church rituals such as taking communion. The Crusades also formed a background to the composition of these romances, although the Grail as a relic never acquired the importance of other symbols of Christ's life. No two versions of the Grail story in the romances are exactly the same, but the romance genre reached something of a peak in Thomas Malory's *Morte Darthur,* published by the printer William Caxton in 1485. Written against the dynastic struggles known as the Wars of the Roses, Malory's romance marks an end to the chivalric lifestyle and the rise of modern nation states. As a printed work, it also signals a shift in the audience who read and absorbed narratives such as the Grail story.

In the following centuries, under the pressure of religious reformation and counter-reformation, the Grail became more secular and much less popular. New networks suited to a rising professional middle class began to replace the aristocratic knightly orders and workers' guilds. This period saw the rise of Freemasonry, and its more speculative cousin Rosicrucianism. Pseudo-history and mysterious symbolism associated with the Crusades and the 'Temple of Solomon' in Jerusalem added antiquity, romance and mystery to the newly created identities of these movements, and the Grail, as a marginal relic tradition, could be absorbed without offending anyone.

The rational thinkers of the eighteenth-century Enlightenment mistrusted the conservative and, from their point of view repressive, tendencies of the old monarchies and traditional religions. To the Enlightenment, with its assumptions of rationality and progress, the European Middle Ages, encompassing roughly the fifth to fifteenth centuries, looked like an aberration, a time of dreadful superstition. Paradoxically this era of rationalism also witnessed the rise of the conspiracy genre. Fear of conspiracy was nothing new, but this period saw the creation of the idea that a cabal could manipulate events behind the scenes. These counter-enlightenment forces in their turn mistrusted the secular and modernizing tendencies of Enlightenment rationality. They too created conspiracies, often benevolent ones, that guarded a 'secret wisdom' capable of causing a social and spiritual revolution. As opponents of the medieval church, the 'Templars' were seen as an evil cabal by one group and as keepers of secret wisdom by the other.

By the beginning of the nineteenth century, the newly available texts of medieval romances began to influence a new Grail literature. They also became part of a phenomenon known as the occult revival. This revival signalled a renewed interest in medieval and Renaissance philosophies such as neo-platonism, and in the writings of groups like the Gnostics of the early Christian period. New disciplines like archaeology and anthropology resulted in new perspectives from which to understand the past. Archaeological excavation in what had once been considered the 'Holy Land' offered a more balanced and rational understanding of biblical events, while anthropology revealed the origins of belief and the process of social evolution. But this too produced a reaction. Archaeological excavations could also reveal the existence of secret cults and long-buried documents, and ancient cultural norms, once thought savage and barbaric, could be transformed into alternative forms of worship driven underground by repression, but preserved via the secret codes of the Grail. All these factors influenced the creation of new versions of the Grail story.

Medieval Grail romances can be confusing and complex, but they share certain themes. Chrétien's story of the Grail, completed and expanded by later writers, introduced a sacred object. Although not initially linked to the Eucharist, it became increasingly sacramental in later versions. Robert de Boron inserted the Grail story into an apocryphal religious history and identified it with the cup used at the Last Supper. Other romances developed the religious theme and transformed the chivalric deeds of knighthood into a sacred quest. With the publication of modern texts, scholarly interest considered whether the Grail episodes constituted a single narrative, and if so, what was its original meaning and purpose. On the whole, opinion favoured a myth about a supernatural talisman, which medieval romance authors never fully understood, yet attempted to explain. This implied that the original Grail story changed during a process of transmission. However, if the texts are read in the sequence in which they were written, the Grail material becomes more not less consistent over time. This suggests another possibility, namely that romance writers adapted diverse motifs into narratives whose meaning was coloured by artistic purpose rather than ancient myth. The question a modern Perceval might ask is not 'whom does the Grail serve?' but 'what is the Holy Grail?' The various chapters of this book consider some of the answers that have been given to this question.

Chapter 1 summarizes the history of the medieval sources and the Grail relics. Chapter 2 examines the way in which the image of the Grail became a vehicle to increase the prestige of medieval Glastonbury and a focus for spirituality in contemporary Glastonbury. Chapter 3 looks at references to the Grail in Welsh literature and to some of its manifestations in Welsh folk tradition. Chapters 4–6 consider some of the theories put forward to explain the Grail, such as the idea that it was originally a Celtic myth or part of a secret tradition guarded by the medieval Cathars or the Knights Templar. These chapters also discuss some modern Grail locations such as Rosslyn Chapel in Scotland, Rennes-le-Château in southern France and Shugborough in England, while Chapter 7 considers how these various interpretations and theories have affected fiction and modern popular culture.

New theories about the origins of the Grail allowed writers to reinterpret it, not as a quest motif found in medieval romance, but as an image of personal and cultural transformation. Theories about secret meanings have their adherents and their detractors, and the number of books published is so vast that it would be impossible to encompass all of them. Alternative histories claim that the Holy Grail holds a key to an esoteric worldview which, once the secret is revealed, will bring about a dramatic transformation. This adds the thrill of a detective story to the adventures of the Arthurian knights, one which involves the reader personally in solving a puzzle to discover a secret. With the advent of mass-market publishing, television and the Internet, these theories have reached a global audience. Various commentators have addressed the truth or falsity of the ideas perpetuated by these theories; others have examined the social or psychological factors that affect people's readiness to invest in this type of knowledge.[1] Much of this writing reflects what have come to be called 'new age' concerns about the accessibility of spirituality, personal development, and the survival of ancient myth and religion. These were not, however, the interests of the medieval men and women who first listened to these romances. This book is concerned with how a tale, which developed in the feudal world of western Europe, has been transformed into a myth of global proportions.

The rise of popular books on the origin and meaning of the Grail is a relatively new phenomenon. Current explanations of the 'Grail story' fuse Celtic myth, dualist heresies, and the initiation rites of ancient mystery religions. Often the authors are non-specialists with an enthusiasm for a subject that outstrips a conventional academic understanding of the sources. They position themselves quite deliberately in contrast with academe, seeking new truths, which, they feel, the academic world ignores. Not surprisingly, numerous book reviews, interviews and rebuttals highlight the shortcoming of theories founded on selective readings of, admittedly difficult, source material to which are added speculations based on notions of history or reality that are, literally, the stuff of myth and legend. Nevertheless, belief in these theories continues despite comprehensive deconstruction of the speculations on which they are based. Such theories involve conspiracies and codes, both of which are an increasing part of the discourse of modern life. This study is concerned less with the errors or the selection of evidence that informs the most cogent criticism of these ideas, than with the reasons underlying their popularity.

In order to understand the emergence and significance of beliefs about the Grail in contemporary culture, it is necessary to look once again at the medieval romances. Recent academic studies stress the character of medieval romance as literature written in a particular context and addressed to a particular audience. Within this framework, Grail studies position the Grail theme as fulfilling the expectations of a courtly elite in a context contemporary with the actual romances. In so far as the Grail had a meaning for medieval readers, this is how it would have to function. This approach is somewhat different from earlier Grail studies, which concentrated on origins. Modern appreciation of the Grail romances began in the nineteenth century. This same period saw the rise of the systematic study of traditional forms of narrative and the idea that they reflected important aspects of human cultural behaviour. Whether the Grail was believed to be a sacred myth, an initiation rite, an archetype or set of beliefs among Celts or Gnostic Christians, the search for the Grail was often the search for its ultimate origin. One of the earliest commentators, the folklorist Alfred Nutt, noted the similarity between Grail romances and traditional myths and legends about objects taken from a supernatural realm.[2] This aspect of the Grail studies remains important, not, as so often in the past, as a way of discovering its origin, but in order to understand how this cluster of mythic and legendary motifs function within traditional folk narratives. This study proposes to revisit this traditional arena in which the Grail legends developed in order to suggest how the traditional categories of myth and legend shaped both the structure of the story and the way in which the narrative was perceived during the European Middle Ages and subsequently.

A category like myth has a wide range of meaning. It can refer to a sacred narrative and to something that is not true. Reinterpretations of real medieval institutions like the Knights Templar and religious sects like the Cathars produced romantic rather than realistic views of these groups. Historians often use the terms 'Templar myth' and 'Cathar myth' in this way. However much they are romanticized and distanced from the actual practices of these groups, these myths embody the ideals and aspirations of their creators. In this sense they form a 'sacred' and meaningful narrative within the context of alternative writing. Another interesting aspect of the Grail phenomenon today is the degree to which popular theories about the Grail function in a similar way to contemporary legend. Essentially a contemporary legend is a realistic-sounding narrative about events (or alleged events) with an ironic, supernatural or mysterious twist. These legends are told, with varying degrees of belief, by a wide range of people. They are an integral part of modern 'folk' culture, but they are not an exclusively modern phenomenon. An event is deemed to occur in real time with real witnesses who left some clue or testimony as to what happened, and the link between event and meaning is what makes them 'contemporary'. We recognize stories about people who buy exotic plants at a local shop only to be bitten by a poisonous spider, or travellers who pick up innocent-looking hitchhikers only to have them turn into axe-murderers. As these stories come at second or third hand, exact details are difficult to verify. A similar mechanism underlies modern Grail legends. Here too all is not as it seems, and the true facts about the Grail can be found one or two informants, or one or two sources, back down the line of research hidden only by a conspiracy. Speculations about the Grail involving secret societies, eccentric documents and codes are a pervasive and influential body of contemporary folklore, and, in this sense, the Grail is both a contemporary legend and a realization of myth.

The claims of these modern Grail legends, particularly relating to the idea of conspiracy, have an explosive quality that requires an immediate response. Contemporary legends such as these can challenge our understanding of the world or attempt to redefine reality in a way that restores the narrator's (or in this case the writer's) control over a situation by finding an acceptable cultural language.[3] These alternative ideas are by definition and by self-proclamation outside legitimized knowledge and as such they evoke strong reactions. Although the responses to alternative theories are still shaped in very traditional ways, they are no longer transmitted by exclusively oral means. New responses are now carried by print and mass media and on the Internet where Grail websites appear and disappear.[4] The Internet is one of the most fruitful areas for Grail traditions. The popularity of the code/computer game format and the speed with which new ideas can spread contributes to its special role in modern Grail legends. The connectivity of the Web is also a breeding ground for conspiracy theory. It encourages users to make connections and the source of ideas becomes untraceable. These ideas now spread from popular theory to popular theory and often by-pass medieval texts. They may be driven by political or commercial agendas, but they suffuse and enliven everyday life.[5] They also provide scenarios that enable readers to adapt to the powerful and impersonal forces that dominate modern society.[6] Because historic codes have directness, and a superficial clarity, which allows us to project our present fears onto an image of the past, they continue to appeal. History becomes a metaphor for otherness, and its secret codes present clear solutions. Instead of the uncertain complexities of history, we get custodians of secret wisdom and ancient cults.

The process of formulating history in terms of a secret cult creates a kind of mythic historicism which has many qualities of narrative. The legend process is complex, and the relationship between a culture and its legendary past is less a matter of whether a belief is true and more a question of how it functions within a complex cultural envelope. The search for 'the folk' as somehow encapsulating the past has given way to a view of society as an integrated social organism. This less fragmented approach allows us to extend our understanding of the dynamics of modern Grail legends. Myths and legends grow out of social contexts, and as such the traditions of the Holy Grail have a rich heritage. Even as a contemporary legend rooted in popular ideas, it still encapsulates a myth about the possession of a supernatural object. It is this that allows it to be reinterpreted in so many imaginative ways. Our examination will take us back to the 1930s and to the fin-de-siècle world at the turn of the nineteenth century. These were times when a revival of interest in the philosophies of magic and the occult melded with an interest in the origins of human culture. Beyond that we will look at the medieval world of the Grail romances and into an even more remote past where so many have placed the ultimate origins of this narrative. The concepts of folklore still provide a worthwhile approach to the material, not in order to understand its ultimate source, but in order to appreciate the complex ways in which the legends developed in the modern world. However diverse the attempts to explain and understand the Grail, it is depicted as somehow greater than any individual retelling. It holds a key to something larger than itself, whether Celtic folklore, archetypes, Gnostic wisdom, or alternative Christianity. What this larger entity is depends on personal interest and worldview, but the process can be understood in terms of legend formation. These factors all play a role in the modern Grail and allow us to bring together alternative history, medieval text, modern fantasy and thriller novels, and the infinitely varied comments on the Internet. What one finds in the Grail castle is largely a matter of personal aspiration, but the journey is shaped by tradition.

CHAPTER 1

Romances and Relics

THE STORY OF the Holy Grail is a rich and complex narrative set in the context of Arthurian tradition and the medieval world of knighthood and chivalry. These romances reflected the lifestyle and aspirations of an elite, the men and women who dominated the feudal world. The narratives produced during this relatively brief period have a universal appeal, and subsequent readers have interpreted them in different ways. Whatever the conclusions about the origins and meaning of the legend of the Holy Grail, however, they are rooted in the texts of the medieval romances.

It can be something of a surprise to readers new to the Grail story, that medieval romances describe the Grail and the adventures of the knights in so many different ways. About a dozen romances include material about the Grail, and they have come to be regarded as a special class of fiction. However, no consistent 'Grail story' ever emerges from these romances, and the Grail episode is not always the main plot line. Chrétien de Troyes's French romance written about 1180 is the earliest literary work to mention it. All subsequent romances which incorporate Grail material are based to some extent on Chrétien's tale. Even this apparently clear starting point can be deceptive. The romances never formed an orderly cycle with one taking up where the other left off. The dates of composition overlap, and it is not possible to establish a clear timeline. Material was borrowed and new themes introduced. Some romances are fragmentary or exist only as prose redactions of the original poetry, while sections, and even whole romances, have been lost. Some writers probably could not read Chrétien's original French poetry, and many would not have had access to all the available sources. The idea of a body of work about an object called the Grail is a recent one, and it is only with modern editions that scholars have had access to all the romances and are able to understand the ways in which they relate to one another.

The fact that no consistent 'Grail story' emerges from the romances is frustrating, and has undoubtedly contributed to the number of speculative theories about its origin. However a basic story outline would be something like the following:

A mysterious vessel or object which sustains life and/or provides sustenance is guarded in a castle which is difficult to find. The owner of the castle is either lame or sick and often (but not always) the surrounding land is barren. The owner can be restored only if a knight finds the castle and, after witnessing a mysterious procession, asks a certain question. If he fails in this task, everything will remain as before and the search must begin again. After wanderings and adventures (many of which relate to events which the young hero failed to understand the first time), the knight returns to the castle and asks the question which cures the king and restores the land. The hero knight succeeds the wounded king (usually called the Fisher King) as guardian of the castle and its contents.

Five knights search for the Grail. Perceval (also called Peredur and Perlesvaus) begins as a gauche boy unaware of his connections with the guardians of the Grail. He fails to ask whom the Grail serves when he first observes the Grail procession. He is reproached for this failing by a loathly damsel figure, and sets out again in despair. After many adventures he meets a hermit and finally accepts his knightly role. He returns to the castle of the wounded king, asks the proper question and takes over the role of Grail king. The suave sophistication of Gawain is a perfect foil for Perceval, but his character is also refined by the Grail search. The two present a contrast between more earthly (Gawain) and more spiritual (Perceval) aspects of chivalry, and many romances alternate descriptions of their adventures. Both visit the Grail castle and fail to ask the correct question and both have a chance to make amends. Sir Bors accompanies Perceval and Gawain on their journey and is the third knight to see the Holy Grail. He is also the one who returns to Arthur's court to recount the events of the Grail adventure. As the best of Arthur's knights, it should really be Lancelot who finds the Grail, but as the Grail quest became more spiritual, Lancelot's adultery with the queen became a problem. Lancelot achieves only a partial vision of the Grail, although it does cure him of madness. Later romance tradition introduced the perfect Grail knight, Galahad, the son of Lancelot and the Grail maiden, daughter of the Fisher King. Galahad is the perfect knight. He occupies the Siege Perilous, the seat at the Round Table intended for the man who will achieve the Grail quest, and his experience of the Grail transforms him completely.

The Fisher King is an evocative image whose interpretation reflects different streams of Arthurian criticism. Is he originally a Celtic deity and ritual figure or is he Christian? In the earliest Grail romance, he is 'Le Roi Pecheur'. Robert de Boron's romance trilogy, *Joseph of Arimathea, Merlin* and *Perceval*, provides background for this pivotal figure. Before the Grail was taken to Britain, Hebron (Bron), the brother-in-law of Joseph of Arimathea, caught a fish and placed it on the Grail table. He became known as the Rich Fisher and is by extension the Fisher King when he becomes lord of the Grail castle in Britain, a title he sometimes shares with his son, Alain. In some romances the Fisher King is identified with the Grail King, in others, they are separate. The Fisher/Grail King is often wounded or sick and can be healed only when the pre-ordained visitor to his castle asks the proper question. The link between the king and land differs depending on the romance. Sometimes the king's sickness is reflected in the state of his kingdom, which has become a wasteland. In the earliest Grail romance, Perceval's failure to ask the question means that the king's wound is not healed, and the land remains barren and undefended. The wasteland motif is frequently invoked in anthropological and ritual inter-pretations as an example of the link between a king and the fertility of his kingdom, and the motif is popular in modern literature as a metaphor for alienation and the emptiness of modern materialism.

Another motif important in ritual interpretations is the relationship between the male characters and a mysterious female figure identified as a sovereignty goddess, the supernatural consort of the rightful ruler. The appearance of these women, whether ugly or beautiful, mirrors the health of the kingdom and the fitness of the king. This figure is represented in the Grail romances by a loathly lady who berates the Grail heroes for their failure to ask the right question, and by various beautiful women who help him and fulfil the function of consort. In some modern treatments of the legend, these characters have merged with notions of the sacred feminine and speculations about a lost goddess culture repressed by Christianity. The figure of Mary Magdalene as the hidden bride of Christ has come to represent this lost sacred feminine in many modern conspiracy treatments of the Grail.

An object referred to as the Grail or the Holy Grail occurs in a number of medieval romances written between the end of the twelfth and the end of the thirteenth century. Despite the vast antiquity claimed for the mate-rial, its appearance in literary form occurred within a single century. The author of the first Grail romance called his work *The Story of the Grail* (*Le Conte del Graal*). We know him as Chrétien de Troyes. No fewer than five Arthurian romances are attributed to him, and the sheer volume of manuscripts containing copies of whole or fragmentary romance texts, with illuminations or without, demonstrate the popularity his works enjoyed.

The Story of the Grail, for example, appears in more than a dozen manuscripts.

Of the author's personal history, we know only what he reveals in the prologues to his works and what we can discern in the texts themselves. Medieval authors often adopted a fictional persona, but some of what Chrétien tells us rings true. The town of Troyes, in the Champagne region of France, may have been his birthplace, and some medieval scholars have detected traces of local dialect in his French. At the very least, it puts Chrétien in the courtly world of north-east France and Flanders in the twelfth century. *The Story of the Grail* was written for Philip of Alsace, Count of Flanders, who went on crusade in 1191. Chrétien would most likely have begun this romance before Philip's departure, and either Philip's death or his own would account for why the romance remained unfinished. Other references indicate that, like his contemporaries, he translated and adapted material. He may have had some contact with the court of the Angevin king, Henry II of England and his queen, Eleanor of Aquitaine. Eleanor's daughter, Marie of Champagne, was also Chrétien's patron and Marie's uncle by marriage was Henry of Blois, an important Anglo-Norman Abbot of Glastonbury (1126–71). The search for Arthur's grave at Glastonbury was prompted by King Henry's interest in the Arthurian legends and the political influence it could bring. Abbot Henry of Blois also had contacts with Geoffrey of Monmouth and William of Malmesbury, both of whom helped popularize the Arthurian legends. These links with Chrétien are tempting if not susceptible to proof, but a writer who evidently wrote for different courts in north-east France and Flanders might well have had moved in similar aristocratic circles in England.[1]

Chrétien de Troyes's *The Story of the Grail* (*Le conte del graal*) was probably composed some time between 1180 and 1190.[2] Copyists, however, often used the name of the hero, *Perceval*. The hero first appears as an immature youth living in the wilderness with his mother, who has sought refuge there after the death of her husband and other sons. Reluctantly his mother sends him off to fulfil his true vocation. A series of misadventures brings him to Arthur's court from which he sets out in pursuit of the Red Knight who has stolen a cup from Queen Guinevere. Perceval becomes squire to a nobleman who advises him on the modest behaviour expected of a knight. He encounters two men fishing in a river; one of them offers him hospitality for the night, and Perceval finds himself at the Grail castle, home of the Fisher King. Before dinner he is presented with a sword, then a youth bearing a bleeding lance crosses the room followed by two more boys carrying candlesticks, and finally a maiden carrying a bejewelled Grail that emits such light, it dims the candles. Mindful of his mentor's commands about modest behaviour, Perceval does not ask his host about these wonders. Next morning he leaves the empty castle and returns to Arthur's court, where he redresses some of the chaos caused by his previous impulsive behaviour. Later, a loathly maiden denounces Perceval for failing to ask the proper question during the banquet, and thereby leaving the king in misery and his land prey to marauders. Both Gawain and Perceval leave Arthur's court. Gawain's search for the bleeding lance parallels Perceval's Grail adventure. On Good Friday Perceval visits his uncle, a hermit, who explains the meaning of the Grail procession. A wafer from the Grail sustained the old king, Perceval's maternal uncle, and his son, the Fisher King who is Perceval's cousin.

The Grail, called *graal*, in Chrétien is not a relic, but a large jewelled serving dish. Nevertheless, the romance calls it 'a holy thing', and it contains the Mass wafer which sustains a wounded king. However, the king's illness is the result of a battle wound, and the land is jeopardized because the ruler is unable to defend it, not blasted in any magical way. Even in its unfinished state, the Grail does not dominate the romance plot completely, and the sword also symbolizes Perceval's development as a knight.

Four attempts, called *Continuations*, were made to complete Chrétien's romance. In the course of these very different attempts to finish the work as the original author might have intended, the Grail gradually became more sacramental.[3] The *First Continuation*, completed some time before 1200 by an unknown author, concentrated on the adventures of Gawain. By this time, the bleeding lance in the Grail procession had become identified with the Lance of Longinus, the Roman centurion who pierced Christ's side at the Crucifixion. A bier with a broken sword was added to the procession, and Gawain was given the task to mend it. On his second visit to the castle, the 'rich Grail' floats about the hall and provides food for all, but Gawain falls asleep and fails to ask the question. The author of the *Second Continuation* (1200–10), Wauchier de Danaing, shifted the focus back to Perceval. Although many adventures do not relate directly to the Grail, they reflect Perceval's growing appreciation of the requirements of knighthood. He sees candles burning in a forest, but does not recognize this as a sign of the Grail's presence. At the Fisher King's castle, maidens carry both the Holy Grail and the lance and a youth brings in the broken sword, although Perceval cannot mend it completely. It was left to Manessier, the author of the *Third Continuation* (1210–20), to complete the adventures of Perceval and Gawain. In this version, the broken sword is as important as the Grail. It wounded both the Fisher King and his brother, and it becomes the means for Perceval to avenge his family once it is repaired. In this procession the Grail is covered, making it resemble even more strongly a chalice covered by the protective paten, as it would be during the mass. The Fisher King explains that the lance belonged to Longinus and the cup was used by Joseph of Arimathea to collect Christ's blood. The Grail makes several appearances. An angel heals Perceval's wounds with it, and, after he avenges his family, he witnesses the Grail procession at the castle. The Grail brings abundant food when Perceval succeeds the Fisher King, and when he dies the Grail, lance, paten, and by implication the sword, go with him. These four objects gave rise to the modern idea of four Grail hallows. In the *Fourth Continuation*, Gerbert de Montreuil (c. 1230) adopts a strong moralizing tone and offers an alternative ending. He takes up the story after Perceval's first failure to repair the sword and interpolates a long series of adventures before Perceval's final successful return to the Grail castle.

The attempts to complete Chrétien's text are a mark of the popularity of the story, but they did not create a smooth and coherent narrative. The same period produced two attempts to explain the background in the form of prologues, in the manner of modern prequels. The *Bliocadran Prologue* (1200–10) presents the history of Perceval's family.[4] His father, Bliocadran, was the last of twelve brothers and after his death in a tournament, his wife took the infant, Perceval, to a forest in an effort to protect him from the dangers of knighthood's fighting code. The *Elucidation Prologue* (1200–10) is an altogether more unusual piece.[5] It begins with a folktale episode about a group of female well attendants, who are raped and whose golden cups are stolen. Folktales about women whose lives are bound up with water sources are fairly common, but not in the Grail romances. In some romances, the Red Knight steals a golden cup from Guinevere, and Perceval goes in pursuit, but in this prologue, Arthur's knights avenge the women. The Grail moves automatically at feasts and brings sustenance to all in mysterious ways. Confused though it is at times, the *Prologue* reflects the events in the *Continuations* rather than the supposed distant, mythic sources of the stories.[6]

Other writers completed the knightly adventures of Perceval and Gawain, which began in Chrétien's romance. Robert de Boron, a Burgundian poet writing in the first decade of the thirteenth century, introduced a significant innovation to the Grail story by identifying the Grail with the cup used by Jesus Christ at the Last Supper. Robert evidently planned his verse romance, *The History of the Grail* (*L'histoire del Graal*), as a trilogy intended to trace the Grail through the wanderings of *Joseph of Arimathea* into the world of Arthur and *Merlin* and through the adventures of Grail knights such as *Perceval*.[7] He completed the first two romances and a prose version, the *Roman du Graal*,[8] follows his planned history of the Grail from its origins in the New Testament Passion story to its achievement by Perceval. According to the only complete surviving romance, *Joseph of Arimathea*, Pilate gave the cup used at the Last Supper to Joseph, and the Grail sustained Joseph in prison. The Joseph of Arimathea material derives from the biblical Apocrypha, specifically part of the Gospel of Nicodemus known as the Acts of Pilate.[9] In the Apocrypha, Joseph is imprisoned, but there is no mention of a Grail. Robert de Boron's verse romance added details and created a kind of apocryphal gospel within the romance to emphasize the role of the Grail.

The Holy Grail is first named at the Grail feast celebrated by Joseph of Arimathea and his followers. Robert de Boron placed this feast at a symbolic midpoint between the institution of the Eucharist at the Last Supper and the Round Table of Arthur's court. The Grail brings joy to all who sit at table, but it also served to distinguish the true followers from the corrupt ones and paralleled the Last Supper story even to an outcast figure. Joseph's brother-in-law, Hebron (Bron), caught a fish for the sacred feast, and it is he who becomes the Rich Fisher and journeys with the Grail to Britain. Alain is chief among Bron's twelve sons and also goes to Britain to await a 'third man' who will be the permanent keeper of the Grail (namely the knight, Perceval), while Joseph returns to Arimathea. In the *Merlin* romance, of which only a fragment remains, the magician constructs the Round Table in imitation of Joseph's Grail table and of the table at the Last Supper, and he sets up the Siege Perilous for the knight most worthy of the Grail. Arthur's knights undertake the quest for the Holy Grail, and the events of the quest follow a pattern similar to Chrétien's romance. Perceval fails to ask the question during his first visit to the castle of Bron, the Fisher King, and his subsequent adventures lead him to the hermit. Perceval finally asks the question which cures the Grail king and takes his place. Merlin, who helped Perceval during his quest, eventually retires to the woods to dictate the story for posterity.[10]

In the *Didot-Perceval*, composed in the second decade of the twelfth century, Perceval occupies the forbidden Siege Perilous at the Round Table.[11] As a result of Perceval's action, the Grail appears, a magic stone splits, and a voice announces the quest to restore order and lift the enchantments. All the knights go on quest, but only Perceval asks the question which cures the Fisher King, repairs the stone and reveals the secret of the Holy Grail. He remains to rule the Grail castle, and the tale continues with Arthur's adventures. Although the romance incorporates elements from the Joseph of Arimathea tradition, the context is Arthur's court and the Grail episode is part of a wider Arthurian saga.

15

Perlesvaus or *The High Book of the Grail* is a French prose romance written at the beginning of the thirteenth century.[12] The author's patron was the crusader lord, Jean de Nesle. Like Chrétien's patron, he too was associated with Flanders and with the Fourth Crusade, but survived long enough to participate in the crusade against the Albigensians. The *Perlesvaus* romance is a dramatic reworking of the Grail legend suffused with Christian fervour and deep symbolic meaning. The romance states clearly that it is the story of the holy vessel called the Grail used to collect the Saviour's blood at the Crucifixion. It opens with Arthur sitting immobile at court uninterested in great deeds. Guinevere's reproaches send him out to find adventure, and he meets Perlesvaus (Perceval). Gawain sees two maidens at the court of the Fisher King; one carrying the Holy Grail, the other a bleeding lance. Gawain remains silent as the Grail appears as a chalice, then as a child, and finally as a crucified king. Lancelot arrives next, but his adulterous love for the queen means that he sees nothing at all. Finally Perlesvaus's sister has a vision of a spirit battle in the cemetery. She hears a voice declare that the Fisher King's evil brother, the King of Castel Mortal, has seized the Grail castle and only the Good Knight, Perlesvaus, can help. The Grail, the bleeding lance and the sword of St John are restored to the Grail chapel. King Arthur and Perlesvaus witness a procession of monks who perform the service of the Holy Grail, one which equates the Grail chalice with the Christian Eucharist. Perlesvaus performs one more deed, killing the black hermit, after which a voice speaks from the Grail chapel and Perlesvaus boards a ship which takes him no one knows where. This romance was adapted into Middle Welsh as *Y Seint Greal* in the thirteenth century.[13]

Wolfram von Eschenbach composed his Middle High German romance, *Parzival*, in the first decade of the thirteenth century.[14] The Grail is a marvellous stone called *lapsis exillus*. The Grail knights are called *templeise* (Templars), although they are not necessarily members of a particular order, especially since there are Grail women as well. Parzival's mother is one of them, thus the hero is related to Arthur through his father, and to the Grail family through his mother. The Grail king, Anfortas, although wounded in the groin, cannot die because of the presence of the Grail. His virgin sister carries the Grail stone, and it shows a message saying that his successor must ask a question on the first night. Parzival observes the procession and the bleeding spear, but says nothing and is reprimanded by Cundrie, the loathly maiden. Later, he learns about his relationship to the people in the Grail castle from the hermit. As in other romances, his story is interspersed with Gawain's adventures, so that the contrast between the two knights, and their very different relationship to the ideals of chivalry, is maintained. In addition Parzival fights with his pagan (i.e. part-Saracen) half-brother. The two are reconciled and journey together to Montsalvasche, the Grail castle, where the hero finally asks what ails Anfortas and becomes Grail king.

Comments on the Grail are scattered throughout the poem. Like Chrétien, Wolfram described events relating to the Grail, but withheld the full explanation to create tension and maintain suspense in the narrative. For Wolfram the 'thing called the Gral' is a stone with the name 'lapsit exillus', the stone by which the Phoenix is burned and reborn. It healed the sick and provided food and drink for the inhabitants of Munsalvaeche, the Grail castle in the land of Terre de Salvaesche. The Grail king, his family and his companions protect the Grail, and only a virgin can carry it. Every Good Friday a heavenly dove renews the Grail's power with a communion wafer, and from time to time messages appear on the Grail stone. Parzival's coming is predicted in this way. Only those who have been called can find Munsalvaeche, and only baptized Christians can see the Grail. When a country needs a ruler, the Grail supplies one. The women are sent out openly, but the men must not be asked where they come from. The Grail king may marry, but the knights atone for their sins by remaining chaste and defending the Grail.[15]

The mysterious phrase, *lapsit exillus*, may be a distortion of the Latin for 'lapsis ex caelis' (that which fell from heaven). It may also be related to the stone, *lapis exilis,* in the Alexander legend which served as a warning against pride. In *Parzifal*, angels learn humility before the stone of the Grail. This may echo a motif in the Alexander legend. When the king attempted to enter the Earthly Paradise, he received a stone, which was both heavy and light, as a lesson about the humility necessary for a just king. This motif also reflects on Anfortas, who is wounded because he violated the code of the Grail guardians, and on Parzival's own inner journey. The powerful Count Hermann of Thuringia was Wolfram's patron, and such themes would have been relevant to the knightly cadres who were Wolfram's main audience. As with many romance writers, Wolfram takes no personal responsibility for the story. Instead he introduced the figure of Kyot, a fictional Provençal poet, who learned Arabic in order to read the discarded Grail story found in a manuscript at Toledo, which had in turn been recorded by a Jewish astronomer. Despite numerous attempts to substantiate the details of Wolfram's origin story, it is a clever storyteller's conceit, but the complex origin tale about lost manuscripts contrasts effectively with Wolfram's claims to be an illiterate master storyteller.[16]

The composition of *the Lancelot-Grail* (The *Vulgate Cycle* or the *Prose Lancelot*) spans about twenty years (c.1215–35).[17] the cycle prepared the way for a new Grail knight, Galahad, and established the fashion for a

Grail cycle about knights who go on a spiritual quest rather than knights who have courtly adventures. It unfolds over a series of romances. *The History of the Holy Grail (Estoire del Saint Graal)* sets up a chain of Grail kings and fisher kings. Joseph of Arimathea and his son, Josephe, convert King Evalach of Sarras, the city of the Saracens, and his brother-in-law, Nasciens. Evalach receives the red-cross shield, while Nasciens's descendant will be the 'bon chevalier', Galahad. Joseph is succeeded as Grail keeper by his son, Josephe, and by his grandson, Alain, the Rich Fisherman who guards the Grail in Corbenic Castle. The land becomes waste when the sword destined for Galahad wounds one of the guardians. Another guardian, Pellehan, receives a thigh wound, while his son, Pelles, fathers the Grail maiden Elaine, who, in turn, became the mother of Galahad. Increasingly, the eucharistic qualities of the Grail are emphasized even though it is still carried by a maiden in the Grail procession. Gawain first sees it as a chalice carried aloft by Elaine, the future mother of Galahad. Its arrival is heralded by a white dove bearing a censer and accompanied by abundant food for everyone except the unworthy Gawain. Bors sees the Grail covered first in white cloth and then revealed in its glory. The healing aspect of the Grail is important in the *Vulgate Cycle*; both Bors and Perceval are healed and Lancelot is cured of madness.

The *Quest of the Holy Grail (Queste del Saint Graal)* focuses on the Grail seekers and their relationship to King Arthur. Galahad claims the Siege Perilous and is awarded the red-cross shield. The appearance of the Holy Grail is attended by sweet odours and plentiful food. A voice announces a quest that takes the familiar romance format of adventures through dark forests and strange voyages to mysterious castles. However, the adventures the knights encounter at Corbenic and Sarras are different. Worldly knights like Gawain are ultimately excluded. Lancelot, the repentant sinner, sees only a partial vision. Bors and Perceval participate fully in the Grail in its eucharistic aspect, while Galahad experiences a final complete union with the divine. When the Grail chalice is elevated during mass, the knights witness a miraculous transformation as images of the Trinity, a child, or the figure of the wounded Christ rise from the Grail. This vision resolves some of the details of earlier Grail processions. For example, the blood from the lance runs into the Grail, and Joseph of Arimathea's son, Josephe, celebrates this mass. Identifying the Grail with the platter from which Christ and his apostles ate the Pascal lamb further reinforces the eucharistic imagery. After Galahad achieves the vision of the Holy Grail at Sarras, a mysterious hand removes the Grail, its covering and the lance.[18]

Vengeance for the death of a kinsman is the main theme in the thirteenth-century Welsh romance, *Peredur*.[19] The Grail is a platter with the bloody head of Peredur's murdered cousin. When the loathly damsel berates Peredur for failing to ask questions, he learns that witches lamed his uncle and killed the cousin whose head is in the salver. These witches instruct Peredur in the craft of war, but he eventually kills them. The *Roman du Graal* (the Post-Vulgate Cycle), composed in the middle of the thirteenth century,[20] traces the origins of the Grail from the Passion story to its achievement by one of the knights. Balin uses the holy lance in the Dolorous Stroke which wounds Pellehan, making him the Maimed King and creating the Wasteland.

Malory distilled the whole of his extensive knowledge of Arthurian romance into *Morte Darthur*, which was completed by 1470 and published by William Caxton in 1485. He includes the episode of Balin and the Dolorous Stroke, the story of Lancelot and Elaine and the conception of Galahad, and 'The noble tale of the Sankreall which is called the holy vessel and the signification of blessed blood of Our Lord Jesu Christ, which was brought into this land by Joseph of Arimathea.'[21] Pellam, the Fisher King, is wounded by Balin's Dolorous Stroke and will not be healed until the coming of Galahad. Lancelot sees the Grail at Corbenic where Elaine, the daughter of the Grail keeper, Pelles, conceives Galahad. Bors and Perceval also experience the Grail at Corbenic. Malory's Grail is described as the vessel in which Christ's blood was collected on the Cross. This may reflect his familiarity with the relics of the Holy Blood at Hailes Abbey in England. Certainly it melds with the view that the Grail is the Eucharist cup that, according to Christian theology, during the Mass actually contained Christ's blood.[22] Sir Thomas Malory's *Morte Darthur* is perhaps the greatest version of the Arthurian legend in English. Caxton's edition introduced the world of courtly deeds to a new audience, and it was the departure point for the revival of the Arthurian legend in Britain in the nineteenth century.

Heinrich von dem Türlin's romance, *The Crown* (*Diu Crône*), dates from about 1240. The list of sources shows that the Grail romances were widely known in the medieval period,[23] but the Grail quest is only one among many adventures with little or no religious meaning. The journey to the Grail castle, where a wondrous feast is set out, reads like a traditional wonder tale. Gawain, the hero, even has the help of a magician's sister who later appears with the Grail. Lancelot is drugged with magic wine, but Gawain, who has been forewarned, witnesses an elaborate Grail procession. Two girls carry candlesticks, two boys carry a spear, from which fall three drops of blood, and two more girls hold an ornate bowl, a lady enters carrying a reliquary containing bread followed by a weeping woman. The lord of the castle explains that this is the Grail, but because of Perceval's failure they, a company of the living dead, will disappear for ever.[24] The romance of *Foulk fitz Warin* (c.1250), set in Shropshire, is known from a later Anglo-Norman prose redaction. The Grail episode occurs at the end of this romance and may have been influenced by *Perlesvaus*.[25] In the *Le Roman de Tristan en prose* (c.1250) the Grail quest draws the most significant of Arthur's knights together. Galahad cures his grandfather, the maimed king Palamedes, by rubbing blood from the Lance on his legs and thighs. Galahad, Perceval and Bors carry the Grail onto a ship and sail to Sarras.[26]

Henry Lovelich's *The History of the Holy Grail*, compiled in the middle of the fifteenth century, is a translation from the French Vulgate, but he adds the burial of Joseph at Glastonbury and stresses Merlin's role as prophet of the Holy Grail.[27] Another English writer, John Hardyng, was a contemporary of Malory. He interprets the *san greal* as a reference to *sang real* (royal blood). After Galahad finds the Grail in Wales, he establishes the order of *Sanke roiall* in Palestine to fight against the Saracens. Perceval brings Galahad's red-cross shield to Glastonbury where Galahad's heart is eventually buried.[28]

In the medieval romances, the Grail has both eucharistic and pentecostal overtones, but it also heals both physically and spiritually. If the source of the Holy Grail theme lies in these literary texts, then the legends associated with the Grail relics introduced new ideas that have influenced a new and vibrant literature.

Faced with an array of chalices, the archaeologist hero in *Indiana Jones and the Last Crusade* chooses a simple pottery cup as the appropriate drinking vessel for a carpenter's son. It is, of course, the right choice, and it enables the modern, wisecracking knight-errant to revive his gravely wounded, but equally modern, fisher-king father. Although Chrétien did not clarify the nature of the shining jewelled *graal,* he hinted that the Fisher King was sustained by sacred food. The mysterious nature of this food may have prompted Robert de Boron to introduce the idea that the Grail was the cup used at the Last Supper. Thus the Grail became associated with sustenance, with a wounded king, and with the Christian sacrament of the Eucharist. Veneration of relics was an important aspect of popular devotion during the Middle Ages and among the most prized were relics associated with the Passion of Christ, the final events of his life, the Last Supper, the Crucifixion, and the Resurrection. In the wake of the Crusades,[29] there were a number of stories about miraculous discoveries, daring escapes and ingenious ways of transporting these precious objects to western churches. However, the Holy Grail was largely absent from medieval relic collections.[30] Those that do exist are relatively modern 'Grails', steeped either in local tradition, or in the imaginative history of Templars and secret societies.

An early reference to the cup of the Last Supper dates from the seventh century when Arculf, a Briton, made a pilgrimage to the Holy Land.[31] He described a two-handled silver chalice in a chapel near Golgotha, the site of the Crucifixion. It is not called a Grail, which is hardly surprising since the description pre-dates the romances by several centuries, but there is already some confusion about its appearance. Arculf's account, based on eyewitness reports, mentioned a silver relic, while an earlier, but less clear, account said it was made of onyx.[32] It is just possible that this description may have influenced the shape and decoration of the famous Ardagh Chalice. This imposing object was found in Ireland in 1868 close to the rath of Ardagh, County Limerick. It was not linked either to the Grail of romance or the actual cup used at the Last Supper, but the story attached to it, namely that the son of a widowed farmer found it while he was digging under a thorn tree, is typical of discovery legends known elsewhere.[33]

The Crusades provided imaginative histories for other Grails. The *sacro catino*, the 'emerald' vessel, was 'discovered' in Caesarea during the time of the Crusades. It was brought to Genoa by the heroic crusader, Guglielmo Embriaco, head of an influential Genoese family. In a fresco on a wall of the Palazzo San Giorgio, he holds the object in his hand. William of Tyre, whose *History of Deeds beyond the Sea* is the source of so many legends about the Templars, mentions that the *sacro catino* was carved from a single emerald. It was found in a mosque in Caesarea and taken to Europe as booty after the Crusade, thus keeping it in the tradition of relics brought back from the Holy Land. An ordinance forbade anyone to touch the *sacro catino* with any metallic object.[34] The *sacro catino* is not precious gemstone, but a shallow hexagonal glass dish, now somewhat damaged and displayed in the cathedral museum of San Lorenzo. It still functions as part of the city's public celebration of its heritage when a copy is paraded through the streets.[35] According to tradition, the damage occurred when the dish was taken to France by Napoleon. At this time it was found to be green glass, not emerald, but eventually it was returned to Genoa.[36] Napoleon often functions in legends as a generic villain, full of crass political hubris, who steals and demystifies some precious object. Some legends attribute the theft of Templar records to Napoleon as well. The destructive or acquisitive propensities of such villains provided a good excuse for loss or damage to 'relics', and other Grail legends use this motif. An alternative version of the *sacro catino* legend locates the discovery in Spain during the wars against the Moors. The Spanish king gave it to Genoese mercenaries, who accepted it in lieu of money in recognition for their help.[37] None of the sources identifies the *sacro catino* with the Grail, indeed it seems originally to have been a valuable rather than a sacred object. However, at the end of the thirteenth century, Jacobus of Voragine, Bishop of Genoa, wrote a historical chronicle about the city's glorious past and transformed the object into an important part of Genoese history. The bishop, writing from a Genoese point of view, described it as the emerald dish from which Christ and his apostles ate the Pascal lamb at the Passover supper the night before the Crucifixion. Emerald was not just a valuable stone, but one with magical and medical associations as well. He cited 'English books' which speak of the Sangraal,[38] thus associating it with the romance motif. In one of those curious, although definitely non-conspiratorial, coincidences that occur in this material, Jacobus of Voragine also compiled a famous collection of saints' lives known as the *Golden Legend* (*Legenda Aurea*) that included the story of Mary Magdalene's voyage to France.

Two seventeenth-century traditions refer to chalices in France. One was apparently looted from a church in the Holy Land during the Crusades and disappeared during the French Revolution.[39] As with so many contemporary legend motifs, the details could be true in that they are contextualized in actual historical events. However, the creation of an imaginative historical context is a common motif in legend formation. At the end of the seventeenth century, another tradition linked the Grail to Glastonbury Abbey and the story of St Joseph of Arimathea, but no object was found until the beginning of the twentieth century.[40] The varying traditions associated with relics, like the *sacro catino*, encapsulate the kind of legendary 'frame' which surrounds so many relic legends. This frame includes a mysterious heritage involving a crusader, a suggestion that the object dates from the time of Christ, a temporary loss, usually at the hands of some famous villain, and a dramatic restoration. A few popular studies have attempted to reaffirm the authenticity of the Genoese relic with the use of modern archaeological techniques. One of the features of alternative investigations is that they are so often attempts to resanctify a relic using the same techniques that demystified it in the first place. Science was one of the means by which the irrational world was 'disenchanted' and brought under secular control in the wake of the Enlightenment,[41] but new techniques of systematic investigation from psychical research to the use of archaeology to validate the existence of seemingly mythical cultures have been brought into play to heal the breach between modern culture and the certainties it had seemingly left behind.

Similar traditions about mysterious heritage and miraculous discovery surround a stone cup, the *santo caliz*, in Valencia Cathedral in Spain. The object is a small agate bowl set in a gilt structure, enabling it to be used as a chalice for celebrating mass. The mounting is medieval, and the agate bowl could be a Greco-Roman artefact, and therefore an object from the

right period. Such chalices were not unusual, but stone artefacts are difficult to date and authentication remains a contentious issue. The account
of how it came to Valencia follows the same legend frame as other candidates for the Grail. The first mention of the *santo caliz*, at the end of the
fourteenth century, records that it was given to the King of Aragon. As
one would expect, less verifiable traditions recount a much older, and
almost certainly imaginative, history. In this legendary history, St Peter
himself took the *santo caliz* with him to Rome. Fear of persecution by one
of the Roman emperors hostile to Christians provided the context for it
being sent to Spain. In this tradition, St Lawrence, rather than Joseph of
Arimathea, is associated with the chalice. Yet another custodian saved the
cup during the Moorish invasions and hid it in a monastery in Catalonia.[42]
The *santo caliz* appears in several Spanish paintings of the Last Supper,
but these were painted only after the legend had developed.[43] There may
be a link between this legend and Spanish royal interest in the Grail romances.
Alfonso V of Aragon, who sold the cup to the cathedral of Valencia in the
fifteenth century, was interested in chivalry and in the Grail romances.
However, even in this account, the chalice is called the cup of the Last
Supper, not the Grail.[44]

Its symbolic links to the central mystery of Christian religion ensure that
the *santo caliz* remains a focus for veneration. However, a self-published
book claims to have found new historical evidence in a seventeenth-century
translation of a lost life of St Lawrence that establishes its authenticity as
the Grail.[45] St Lawrence was the saint who allegedly brought the chalice
to Spain, and the seventeenth century was exactly the period when the
santo caliz legend was created. Such sources attest to the way these objects
continue to be valued as a focus for pious veneration or national pride,
but as proof of authenticity, they remain problematic.

The beginning of the twentieth century was a fruitful period for Grail
objects. A damaged medieval wooden bowl, known as the Nanteos cup,
was identified with the Holy Grail. Like so many others, this Welsh legend
featured escaping monks, secrets, tunnels and even a crusader.[46] About the
same time, an antique glass dish came to light just outside Glastonbury,
England. It was concealed at a local spot called Bride's Well, where it was
rediscovered by the family and friends of a mystic, Wellesley Tudor Pole.[47]
Two other objects, both associated with the important classical city of
Antioch, were put forward as candidates for the Grail in the 1930s. One
is a glass *krater*, a drinking cup, fitted into a protective leather case which
was displayed at an exhibition of artefacts from 'Palestine and the Bible
Lands' in London. According to a somewhat vague tradition, a crusader
brought it back from the East.[48] The other is a magnificent silver-gilt object.

It was originally identified as a Eucharist cup and was probably crafted at one of the workshops near Antioch about the sixth century. Gustavus Eisen, a colourful but respected antiquary, identified it as the Holy Grail, and it was displayed, with a certain amount of fanfare, in the Hall of Religion at the Chicago World's Fair of 1933–4.[49] It is now among the Byzantine artefacts in the Metropolitan Museum of Art in New York.[50] The highly crafted adornment depicts men sitting among a running motif of vine and grapes. The figures may represent either the apostles or the classical philosophers whose work was thought to prefigure Christianity. The object is probably a liturgical lamp rather than a chalice, and this would suggest that the object reflects the idea of Christ as the light of the world. The decoration may echo the idea of Christ as the vine and Christians as the branches, rather than the Eucharist and the Last Supper. The journalist and novelist Thomas Costain used it as the model for his historical novel, *The Silver Chalice*, in the 1950s. In the novel, Joseph of Arimathea commissions a young pagan silversmith to provide a silver chalice to house the cup used at the Last Supper. The young silversmith seeks out the followers of Christ in order to sculpt their likenesses for the chalice. Naturally, he finds both adventure and romance with a beautiful Christian girl.[51] As with other fictional accounts of the Grail, there is a crossover into popular belief, and this object is still occasionally identified with the Holy Grail. A small stone cup, possibly a Roman make-up pot, supposedly found concealed in a statue at a British country house, Hawkstone Hall, in Shropshire, has been put forward as another modern Grail candidate. The account of its unmasking is full of mysteries, codes and exciting discoveries, all of them overlooked by establishment historians and academics. Soon after the existence of the Hawkstone Grail was published, the head of an Italian Templar organization claimed that he owned a similar cup and that this was the 'real' Holy Grail.[52]

Inevitably perhaps, popular works of mystery and conspiracy overlap. The Grail legend shares motifs with other mysterious relics, like the Spear of Longinus and the Shroud of Turin. The bleeding spear, which appears in several versions of the Grail procession, was usually identified in the romances themselves as the lance belonging to a Roman centurion, Longinus. By the fourth century, the Roman soldier who pierced Christ's side as an act of mercy to end his suffering was called Longinus. Later tradition makes him a blind centurion who was cured by the power of the Holy Blood and converted to Christianity. Critics of mythic interpretations of the Grail legend point out that the Longinus legend was very popular, and the details fit the idea of a lance dripping blood more closely than pagan Celtic story motifs.[53] As a relic, the Holy Lance had a miraculous history of its own.

More than one candidate claimed to be the 'true' lance,[54] and various traditions assign ownership to Constantine, Charlemagne and subsequent Holy
Roman emperors. In contemporary Grail legends, the nature of the lance
has changed. Possession ostensibly conferred occult power, which, added
to other talismans, such as the Grail, would increase.

If the legends surrounding the spear and the Grail evoke a conspiracy
by a sinister elite to harness occult power, the link between the shroud of
Turin and the Grail illustrates the converse, a conspiracy by the establishment to conceal an unorthodox secret from ordinary people. The shroud
of Turin is supposedly the linen cloth in which Christ was wrapped for
burial and bears a seemingly miraculous image of him. When carbon dating
revealed that the cloth and its image were created during the medieval
period, a flurry of books appeared defending its authenticity.[55] Scientific
methods had demystified the shroud, and a new genre of books appeared
advocating the use of just those scientific methods in order to re-enchant
the relic and restore its authenticity and spiritual authority.[56] One approach
explained the image on the shroud as evidence that Leonardo Da Vinci
(1452–1519) was a pioneer in photography who held unorthodox religious
beliefs.[57] The artist's extensive notebooks contain no substantial references
to religion. This silence has been taken as an indication that he held
unorthodox beliefs, and some writers have examined his religious paintings to search for evidence of these beliefs. Neo-Cathar writers like Joséphin
Péladan also linked Leonardo to heretical sects and unorthodox ideas.[58]
Hints about a conflict between Leonardo's science and Church orthodoxy
date back to the first biography written by Giorgio Vasari in the sixteenth
century, and later art historians developed the image of the romantic genius
in conflict with the establishment. Specific traditions have become attached
to individual paintings. One popular legend about his painting of *The Last
Supper* pre-dates speculation about whether the figure next to Jesus is male
or female. It recounts how Leonardo modelled the figure of Jesus on that
of a handsome young man, and when he came to paint the traitor apostle,
Judas, he used the same model, whose face had become marred by corrupt
living. As so often with this kind of legend formation, the idea that
Leonardo painted an alternative religious message involving the Grail in
his painting of *The Last Supper* is not a shocking new revelation, but rather
a further development of a legend already in existence.[59]

Popular medieval pilgrimages were associated with relics of the Holy
Blood at Fécamp Abbey in France, Bruges in Belgium and two English
sites, Hailes Abbey in Gloucestershire and Westminster Abbey in London.
The relic of the Holy Blood in Bruges was linked to a crusader legend, as
are many of the modern Grail legends. An annual procession has taken

place since the fourteenth century, and like the *sacro catino* in Genoa, it is important as a marker of civic identity. Today the procession, and indeed interest in the relic, is undergoing a revival. One website describes the relic housed in the Basilica of the Holy Blood in Bruges as 'a venerated relic of Christ whose origin is a mystery worthy of Indiana Jones'.[60]

The relics at Hailes Abbey and Westminster Abbey became casualities of the English Reformation; it is possible that the relic at Hailes Abbey may have influenced Thomas Malory's thinking on the nature of the Holy Grail. Malory's own home was not far from Hailes Abbey. In his reworking of Arthurian tradition, Malory follows his source, the *Queste,* in setting the Grail firmly in the context of the Eucharistic practice and the biblical story of Christ's Passion. It is a reminder of the Last Supper and of the miraculous change of wine into the blood of Christ. Malory's understanding no doubt reflected that of lay readers at the time. Barely a decade after this, Henry Lovelich translated one of Malory's main sources, the *Lancelot-Grail.* He used the term 'Sank Royal' or 'royal blood'.[61] Malory and Lovelich's characterization of *sanc real* was still within the context of a lay understanding of eucharistic doctrine and practice prior to the Reformation, but the idea of *sang real* as holy/royal blood took a dramatic turn in the 1980s with the publication of an ingenuously speculative and popular example of the conspiracy genre, *The Holy Blood and the Holy Grail.*

Narratives associated with Grail relics follow a strikingly similar pattern in which code, revelation and secret message are dominant themes. The early history of these objects is always shrouded in mystery, but a line of custodians, linked by equally mysterious coincidences, leads back to some important figure. In the absence of clear documentation, it is this line of custodians who provide a connecting thread linking the elements of the legend. The story of the *santo caliz* leads back to St Peter through Spanish kings and saints, and the *sacro catino,* found in the Holy Land, allegedly was brought back by a crusader. Templars and crusaders are popular candidates for custodians in other variants of these legends, and the chaos of the Crusades or the confusion surrounding the trial of the Templars provides an explanation for the absence of clear documentation. Invariably, the Grail comes into the possession of its present owner in dramatic or mysterious circumstances. The last survivor among the guardian monks supposedly gave the Nanteos cup to the Powell family, while the stone cup was presented to the head of the Italian Templars by his father-in-law. At Glastonbury and at Hawkstone, one owner deliberately concealed objects, only for them to be found much later. Shugborough illustrates how cross-fertilization produces new legends. As a Grail mystery, it is developed from other alternative work, not from any of the traditions associated with its creation.

Legend formation is a dynamic cultural process. The search for the Grail as a real object appeals to a need for the supernatural in a sceptical and secular age. The *santo caliz* remains in an active pietistic context, and cures are associated with the Nanteos cup in Wales, but modern Grail relic traditions are more concerned with authenticity than with miracles. Modern Grails invoke the scientific validity of disciplines like archaeology as a means of authentication. Despite the fact that their discovery involved an element of chance or mystery, the Great Chalice of Antioch and the glass bowl discovered at Glastonbury were viewed as archaeological antiquities, even when experts who examined these objects disagreed about dating or provenance. If the power of these relics has been neutralized by the rise of science and reason, then science and reason can be used to reveal the hidden and suppressed truths inherent in them once again. They can be re-enchanted for the modern world and regain the power of transformation.

CHAPTER 2

The Grail at Glastonbury

GLASTONBURY TOR, WHICH dominates both the town and the surrounding area, is one of those natural features that seem intrinsically mysterious. It rises above lush farmland created by centuries of land drainage, and its steep sides give it the appearance of isolation, an effect reinforced by the ruined medieval chapel that crowns it. Before the surrounding land was drained, the Tor would have been an island surrounded by marshland and tidal pools. There is evidence of human exploitation of this environment well before the Christian era, although the distinctive lake villages were established only about 50 BC. The area became a prosperous agricultural, fishing and trading centre for south-western Britain and provided a context for the earliest Glastonbury legends. The mystic Dion Fortune, writing in 1934, described the 'many different roads' to Glastonbury as the high road of history, the upland path of legend and the mystical secret road of the soul.[1] Each leads to a very different place, but no consideration of the legend of the Holy Grail can be complete without understanding its connection to the many aspects of Glastonbury and its environs.

The history of the abbey begins with the legendary grant of twelve hides. This is a not uncommon origin legend, in which a land grant is maximized by cutting something into strips to enclose a much larger area. It illustrates how legends shaped events at Glastonbury even at an early stage. It was one of the richest houses in England until a disastrous fire in 1184 gutted many buildings and destroyed both the library and the old church. As saints' cults provided both prestige and income, the creation of cults attached to Arthur, Joseph of Arimathea and the Grail may reflect a need to re-establish the abbey's position. At the same time, the Anglo-Norman Angevin kings were also attempting to consolidate their position as British rulers, and this wider process of national mythmaking was expressed in the writings of Gerald of Wales and William of Malmesbury. The death of Henry II in 1189, one of

the abbey's most important patrons, may have further stimulated the establishment of Arthur's cult at Glastonbury, while traditions about Joseph of
Arimathea provided another link between medieval Arthurian traditions and
the abbey's early history. The town enjoyed brief fame as a spa centre
in the eighteenth century, but it was not until the late nineteenth century
that the religious aspect of Glastonbury began to revive with the development of the Chalice Well area at the foot of the Tor, and the eventual
purchase of the abbey ruins in 1907 by the Church of England. This period
also witnessed the emergence of a group of people within Glastonbury who
identified themselves with an ancient system of beliefs embodied in the landscape and history of the town and its environs.

When William of Malmesbury wrote an account of the abbey at the
beginning of the twelfth century, he found an institution already steeped in
tradition. It had been established as a Benedictine monastery in the seventh
century, but its association with British Christianity pre-dated the arrival of
St Augustine of Canterbury, according to tradition the founder of the English
Church. After a century of Danish raids, the abbey church was rebuilt and
enlarged in the tenth century under the influence of St Dunstan. He transformed it into a centre for Saxon spirituality, and the tradition of royal
burials was established with the interment of several Saxon kings. This
wealthy abbey was associated with key events in the spiritual history of
Britain, such as the coming of early British Christian missionaries, the threat
of Danish raiders, the conversion of the Saxons, and the transfer of this
legacy to the Normans. These events had already attracted a wide spectrum
of legendary material,[2] and the new Norman abbots were keen to maintain
that wealth and extend its prestige. William of Malmesbury's *De Antiquitate
Glastonie Ecclesiae* was written between 1125 and 1135 and probably
commissioned at the behest of the then abbot, Henry of Blois.[3] William's
account provided the earliest complete history of the abbey, based on material in its well-stocked library, his own observations and, no doubt, information of a more traditional nature gleaned from the monks themselves.
William was a careful historian with a keen and critical perspective on the
written sources, as well as on what the monks told him. It is clear that he
visited the churches in Glastonbury personally to examine the existing
monuments, and a significant number of his observations have been confirmed
by archaeology.[4] He placed the abbey's founding before St Augustine's mission
to convert the English in 597 – this was crucial to Glastonbury's claims to
precedence over other religious foundations. William's original account makes
no mention of Arthur, Joseph of Arimathea or the Grail, which suggests
that these were not part of the history or the legends associated with
Glastonbury at the time.

William's account was further elaborated as the abbey's importance grew. The revisions made in the middle of the thirteenth century contain much of what today constitutes the legendary history of Glastonbury. This later version started with the supposed conversion of Gaul by the Apostle Philip, who then sent twelve disciples on a mission to Britain under St Joseph of Arimathea. This event supposedly took place in AD 63, the fifteenth year after the Assumption of the Blessed Virgin, the patron of Glastonbury Abbey. A sympathetic pagan king, Arviragus, gave the missionaries land around Glastonbury Tor, a place called Ynys Witrin by the native Britons, and subsequent kings added to this, creating the Twelve Hides of the original foundation. This community of twelve hermits was directed by St Gabriel to build a church, and Christ himself dedicated this first Christian church in Britain to his mother. After the death of the last hermit, the site reverted to wilderness until another pagan, King Lucius, asked Pope Eleutherius to send missionaries to undertake the conversion of Britain. Two new missionary saints, Phagan and Deruvian, rebuilt the *vetusta ecclesia* (this Latin phrase, meaning 'the oldest church', described the original church at Glastonbury). In the fifth century, Patrick, later confused with the apostle to Ireland, became the first abbot of a proper monastery, Glastonbury Abbey. In support of this, a later expanded version of the *De Antiquitate* cited a conveniently detailed foundation charter, which not only summarized the early history but also listed the indulgences to be gained by contemporary pilgrims (that is, those visiting in the thirteenth century). The source for this rather too convenient information was a mysterious book supposedly discovered by St Patrick in the ancient church on Glastonbury Tor dedicated to St Michael by the missionaries Phagan and Deruvian. The charter listed further indulgences and other saints, among them Bridget, Gildas, David and Columba, who supposedly came to Glastonbury and whose relics were there.

The foundation charter, with information about indulgences and about the church on the Tor so suspiciously useful to the thirteenth-century abbey, is missing from William of Malmesbury's original account. William cited 'annals of good credit' for the King Lucius story, although he seemed a little surprised that a pagan king would call for missionaries from a new religion like Christianity. William accepted the importance of Glastonbury before the mission of St Augustine in the sixth century, a period which is so often linked to Celtic Christianity, and listed a number of saints and dignitaries buried there. His source for this information was two 'pyramids', perhaps early memorial crosses, located near the monks' graveyards, which recorded the names of people buried there.[5] He is less precise about the supposed burials of saints like David, Gildas and Bridget, and he is cautious about the role of St Patrick, saying only that he returned to Glastonbury after converting the Irish. Even so good a historian as William occasionally gets confused. This Patrick was probably an early bishop, not the famous Irish saint, and it is unlikely that either the Welsh David or the Irish Bridget was buried at Glastonbury.

The Glastonbury legends concerning Arthur, Joseph and the Grail reflect the changing fortunes of the abbey itself, and their authenticity is necessarily coloured by this. Origin legends were an important strategy in establishing monastic status – just as modern Grail legends use similar techniques in forging connections with ancient secret traditions. The disastrous fire, which severely damaged the abbey in 1184, was the catalyst for the next stage of legend-making. The extensive restorations paid for by a royal patron, Henry II, were jeopardized by his death, since his son, Richard the Lionheart, had very little interest in the project. At the same time, the prestige, and even the independence, of Glastonbury was in danger of being overwhelmed by the diocese of Bath and Wells. Competition for patronage and ecclesiastical status therefore form the background to the finding of the bodies of Arthur and Guinevere in 1191. As the king's burial place on the Isle of Avalon, Glastonbury became central to the developing Arthurian legend, and Arthur's story became a national myth localized in Britain.[6] This bolstered the abbey's status and forged closer links with the royal family. The inevitable mixing of ecclesiastical and secular legends had consequences for the development of the Holy Grail tradition.

By the mid-thirteenth century, the story of Joseph of Arimathea began to appear in the abbey's foundation legends. Two things facilitated this new inclusion. King Arthur was already an established presence there, and the Grail romances had absorbed the apocryphal legends of Joseph, recasting him as an apostolic saint carrying the Christian message to the West. According to the biblical account, Joseph of Arimathea obtained Christ's body from Pilate and buried it in his own tomb. The apocryphal accounts, which were popular during the first to the third centuries of the Christian era, considerably expanded Joseph's role. He became closely associated with the risen Christ and the Holy Virgin Mary, and with the apostolic mission of the early Church. In the Apocrypha, the imprisoned Joseph was miraculously sustained by his faith, but there is no mention of the Grail. Robert de Boron's romance, however, specified that the Grail was the vessel used at the Last Supper and that Joseph, after a number of adventures, travelled westwards to 'vaus D'Avaron'. In this romance, Joseph resembles a New Testament version of Moses leading his followers to a promised land. Indeed, in the symbolic Grail feast presided over by Bron, a character called Moyses is deemed unworthy of the new Grail mission. Robert de Boron wrote at the end of the twelfth century, about the time that Arthur's grave became part of the Glastonbury pilgrim experience, and 'vaus D'Avaron', Joseph's goal, became equated with Avalon, and by extension Glastonbury. Other Grail romances, the *Continuations* of Chrétien's *Perceval*, the *Perlesvaus*, the *Vulgate Cycle* and the *Estories del Saint Graal* developed Joseph's British connections and furthered his links with the Grail and the Grail keepers.

Two medieval forgeries offered further support for Glastonbury's claims. The Charter of St Patrick attributed the origin of Christianity in Britain and the building of the *vetusta ecclesia* at Glastonbury to the efforts of twelve disciples of the apostles Philip and James. The site was rediscovered by Phagan and Deruvian, and the account provided a popular alternative to the more sober history of William of Malmesbury.[7] Joseph's story, both as founder of Glastonbury and as custodian of the Grail, was interpolated into this,[8] despite the fact that secular Grail romances, rather than hagiographical and chronicle literature, carried the story of Joseph and the Grail. In the middle of the fourteenth century, Edward III, another king with Arthurian interests, occupied the English throne. In 1345, a royal writ was issued to John Blome of London to search for St Joseph's body. Despite an unsubstantiated report of a discovery, nothing was actually found.[9] About this time, the Grail romances began to influence the chronicles and references to Joseph, Glastonbury and the Grail begin to appear in historical and genealogical documents.

The second forgery is the Prophecy of Melkin. In his description of the antiquities of the abbey (*Chronica sive antiquitates Glastonienses Ecclesie*), John of Glastonbury referred to an ancient prophecy by someone he calls Melkin the bard, which claimed that the discovery of Joseph of Arimathea's tomb would bring great blessings. John's account claimed that Joseph was buried at Glastonbury together with two white and silver vessels filled with the blood and sweat of the prophet Jesus ('*duo fassula alba et argentea cruore prophete Ihesu et sudore perimpleta*'). Melkin's prophecy linked the miracles with the finding of Joseph's tomb, rather than the contents of the cruets, but historians and antiquarians with an interest in the Grail invoked Melkin as an authority well into the eighteenth century. These include John Hardyng, who included the Grail in his verse chronicle, the Tudor antiquarian John Leland, John Capgrave, who added a late life of Joseph to his collection of English saints' lives, and Archbishop James Ussher, who referred to both Joseph and the Grail in his treatise on the antiquity of Christianity in Britain. There is broad agreement among them that Melkin was born in Wales, trained as a bard, lived either before Merlin or during the time of Maelgwn Gwynedd, a British king whose *floruit* was the sixth century. The Grail in the Melkin/John of Glastonbury account has become two cruets, relics of Christ's Passion rather than the mysterious object associated with Joseph in the romances. Since romance accounts of Joseph and the Grail are the sources for the Glastonbury references, the Melkin prophecy is probably a later interpolation. Perhaps John of Glastonbury created it to give substance to his claims about St Joseph.[10] Most references to Melkin's prophecy in antiquarian histories depend on one another, and only John Leland, who had access to Glastonbury's library before the Dissolution and claimed to have seen books by Melkin, offers any support for a Melkin tradition independent of John's *Chronicle*.[11]

Melkin is often equated with the historical British king Maelgwn Gwynedd. Although this is not impossible, Maelgwn in Welsh tradition embodies the overweening pride of secular power, and Welsh sources do not refer to him as a bard or a prophet.[12] This suggests that the prophecy, while complex, is not rooted in Welsh tradition and is more likely part of the Glastonbury legend itself. Gerald of Wales recorded that an unnamed 'British soothsayer', totally unknown in Welsh tradition, prophesied the discovery of Arthur's grave at Glastonbury. This may have provided a model for the later creation of Melkin's prophecies regarding St Joseph of Arimathea. Another attempt to unravel the Melkin prophecy by the historian of witchcraft Margaret Murray illustrates the degree to which scholarly investigation and legend-making are intertwined in the story of Glastonbury and the Grail. Murray's work has been a seminal influence on the rise of modern Wicca at Glastonbury and elsewhere. She went to Glastonbury to recuperate from exhaustion after the First World War. Here she experienced a crucial insight which stimulated her work on the survival of a witch cult in western Europe. There is no mention in her autobiography of any contact with the 'Avalonians' who created the modern mystical Glastonbury, but it is difficult to imagine that such an enquiring mind, and one so interested in archaeology, did not at least take notice of events. By the time of Murray's sojourn in Glastonbury, the people associated with the Grail relic found at St Bride's Well would have died or left. However, the influence of Frederick Bligh Bond (an architect associated with the excavation of the abbey and with mystical theories about its past) on mystical discoveries was still strong, and both he and Murray were archaeologists. She wrote her one article on the Grail tradition, specifically the Melkin prophecy, at Glastonbury. Murray suggested a Coptic original for the text and sought clarification on this from another prominent Arthurian scholar, Professor John Rhŷs.[13] However little this tells us about the background to Melkin, such details reveal the far-reaching interest in the Grail at the time.

The factors that favoured the development of the Joseph legend are less clear than those surrounding the finding of Arthur's body. The very stability of Glastonbury's prestige may have meant that there was no necessity to exploit traditions about Joseph after the discovery of Arthur's grave. The rise in popularity of the Joseph legend occurred later, in the fourteenth century, at a time when the abbey's power and influence, under Abbot John Chinnock (1375–1420), were at their height and not in need of additional pilgrimage income. The revival of interest in this saint and his connection with the abbey may reflect the increased religious tension across Europe and a growing nationalism in the political struggles between England and France. Whatever the motivation, Abbot Chinnock added Joseph of Arimathea to a triptych of the deposition of Christ from the cross, which he placed in the restored chapel of St Michael. This same abbot also sponsored John of Glastonbury's *Chronicle,* which recounted the fully developed legend of St Joseph depicting him and his eleven followers as the founders of Glastonbury in AD 63,[14] replacing the earlier origin legend about the missionary saints, Phagan and Deruvian. The St Joseph legend as it developed in the fourteenth century may also have countered the attempts to establish St David as the earliest saint to convert Britain, and even, perhaps check Owen Glyndwr's claims for an independent Wales with an independent Welsh Church.[15]

The writings of the Apocrypha expanded Joseph's brief appearance in the Gospel accounts, involving him more closely with the early Christian message. In the French Grail romances of the late twelfth and early thirteenth centuries, he was transformed into an apostolic figure associated with one of the primary relics of Christ's Passion, the cup of the Last Supper. Much later, he became the founder of Glastonbury Abbey. The fictional 'Prophecy of Melkin' gave suitably mysterious hints as to the location of Joseph's grave, and two searches were made for it. Neither the first search in the fourteenth century, nor the second search carried out during the abbacy of John Chinook in the fifteenth century, produced a clear result.[16] However, the story of Joseph's apostolic mission to Britain was fully developed by the time Abbot Chinnock ordered the restoration and rededication of a chapel to St Michael and St Joseph. This and other events were recorded on *magna tabula,* large manuscript sheets fastened to wooden frames that provided information for pilgrims at many ecclesiastical sites.[17] Although built up over a considerable period from various non-historical sources, the Joseph legend provided the basis for a conversion story in Britain which pre-dated the founding of the church at Rome. It had its political uses in establishing the precedence of Glastonbury in England and in bolstering the integrity of a national church at important European

Church Councils. After the Reformation, it continued to provide support for the idea that a Protestant British Church had been established earlier than its Roman Catholic rival, and eventually the legend could be adapted as a foundation for the ecologically sound, pro-pagan institutions of the modern Celtic revival.

The legend linked Joseph of Arimathea with the national hero, King Arthur. The historical arguments centred on Joseph's apostolic mission rather than his connection with the Grail. In the Glastonbury version of the legend, Joseph has two cruets, one containing sweat, the other blood. This double relic kept the story in line with the accepted version of the translation of the Precious Blood relic to England, an account that included the apocryphal details of Joseph gathering Christ's blood and sweat and a purely English elaboration in which he sent these relics to the English king. This meant that Glastonbury, like Hailes Abbey in Britain and Fécamp in France, possessed a relic of the Holy Blood.[18] Early sources were aware of Joseph of Arimathea as the founder of Glastonbury/Avalon, but the Grail is seldom mentioned, and when it is the reference is usually to one of the romances, not a relic.[19] In the fifteenth century, however, an English chronicle writer, John Hardyng (1378–1465?), fused the Glastonbury tradition with romance material related to the figure of Galahad.[20] Several aspects of Hardyng's story anticipate the mix of legend-making, antiquarianism and creative use of the past that characterizes many of the modern Grail theories. At first glance, Hardyng's main concern, namely England's right to rule Scotland, seems to have little to do with either the Grail or Glastonbury. However, in an attempt to strengthen his case, he gathered and presented evidence to successive kings in an effort to urge them to assert their authority. The so-called evidence was in fact his creation and had little effect on royal policy. However, his chronicle did influence Thomas Malory's account of the Grail story.[21]

Hardyng, like so many proponents of dubious Grail theories, invoked the supposed antiquity of the story of Joseph of Arimathea to substantiate England's claims, thus anticipating modern theories in using legendary fiction to support fact. One of his sources was the *Vulgate Cycle,* but in Hardyng's version, Joseph presented a shield with a red cross to Arviragus, the converted pagan king from whom he received the land on which Glastonbury Abbey was founded. Galahad later found this shield in Avalon/Glastonbury. In Arthurian literature, Galahad's arms do indeed have a red cross but, uniquely in Hardyng, and probably an invention of his own, Glastonbury becomes the place of origin for the cross of St George, patron of the English nation. According to Hardyng's chronicle, Galahad carried the shield during his Grail quest to the Holy Land, where he founded a chivalric order, the Sanke Roiall. Hardyng thus demystified the Grail and interpreted it as 'royal blood' (Sanke Roiall): he was a soldier rather than a scholar, with little interest in the Grail as either an orthodox or heterodox eucharistic symbol;[22] nor did he have the backing of a modern publicity machine, and never received what he considered adequate compensation for his hard work. His treatment is a reminder that responses to these romances have always varied. In interpreting *sang real* as 'royal blood' and associating Galahad with a chivalric order, he anticipated by several hundred years one of the most influential developments of popular Grail scholarship in the twentieth century. Another writer, Henry Lovelich, also used the *Vulgate Cycle* as the basis for an English translation, the *History of the Holy Grail*. It is a close translation of the source, which makes the deviations in relation to the Joseph story all the more interesting. Lovelich relocated the story of the red-cross shield to England and claimed that St Joseph was buried in 'the abbey of Glas that tyme was Cald/which Abbey of Glastyngbery now men hald'.[23]

A fully developed life of St Joseph of Arimathea is absent from the standard work on British saints compiled in the fourteenth century, and a life of this saint, based on John of Glastonbury's *Chronicle*, appeared only in Wynken de Worde's edition of saints' lives in 1516. Other traditions and relics were associated with him, such as a miraculous cross at Old St Paul's, and a possible grave site at Montacute near Glastonbury.[24] However, this is the legend of Joseph, Glastonbury and the Grail that has survived and indeed developed since the fifteenth century, attracting in its turn traditions about the Glastonbury thorn and Chalice Well. The last abbot, Richard Whiting, had been appointed by Cardinal Wolsey and was executed during Henry VIII's campaign to dissolve the monasteries. This period of disruption has provided fertile ground for legends, then and now. In the eighteenth century, the Glastonbury thorn was transformed into St Joseph's thorn planted on Werall (now Wearyall) Hill. Several modern traditions are even more closely related to the Grail myth. Among these is the transformation of St Bride's Well, in an area known as Beckery, into an ancient source of the divine feminine whose symbol is a cup.[25] The Chal(c)welle (i.e. Chalk-well) has become Chalice Well, the final resting place of the Grail. This well was not associated with medieval pilgrimage activity, but with the eighteenth-century vogue for 'drinking the waters'.[26] However, a Roman Catholic order bought the well and adjacent property in the 1880s, and their presence helped to establish a sense of longstanding religious history. It became a centre for theatre and the arts, and the property changed hands again when the Chalice Well Trust acquired it in 1959. Frederick Bligh Bond designed the cover for the well. The curving art nouveau plant designs combined with a yin–yang symbol mix eastern thinking and Celtic magic in a manner that has characterized the eclectic spirituality of the place since the late nineteenth century. This impression is reinforced by the recent popularity of the adjacent White Spring Café and its attendant goddess tree that now encloses an artesian well.[27]

MODERN GLASTONBURY

The remains of Glastonbury Abbey were handed over to the Bath and Wells Diocesan Trust in 1909, accompanied by a degree of fanfare and the belief that it might herald a new era. Indeed so it proved. The group of mystic visionaries who were attracted to the place had rather unusual ideas about how Glastonbury should embrace this new era, but, whatever their differences, the Grail was an integral part of their vision. Scholars of the late nineteenth century focused on the origin of the Grail in mythic tradition and on its development in medieval literary texts. Others, however, believed that the Grail was a real object whose survival would benefit contemporary society and, more importantly, alter the future. Nowhere is this stronger than in the traditions that developed at Glastonbury during the first half of the twentieth century. For some of these mystics and social visionaries Glastonbury itself was the setting; for others the vision had a global spiritual dimension. They had differing views of what the Grail was – a Christian relic, a powerful talisman, or an occult force – but they all held the conviction that it would transform society. Among them were Arthur Goodchild, who advocated the idea of the sacred feminine in British spirituality, Wellesley Tudor Pole, the founder of the Chalice Well Trust, the Reverend Lionel Smithett Lewis, a firm believer in Glastonbury as an early Christian site, Alice Buckton who first converted the area around the Tor into a spiritual centre, the architect Frederick Bligh Bond, the occult writer Dion Fortune, and the artist who wrote about the Glastonbury zodiac, Katherine Maltwood.

The Glastonbury myth had been developing since the twelfth century. It was not a sustained or continuous phenomenon, but rather a response to periods of need. In the late nineteenth century, there was a general concern with the spiritual dimension of life and in the global connections of different types of belief. The revival of interest in things medieval, and the rise of Christian spiritual renewal in Britain, also contributed to the esoteric and mystical development of modern Glastonbury as the successor to the pagan Avalon. The link between the two has become so well established that many writers feel there is little doubt that it was a pagan centre before it was Christian. Dion Fortune's *Avalon of the Heart* all too easily transmutes into an Avalon of pure fantasy. The prehistoric settlements in the region do not give clear indication of its sacred meaning, or indeed if it had one at all, and even the earliest monastic settlements are too late for many of the foundation legends that have been put forward. The scholarly work that has been done on Glastonbury's archaeology and its place in Arthurian literature does not support the idea either of a druid stronghold or a primitive Celtic Church with a developed nature-oriented cosmology. However, these traditions make Glastonbury a potent spiritual force, and where these exceed, or even conflict with, the limitations of archaeology, history or literary studies, the possibilities inherent in these undoubtedly attractive ideas can all too easily override the cautions of scholarly investigation.

One such idea is that Joseph of Arimathea established the first Christian foundation in Britain at Glastonbury soon after the Crucifixion; another is that it is 'the Isle of Avalon', the burial site of Arthur and Guinevere, and the third that it was an ancient goddess place, a centre for the sacred feminine. The thread linking these traditions is the story of the Holy Grail, which initially fused the apocryphal legend of Joseph of Arimathea with medieval Arthurian romances to provide an apparently historical narrative supporting the primacy of the British Church. Certain writers saw the Glastonbury myth as a metaphor for a newly emancipated and spiritually enlightened mankind in tune with nature. For them, myth had meaning for the inner evolution of mankind. Glastonbury became a place where they could relocate eastern spiritual ideas, as interpreted by the newly popular teachings of the theosophical movement, into a specifically western mystery tradition linking a distinctive Celtic paganism with a distinctive Christian heritage of Britain.

At the end of the nineteenth century, Dr John Goodchild, acting on a psychic vision, placed an antique glass bowl in a well on the outskirts of Glastonbury dedicated to St Bride. It was uncovered several years later by members of the Tudor Pole family and their friends. Goodchild, a wealthy Victorian doctor, acquired two glass curios which had (allegedly) been found bricked up in a building on the site of an early Christian settlement in Italy.[28] The doctor's antiquarian interests had a distinctly mystical cast which focused on the origins of spiritual life in the West. Goodchild's book *The Light of the West: An Account of the Dannite Settlement of Ireland*[29] presented a spiritual philosophy based on the existence of archetypal realities that reflected ideas about the power of the human psyche. He was influenced, at least indirectly, by the ideas of the Hermetic Society, an offshoot of the more orientalist Theosophical Society, which aimed at restoring the connections that had once existed between Christianity and classical mythology. *The Light of the West* suggested that the Tuatha Dé Danann of Irish mythology were in fact real inhabitants of ancient Ireland who, in the person of their High Queen, Mor Rigan, venerated the female aspect of the deity. These 'Dannite' people of Bride belonged to a world-wide mystery cult which anticipated Christianity. Although knowledge of the Mor Rigan as a real queen had vanished completely, according to Goodchild, and only the memory of a battlefield goddess remained, the veneration of the sacred feminine and the wisdom enshrined in its mystery religion had passed on to the figure of Bride (St Bridget). In Goodchild's spiritual world, the pagan female divinity symbolized by the cauldron (i.e. Grail) blended with the male principle of Christianity, the sword of Christ. The message of Christianity and its sacred relics was carried to Britain soon after the Crucifixion. Many Celtic priests were druids and all druidic and bardic wisdom in Britain derived from this mystery cult in which women had an esteemed place. The belief that Celtic paganism centred on the worship of the goddess and that the Celtic Church was sympathetic to paganism have become influential ideas in modern spirituality movements, especially at Glastonbury.

In effect, Goodchild located the context for the spiritual evolution of mankind, so central to the theosophical thinking of the day, in the West rather than the East. His interest in classical antiquity was coloured by his belief in the mystical nature of early Christianity. In Rome his interests centred on a fourth-century mosaic in the church of Santa Pudenziana, named after St Pudens, a Roman senator whose house formed the original core for the church. He was attracted to the antiquity of the site and inter-preted the inscriptions and the symbolism of the mosaic as evidence for the existence of a matriarchal, druidical Christianity with centres in Ireland, Rome, and most crucially for the development of the modern Holy Grail legend, Glastonbury. According to Goodchild, the Roman Church had been founded by the wife of the Roman senator, a woman brought up in the spirit of pagan Celtic feminism. He believed, even though he never called it the Holy Grail, that the cup purchased in Italy had played a crucial role at the beginning of Christianity and, in the coming age, it would redress the imbalance between masculine and feminine spirituality.[30] He accounted for the lack of evidence for this goddess-centred civilization by saying that the stories had to be disguised in the face of hostile Christianity (i.e. Latin Christianity). The idea of deliberate concealment in the face of a hostile force is a legend motif, which frequently reappears in the context of the

Grail legend. Indeed, many of Goodchild's ideas about coded pictorial images, *gematria*, hidden messages in ancient sources and controversial links between mythical and historical figures anticipate and influenced some of the ideas that have found their way into modern theories and novels.

Just before *The Light of the West* was published in 1898, Goodchild had another psychic experience. The cup (as he referred to it) he now regarded as directly linked with Jesus Christ, although he himself never said it was the Holy Grail and indeed resisted this identification. Following the impulses of his psychic vision, Goodchild concealed the object at St Bride's Well outside Glastonbury and waited for the prophesied rediscovery. It was a long time in coming. Several years later, he visited the site with his friend and fellow Celtic enthusiast, the Scottish writer William Sharp. They apparently found a 'token' left by a young Bristol woman, Katherine Tudor Pole, and in September 1906 the cup was rediscovered amid intense psychic activity. Katherine's brother, Wellesley Tudor Pole (1884–1968) experienced a vision of St Bride's Well and the cup, although the object was actually found by their friends, Janet and Christine Allen.[31] Goodchild never denied that the cup had been bought in Italy. However, he shared his thoughts about its sacredness with the Tudor Poles and their friends who, initially at least, believed that they had found the Holy Grail of legend.[32] Janet Allen recalled the deep feeling of reverence that she experienced when she realized 'that the Vessel we had brought to light was the Holy Graal'.[33] Wellesley Tudor Pole shared his beliefs about the object, a shallow glass bowl rather than a cup, in his correspondence with the novelist Rosamund Lehmann. They have a distinctly millennial cast, which, for him, 'prepared the Way for the Coming of the Holy Graal'. According to his recollections, his interest in Glastonbury had begun early: 'almost from the first year that I was there on pilgrimage, I have felt that a great find was about to take place, and I have dedicated myself to a search for the "Holy Graal"'.[34] He believed that the ancient wisdom of the Grail had been taught to initiates of ancient mystery religions, and the talisman had reappeared at a crisis point in the development of civilization.

Attempts were made to verify the date of the cup.[35] Experts were cautious, but not dismissive. Someone who did believe that this was the Grail itself, at least initially, was Archdeacon Basil Wilberforce, canon of Westminster Abbey, grandson of the anti-slavery campaigner and son of Samuel Wilberforce, who opposed Huxley in the Darwinian debate in Oxford. Wilberforce was a respected man and open to new ideas. Tudor Pole already knew Wilberforce, and when he brought the cup up to London the archdeacon introduced him to, among others, the American novelist Mark Twain and Sir William Crookes, scientist, specialist in glass and former president of the Society for Psychical Research. Both were impressed with Tudor Pole's sincerity, and Wilberforce arranged a more public gathering of specialists to which the press were invited. The occult historian and ritual magician A. E. Waite saw the object at the Wilberforce home in London. Although his own position was that the Grail was not a material object, he too was impressed.[36] Media reporting was relatively restrained, and it is perhaps a tribute to Wellesley Tudor Pole's character that it never got out of hand. Neville Meakin, a prominent member of the Stella Matutina Temple, an offshoot of the occult movement known as the Golden Dawn, approached Tudor Pole, claiming to be a descendent of King Arthur. This claim resonated strongly with the Pole family, who had adopted the name Tudor believing that they were related to Owen Tudor, grandfather of Henry VII, founder of the Tudor dynasty. Various psychics also made contact with Wellesley Tudor Pole, and one particular development foreshadows later Grail conspiracies. A psychic claimed that the Roman Catholic Church had bribed people to spy on Tudor Pole, because the Church was worried the discoveries at Glastonbury posed a threat to its power. As the details about when the object had been acquired and placed in St Bride's Well were well known, there was a potential conflict with the Glastonbury legend of the Grail coming to Britain soon after the Crucifixion. Neither the psychic experiences of the finders nor the investigations of the specialists ever really resolved this. As is so often the case with attempts to date relics of this kind, expert opinion never reached a consensus about the authenticity of the glass bowl. Opinion favoured a modern date, but just enough ambiguity remained, so that people who were inclined to believe could feel there was a possibility that the object was truly early and therefore might be real.

Through it all, Tudor Pole and his circle remained convinced of its sacredness. At least for the time it was in Bristol, they saw themselves as a sacred priesthood, or priestess-hood would perhaps be more accurate, witnessing the dawn of a new flowering of spirituality. For almost a decade, the glass bowl remained in a specially decorated oratory. Katherine Tudor Pole and the Allen sisters conducted private services and kept notes, but eventually the group went on to other things. Christine Allen married the Scottish painter John Duncan, but returned to be the first Warden of the Chalice Well Trust. Dr Goodchild died in 1914, and Janet Allen eventually converted to Catholicism. Wellesley Tudor Pole served in both world wars. His ongoing psychic experiences and his feelings about the horrors of war led him to urge a national observance of the 'silent minute', which still remains a mark of public respect. As time passed, he too became more cautious about identifying the object found in Bride's Well with the Holy

Grail, but he never gave up his belief in its power. Pole founded the Chalice Well Trust at Glastonbury, and after his death in 1968 the bowl was placed there, where it remains.[37]

The founding of the Chalice Well Trust involved another pioneer in the modern revival of Glastonbury, Alice Buckton (1867–1944).[38] She too had met Wellesley Tudor Pole through Archdeacon Wilberforce, and in 1912 she bought the Chalice Well site in order to establish a centre to foster theatre performance and the arts and crafts. She had a keen interest in children's education, in particular in developing their aesthetic sensibilities as an avenue to spiritual enlightenment, and it was her wish that the site become an international centre for healing and spiritual ease. After her death in 1944 her ashes were scattered on Glastonbury Tor, and another important local figure, the Reverend Lionel Smithett Lewis, conducted a memorial service for her at St John's Church, Glastonbury.[39] Alice Buxton's plans were never fully realized until the establishment of the Chalice Well Trust in 1959. However, her attitudes to the spiritual potential of art overlapped with those of Frederick Bligh Bond, an architect influenced by the principles of the Arts and Craft movement, who was closely associated with the archaeological excavations at Glastonbury. As we have seen, he it was who eventually designed the cover for the Chalice Well with interlocking symbols representing male and female spirituality.

Frederick Bligh Bond (1864–1945) was appointed to oversee the excavations at the abbey in 1908, under the auspices of the Somerset Archaeological and Natural History Society. Bond was a respected architect and, in one of those odd coincidences, a cousin of another scholar interested in the Grail, Sabine Baring Gould. He was also a member of the Society for Psychical Research and attempted to recover information about the abbey through psychic channelling, a technique still used by alternative investigators. Bond's channeller, 'John Alleyne', aka Captain John Allen Bartlett, was a fellow member of the Psychical Research Society. Through Bartlett, Bligh received messages via automatic writing from long dead monks of Glastonbury, known as the 'Watchers'. Bond insisted that a monk, one Johannes Bryant, helped him locate features of the abbey buildings. Bond never claimed he was communicating with the dead, rather that he was accessing a universal cultural memory.[40] This attitude was influenced by the work of Catherine Crowe, who in 1848 had published a fascinating and controversial study on the paranormal.[41] The sessions followed the strict principles laid down by the Society for Psychical Research, and there was no suggestion of fraud. However, the mixture of rudimentary Latin and 'olde' English did not convince the doubters when the results were eventually published. Bond discussed his ideas about *gematria* with Goodchild in the years before the latter's death in 1914. It was his belief that medieval church builders at Glastonbury had used occult *gematria*, allegedly the ancient science of sacred geometry based on hidden mathematical formulas in the Old Testament, and this echoed the techniques Goodchild had used to interpret the mosaic at Santa Pudenziana in Rome, but it did not endear him to archaeologists or Church officials, like the formidable Dean Robinson of Wells Cathedral. Bond was a good field archaeologist, although considerable information about the abbey was already known from existing records. In any case, it was the meanings he ascribed to what he found that dismayed his colleagues. The more specific he became about his ideas that Glastonbury was a 'cipher in stone' and had been built according to sacred geometry, the more difficulties he had with archaeologists and Church officials; and his own personality did not help matters.

However dramatic, Bligh Bond's assertions always remained within the context of Christianity, unlike those of Dr Goodchild and Dion Fortune, which blended Christianity with elements of Celtic paganism. Like many who embraced the principles of the Arts and Crafts movement, he had a romantic view of the medieval period, seeing it as a time when craftsman understood the dignity of their labour and Christianity was uncorrupted. Bond did not immediately connect the abbey with the Grail. Despite his friendship with Dr Goodchild, he was initially sceptical about the cup found at St Bride's.[42] However, secrets and spiritual rebirth were very much in the air at the time, and soon Bligh Bond's own spirit guide, 'Johannes', hinted at a treasure buried at Glastonbury. In 1918 Bond published *The Gate of Remembrance*, a mixture of archaeology, his theories about automatic writing, the spiritual capabilities of the human mind and predictions about global war.[43] Millennial tracts about the First World War were not unusual and not a few of them invoked the Holy Grail. The Anglo-Welsh writer Arthur Machen included such themes in short stories, whose technique of reportage caused them to be treated as real occurrences. The Scottish folklorist Lewis Spence wrote a tract that mingled his ideas about a mystery religion in Atlantis with the Holy Grail.[44] This mix of alternative science and archaeology unsurprisingly annoyed both Church and archaeological authorities, and Bond was sacked. Much later, when Bond was lecturing in America, 'Johannes' revealed through another psychic that the Holy Grail was part of the Glastonbury treasure. These automatic writings were subsequently published as *The Glastonbury Scripts*, but by then Bond's paranormal interests had marginalized him in relation to the ongoing excavations at Glastonbury.[45]

Dion Fortune's life also weaves into the tapestry of mythic Glastonbury.[46] Born Violet Mary Firth in Llandudno, Wales in 1890, she adopted the family motto 'Deo Non Fortuna' (By God, not by Chance) as her magical name when she joined the Hermetic Order of the Golden Dawn and soon became known as 'Dion Fortune'. Her interests focused on the perceived overlap between psychology and the occult with a strong dose of esoteric Christianity. The events she described in her books, such as *Avalon of the Heart*, were filtered through her esoteric vision and not intended as an accurate record. She called these seekers after truth the 'Avalonians', in contrast to the ordinary residents of Glastonbury. Although the term Avalonian had been used before to describe Glastonbury,[47] Fortune articulated a new identity for this very diverse group. Her work reflected the fusion of various influences in Glastonbury, more so perhaps than individual contributors such as Goodchild, the Allen sisters, the Tudor Pole family or Bligh Bond realized. She recalled a visit to Glastonbury Abbey with Frederick Bligh Bond and discussions about the cup at Bride's Well, but her aims were broader than just the Holy Grail legends.[48] For Fortune, Glastonbury was one of those places where the 'veil is thin'. Here, where the pagan Tor and its well stood near a Christian abbey, she found a resolution for her particular view of the occult world, the 'Fraternity of the Inner Light', a mystic society at Glastonbury aiming to reconcile native paganism with established Christianity. At the very least, Fortune provided a link between Glastonbury and other spiritual explorers like the Rosicrucians, the Freemasons, and the theosophists of the Order of the Golden Dawn.[49]

Speculations about the object from St Bride's Well and its relation to the Joseph legend are themes that thread their way through the development of Glastonbury as a modern pilgrimage centre. They are not, however, the whole story. A very vocal and articulate strand in this history viewed Glastonbury as an ancient Christian centre, and a tension between Christianity and notions of paganism permeated Glastonbury theories in the early part of the twentieth century. A booklet about the Nanteos cup in Wales had appeared only two years before Dr Goodchild's bowl was discovered at Bride's Well. Tudor Pole was dismissive of the Nanteos cup, while Arthur Machen had a decidedly negative view of Tudor Pole's 'Bristol Grail'.[50] The claim that Britain was one of the first nations to be converted to Christianity through the efforts of St Joseph of Arimathea was used to bolster the ecclesiastical influence of Britain during the fifteenth century. It also formed part of the Reformation narrative of British Christianity, offering a basis for *true*, that is, not papist, Christian worship in Britain. By the twentieth century, the stability of English Protestantism was well and truly assured, but the story of Joseph and the Grail, with the added millennial spin given it in the wake of the Reformation, was used to construct a new spiritual primacy. Once again, Glastonbury would provide a paradigm for modern British/Celtic Christianity, and this was exactly the aim of the Reverend Lionel Smithett Lewis, vicar of Glastonbury.

Interest in traditions relating to the Holy Grail had waned both in ecclesiastical and literary sources after the Reformation, but they had not entirely disappeared. During the seventeenth century, the Archbishop of Armagh, James Ussher (1581–1656) referred to the Holy Grail in his book, *Britannicarum ecclesiarum antiquitates*. At first glance a reference to an object associated with the Last Supper in fictional medieval romances is somewhat unexpected in a Protestant polemic.[51] Ussher's term as Archbishop of Armagh spanned the difficult transition period from the reign of Elizabeth I to the establishment of a Stuart monarchy. As a historian and a churchman in the immediate aftermath of the English Reformation, Ussher was aware of the need to create a credible historical case, as well as a sound theological one, to support the authority of Protestant Christianity in Britain. He was among the foremost scholars in the seventeenth century, when theology and the study of Greek and Roman classics still dominated academe. His association with the calculation of the date of creation from biblical references has left an undeserved impression of naivety: his aim was to expose the errors of Roman Catholicism, which was strong in Ireland, defend the Stuart dynasty and justify episcopal (not papal) succession – this explains his interest in the early history of Christianity in the British Isles. Ussher's historical studies were directed at strengthening the position of the Anglican Church against Roman Catholic claims to be 'the only true successor of the church of the apostolic Era'.[52] He adopted as his historical model the classical metaphor of successive ages spiralling downwards from ancient purity to modern corruption. History was essentially a record of decadence from a bygone golden age; the only escape was through the millennial transformation of the end of time. For Ussher, the first three centuries of early Christianity were a period of primitive purity, but increasing clerical power brought corruption. The light of true Christianity was, however, kept alive by groups like British Christians. Although no longer used as a model by modern historians, this devolutionary view of history coupled with millennialism, the idea that the past contains the key to saving the future, remain popular with revival movements.

The millennial tone of Ussher's work would have appealed to those Glastonbury writers who believed that the place was to be the centre for a vast spiritual transformation of mankind. Ussher published a treatise tracing the descent of the churches of the West from apostolic times, and in 1639 his study of the antiquities of the British churches, *Britannicarum ecclesiarum antiquitates,* appeared. It is this work that influenced Lionel Smithett Lewis, vicar of Glastonbury, and one of the most fervent believers in its special history. Ussher made clear that his sources regarded the Graal as a work of romance fiction, and his comments on Malory's description of the Sangreal in the 'fabled' *Acts of King Arthur* are cautious: 'qui Sangreal vocum hic usurpat ad Sanguinis realis'.[53] He used other terms, such as *catino* and *gradalis,* when describing the vessel used by Christ with his disciples.[54] Ussher was concerned with St Joseph's apostolic mission rather than the Grail. England had chosen the martial George as its patron saint, so there was room for developing the Joseph legend to balance out the missionary patron saints of other nations, such as Patrick, David, Denys, Andrew and James. Prophecies were attributed to Ussher soon after his death, and his reputation began to change from historian and Protestant cleric to that of prophet.[55] These prophecies were available in modern editions for Lewis's own research.[56]

Unlike many who flocked to Glastonbury at the turn of the twentieth century, the Reverend Lionel Smithett Lewis was firmly in the Christian world, albeit a very romantic one. He revived the Glastonbury thorn ceremony and wrote his own history of Christian Glastonbury. Lewis's defence of the legend of *St Joseph of Arimathea at Glastonbury* began as a sixteen-page pamphlet and went through six further editions and enlargements until 1955 when the last (seventh) edition appeared posthumously. During the intervening years, Lewis continued to research what he sincerely felt was evidence for Glastonbury's claim to be the earliest Christian foundation in Britain. His enthusiasm and energy were prodigious. Along with his own research efforts, he included all possible references to Glastonbury, Joseph and the Grail culled from chronicles, folklore and anecdotes recounted by friends and like-minded correspondents. The references taken from Archbishop Ussher in his quest for material supporting the primacy of Glastonbury are based on a translation by one such enthusiastic correspondent, and they are summarized in an Appendix to the last edition of his work.[57] His widow, who had a hand in this final version, regretted that it had not been possible to trace all the correspondents.[58] Lewis's enthusiasm was not, however, matched by clear critical judgement. He accepted almost any element of folklore as preserving an ancient practice and ignored the problem posed by late interpolations. To use a modern analogy, Lionel Smithett Lewis's work is not unlike an Internet chat room. People wrote to him with suggestions and anecdotes, which he included. Modern and ancient traditions appear cheek by jowl, so that the perspective of the book never rises above the shared perspective of the writer and his fellow enthusiasts.

Attitudes to Glastonbury, its history and its archaeology changed dramatically over the period of thirty years between the first pamphlet and the final edition, but Lewis's views remained constant. The publication of a booklet at the beginning of the twentieth century linked a medieval wooden bowl found at Strata Florida Abbey in Wales, called the Nanteos cup, with an ambiguous and evocative prophecy that 'the church shall claim its own'. Lewis favoured the Nanteos cup over Goodchild's glass bowl as the best candidate for the true Grail. In the 1930s he contacted the owner, Mrs Powell, about her 'Grail', and his correspondence with her is among the family papers held at the National Library of Wales. As part of his attempts to convince her to 'return' the 'Grail' to Glastonbury, he gave her a copy of Ussher's prophecies, which is a likely source for the prophecy attached to the Nanteos cup. He also put her in touch with Crookes, who examined Tudor Pole's glass bowl. What became of this contact is not really clear, since Lewis's request fell on deaf ears: Mrs Powell decided to keep her cup at Nanteos.[59]

A medieval French romance containing a tantalizing link with Glastonbury, *Perlesvaus*, was made available to an English reading public as the *High History of the Holy Grail* by the poet, artist and medieval enthusiast Sebastian Evans.[60] Evans (1823–1908) wrote poems with Arthurian and medieval themes, and his translations provided accessible texts for the ever-expanding audience for medieval literature.[61] His family included prominent antiquarian scholars, like his father,[62] his brother John Evans, President of the Royal Society of Antiquaries, and his nephew, Sir Arthur Evans, who excavated and restored the Minoan sites on Crete. Sebastian Evans wrote a treatise on the meaning of the Grail,[63] but his real relevance for the modern Grail legends lies in the way in which his *High History* affected others. His influential translation included the interesting colophon linking the romance with Glastonbury. 'The Latin from whence this History was drawn into Romance was taken in the isle of Avalon in a holy house of religion that standeth at the head of the Moors Adventurous, there where King Arthur and Queen Guinevere lie.'[64] The correspondence between Rosamund Lehmann and Wellesley Tudor Pole referred to a 'Third Man' whose appearance heralded the spiritual resurgence that was anticipated by finding the glass object at St Bride's Well.[65] This figure was almost certainly influenced by the expected Good Knight in the medieval *Perlesvaus* romance. In Terry Gilliam's fantasy film *The Fisher King* (1991), the character of Parry, a traumatized medieval history professor (played by Robin Williams), shows the cynical Lucas (played by Jeff Bridges) a copy of a book, *The High History of the Holy Graal*, which reveals the location of the Grail at the home of a New York millionaire. Evans's book provided the theosophist and artist Katherine Maltwood with the 'Ariadne's thread' that led her through the Glastonbury zodiac.[66] While working on illustrations inspired by Sebastian Evans's translation of the *High History of the Holy Grail* in the summer of 1929 she had a sudden insight that Glastonbury itself was the subject of the Grail story. The colophon referred to a possible manuscript source in the abbey library, not to the origin of the romance episodes themselves, but Maltwood and others interpreted it in this way.[67] Maltwood projected the Grail story so completely on to the physical landscape of Glastonbury that she believed an ancient zodiac was imprinted on the land. She described this zodiac in theosophical terms, linking it with eastern civilizations and the prospect of evolution into a higher plane. She never made it clear who constructed these effigies; rather, she implied that they were natural, a spontaneous creation of the sacredness of Glastonbury itself.[68] Her friend, the Welsh scholar, Mary Williams, expanded this, identifying the Tor itself as the Grail.[69]

MEDIEVAL SOURCES

In her reliance on Evans's translation, Katherine Maltwood forged a new, but probably unwitting, link between the medieval sources and their modern interpretation. Details in a colophon to one of the *Perlesvaus* manuscripts may provide a real, if somewhat tangential link, with Glastonbury.[70] The colophon states that the Latin text from which the romance was taken came from a holy religious house on the 'isle of Avalon' and refers to the burial site of King Arthur and his queen.[71] In the romance, Lancelot visits the Lady Chapel at Glastonbury after he learns that Guinevere has been buried near the grave of Arthur's murdered son, and that a grave for Arthur has also been prepared there. The colophon and details of Lancelot's pilgrimage to Guinevere's grave imply knowledge of the finding of two graves at Glastonbury in 1191. In another episode in *Perlesvaus*, a squire robs a chapel in a dream and awakes with a fatal stab wound from the dream knight who guards the dream chapel. A Latin version of this adventure exists in a fourteenth-century anthology about the deeds of King Arthur compiled at Glastonbury, and another version of the same story was included in the mid-fourteenth-century chronicle of John of Glastonbury.[72] The Shropshire author of the late thirteenth-century *Romance of Fouke fitz Waryn* also added this story from the *Perlesvaus* romance. Although these intriguing connections do not support the idea of an actual Grail at Glastonbury, the abbey may have owned a copy of the *Perlesvaus* romance. Fragments of a text of the romance have been found at nearby Wells Cathedral.[73] Grail scholars have attempted to resolve these local connections, although no consensus has yet emerged. One suggestion is that Robert de Boron based his story on a Glastonbury source or that the *Perlesvaus* romance originated in Glastonbury. Mary Williams, a Welsh-speaking scholar and one of the earliest to compare the French and Welsh romances, went so far as to identify the author of *Perlesvaus* as a Welshman. While this is unlikely, Glamorgan scribes had access to Glastonbury materials and exemplar, since the Welsh translation of *Perlesvaus* may have come from there.[74]

Geoffrey of Monmouth described an otherworldly place which he called *insula Auallonis* and *insula pomorum* in *Historia Regum Britanniae* and *Vita Merlini* respectively, although he did not equate Avalon directly with Glastonbury. However, the place has been associated with ideas about a Celtic otherworld, and this identification is central to assumptions about its sacredness. It provides a link to a magic Celtic other world, and this reinforces the popular idea that the source of Arthurian traditions, no matter how late, can be grounded in the world of Celtic myth. The ability to link Glastonbury with an older Welsh (i.e., British Celtic) concept of a benevolent other world presided over by a health-giving female presence is important for many Grail theories, which see Glastonbury as a source of ancient spirituality. Such suggestions have been made in the confident assumption that cultures with a Celtic base, like that of Wales, were sufficiently conservative for ancient strata to remain uncontaminated by outside influences.

Connections with a Celtic other world presided over by a healing, supernatural female are not as clear as those looking for ancient meanings might once have assumed. The process by which these mythic traditions came to be fixed in early Welsh tradition, and later transmitted to the courtly romance culture of Anglo-Norman France and beyond, is necessarily full of speculation, and needs to take account of the fact that Wales was a far from inward-looking Celtic society. The dates of Welsh manuscripts containing vernacular Arthurian material are comparatively late, and Arthurian traditions from other sources, notably French romance, were incorporated into Welsh. There is a surprising dearth of references to *Ynys Afallach* and *Ynys Wydrin* in earlier native Welsh literature, and those existing references may be dependent on written rather than oral sources. The name 'Glastonbury' was borrowed into Welsh as *Glasynbri*,[75] and refers specifically to the abbey. The other two names, *Ynys Wydrin* (the island of glass), *Ynys Afallach* (the island of apples), may contain trace references to an earlier British Celtic site. Afallach appears as a personal name in Welsh genealogies and in a collection of Welsh lore known as *The Triads of the Island of Britain*.[76] This personal name is a likely origin for Avalon (Lat. *Auallonus*), and provided Geoffrey of Monmouth with the source for *insula auallonis* in his twelfth-century *Historia Regum Britanniae*. 'Ynys Afallach' could mean either 'Afallach's island' or 'the island of apples', and it appears in the *Brutiau*, thirteenth-century translations of Geoffrey's *Historia*, in this context. Gerald of Wales discussed the origins for Glastonbury as part of his account of the finding of Arthur's grave. He identified *insula Auallonis* with Glastonbury, and derived the name from the glassy blue colour of the river. According to Gerald, *glas* in English equates with *gwydyr* in Welsh, hence *Ynys Wydrin* (the island of glass). However, *Ynys Wydrin* is a rare occurrence in Welsh vernacular texts and may actually have been invented to explain the English name rather than being an older Welsh source for it.[77] The terms may have been imported into Welsh tradition rather than derived from it. Certainly the lack of examples before the influential works of Gerald of Wales and Geoffrey of Monmouth underlines the need for caution regarding the early origins of native Welsh Arthurian traditions.[78]

Whether a historical Joseph of Arimathea ever came along the road to Glastonbury is frankly unlikely, yet the romances present just such a story. Robert de Boron's work incorporated the legend that Joseph, a favoured disciple and a relative of Christ, took the Holy Grail westwards. This tradition was in circulation by the end of the twelfth century, and, within a hundred years, it was further developed in the *Vulgate Cycle*. This more elaborate version, claiming to come direct from Christ himself, described how Joseph collected the blood that flowed from Christ's wounds in a vessel known as the Grail and how Joseph's family left the Holy Land a few years after the Crucifixion and founded a Christian community in Britain.

Medieval writers used the Grail romances to bring Joseph to Glastonbury, but never asserted that he brought the Grail. Indeed the Holy Grail element was largely left out as belonging to fiction.[79] Finally, John of Glastonbury linked Joseph, the Grail bearer in the romances, with traditions of St Joseph at Glastonbury by adapting the story claiming that Joseph brought two vessels, one containing the blood, the other the sweat of Christ. This transformed the Grail into a more plausible relic of the Holy Blood. Its real impact as history was felt much later, in the fifteenth and sixteenth centuries, when the legend was embellished once again and Joseph was presented as an early missionary who established Christianity in Britain soon after the death of Christ. The claim that Britain was one of the first nations to be converted to Christianity through the efforts of St Joseph of Arimathea was used to bolster the ecclesiastical prestige of the British Church after the Reformation. Later (sixteenth- to eighteenth-century) references to the St Joseph legend and Glastonbury's position as the earliest centre of Christianity occasionally mention objects that Joseph brought with him, but interest in the Grail as it is described in the romances, namely an object associated with knightly quests, became a feature in the traditions surrounding Glastonbury only as part of a more general revival of interest in all things Arthurian in the nineteenth century.

The road to Glastonbury is crowded with interesting people such as William of Malmesbury, who wrote the first account of its antiquities, Gerald of Wales, who described the finding of Arthur's grave, and John of Glastonbury, who wrote up the legends of St Joseph. Then there are the abbots of this powerful religious foundation, men like Beere, Chinnock and Whiting, and ambitious English kings, like Henry II and Edward III, who encouraged the cult of St Joseph and who advanced the prestige of the abbey. The revival of the abbey's importance in modern times is full of equally interesting people with a quite different agenda. Lionel Smithett Lewis comes closest perhaps to the Christian spirit of the medieval world, while Dion Fortune and Alice Buckton wanted to establish a spiritual centre with universal relevance. Dr Goodchild, the Tudor Pole family and their friends were directly concerned with the Grail itself, while Frederick Bligh Bond excavated and restored the abbey buildings and attempted to look back into its intangible heritage. Many people have come to Glastonbury, and the process is ongoing. Ideas about the Grail are mystical, idiosyncratic and often very complex. No consensus was ever reached about its meaning, but the picture is nevertheless an intimate one full of actual visits to the place and frequent interchange of ideas at a personal level. In the twentieth century, however, with the advent of mass marketing and the Internet, Grail theories moved away from Glastonbury and the purely local interests of the relic legends to become global.

CHAPTER 3

The Grail in Welsh Tradition

'SUDDENLY HE COULD see two lads entering the hall, and from the hall they proceeded to a chamber, carrying a spear of huge proportions, with three streams of blood running from its socket to the floor. When they all saw the lads coming in this way, they all began weeping and wailing so that it was not easy for anyone to endure it. The man did not explain to Peredur what that was, nor did Peredur ask him about it. After a short silence, suddenly two maidens entered with a large salver between them, and a man's head on the salver and much blood around the head. And then they all shrieked and wailed so that it was not easy for anyone to stay in the same building. At last they stopped, and remained sitting as long as it pleased them, and drank. After that a chamber was prepared for Peredur, and they went to sleep.'[1]

This is the moment that Peredur, the aspiring young hero from the wilds of Wales, sees the mysterious procession so often identified with the Grail. The text of the Welsh tale, *Peredur vab Efrawg*, is included in the collection of medieval Welsh tales known as the *Mabinogion*.[2] This is the only description of the Grail procession in a Celtic language not translated from a French romance. That the Grail originated in the mythological traditions of the Celts has been one of the most potent driving forces in our understanding and interpretation of the medieval romances. A striking feature of this description is that it does not use the word 'Grail' (Welsh *graal*), but a very ordinary word, *disgyl*. The story of the Holy Grail in Britain often reflects an anachronistic belief in its importance. The fusion of traditions about Arthur, St Joseph of Arimathea and Glastonbury began in the twelfth century and continues to the present day. However, during the nineteenth century, the Celts, and of course this included the Welsh, became an important element in an emerging British identity, and at this time the first florescence of Grail scholarship connected Celtic myth with the Grail quest.

Revival of interest in the medieval narratives of Wales owes a great debt to Lady Charlotte Guest (1812–95), who translated the tales known as the *Mabinogion*. In the dedication addressed to her sons, she expressed the hope that these 'venerable relics of ancient lore' would imbue them with a 'chivalric and exalted sense of honour and fervent patriotism'.[3] Guest presented the tales as part of an ancient tradition whose high moral tone could provide an example for the modern world.[4] Her romantic attitude to chivalry as a moral code reflected both the growing Victorian confidence in itself and its British national heritage, and a patriotic fervour towards Welsh antiquity. Her approach also anticipated something of the comparative method adopted by later evolutionary folklorists and anthropologists. She identified 'native' *Mabinogion* tales that portrayed the heroic actions of the war-bands of early British and Welsh kingdoms. These tales had linear plots that were close to oral storytelling. However, the Welsh Arthurian romances, which included *The Story of Peredur Son of Efrawg*, originated as heroic native Welsh tales, but subsequently acquired the trappings of courtly love and knightly adventures from Norman culture.[5] The belief that Arthurian romance could be explained in terms of earlier, more primitive, narratives was to dominate Grail studies in the decades after Guest's translation. At the beginning of the twentieth century, Alfred Nutt, another prominent figure in Celtic and folklore studies, published his own introduction to her translation, which reinforced the idea that Arthurian romances were to be understood as developments of earlier native storytelling.[6]

Peredur's tale begins in a wild forest where he lives with his mother, who hopes to protect him from the world of chivalry that destroyed her husband and other sons. The untutored boy is strong and adventurous, swift enough to herd wild animals among the domesticated ones, but too gauche to know the difference. Inevitably he meets some knights and burns with the desire to emulate them. As he leaves his mother's care, she gives him some advice which, in his bumptious naivety, he takes too literally. He arrives at Arthur's court where he is both praised and taunted. He kills a rogue knight with his javelin and clothes himself in the armour of his defeated foe, thus taking on the appearance at least of knighthood.

Like all romance heroes Peredur embarks on a series of adventures. He visits the castle of an unknown uncle, who advises him on knightly restraint. Just as the impulsive Peredur followed his mother's advice too literally, he reacts to his uncle's advice too carefully. He meets a man fishing by a lake and dines with him in a castle. With his immense strength and knightly potential, Peredur strikes a sword against an iron column. On the third stroke, the sword fails to repair itself, and his uncle declares that Peredur has not yet acquired his full strength. Later he witnesses a mysterious procession: two youths carry a bleeding lance, while all lament; but Peredur asks no questions. Two maidens bring a salver with a bloody head and all lament, but again Peredur asks no questions. Next day Peredur's sister berates him for his silence. The witches of Caer Loyw complete his martial education, before he eventually returns to Arthur's court. From there he sets out on a hunt and further adventures full of marvels – noxious beasts, self-operating game boards, supernatural opponents, and a beautiful woman, the Empress of Constantinople, with whom he lives for fourteen years. This is where the narrative ends in the shorter version of the tale. However, elsewhere, Peredur has further adventures. These bring him back to the Castle of Wonders, where the meaning of the mysterious procession is explained to the young hero, who is now a worthy knight. The head belonged to his cousin, murdered by the witches of Caer Loyw, and the tale concludes with the defeat of the witches.

The bloody head in the salver and the bleeding lance in the procession at the Castle of Wonders differ from other versions of the Grail; if indeed this can be considered a Grail procession at all. The bloody head on its salver is explained as a survival of a pagan Celtic cult of the head, and the procession in the Welsh romance has often been presented as an ancient form of the story. The archaeologist Anne Ross argued that a head cult was a central feature of Celtic religion. Despite the numerous and often striking depictions of heads in Celtic contexts, the pervasiveness of such a cult is not without its critics.[7] The incident in *Peredur* could, for example, be interpreted as a reference to the story of John the Baptist. The sword used to behead this saint is one of the objects sought in other Grail romances.[8] Peredur does not actually seek the Grail. Vengeance seems to be the dominant theme of the tale. This is accomplished when Peredur avenges his uncle's death by killing the witches of Caer Loyw (Gloucester). Nevertheless, the link between the bloody head on its salver and the Grail story is of long standing in Grail criticism, and changing critical perspectives on *Peredur* among Welsh scholars reflect in microcosm changing perspectives on the Grail itself.

Peredur vab Efrawg is one of the *Tair rhamant* (lit. three romances) included in the *Mabinogion*. The fact that these tales are, and probably always will remain, linked together says something about the continued strength of our perceptions of Arthurian literature. The existence of the Peredur tale was an important element in constructing a Celtic source for the Grail story, as it apparently provided the culmination for a series of linked motifs scattered throughout other *Mabinogion* tales. These include episodes from the tale of *Branwen*; the life-giving cauldron of regeneration (*peir dadeni*), the fatal wounding of Bendigeidfran with a spear, and the appearance of his head at two otherworld feasts. In the tale of *Manawydan*, Rhiannon and her son are trapped in the otherworld after touching a golden bowl, and the kingdom is laid waste. Vessels providing abundant food are among the objects sought for the wedding of *Culhwch and Olwen*. In *Lludd and Llefelys*, a horrific scream every May Day causes barrenness throughout the land. In *Owein or the Lady of the Well*, the hero wins a bride and a kingdom after he defeats an armed warrior who appears when water is poured from a bowl at a magic well. Although these motifs fulfil a variety of functions in the medieval tales, theories about Celtic origin subordinate them within the Grail story as late reflections of an ancient myth. This myth concerned a magic cauldron in the gift of a goddess of sovereignty who bestowed it on a hero. Abundance and fertility flowed from the successful union of the hero and the goddess; failure resulted in barrenness. For scholars convinced that the Grail had a Celtic origin, the Welsh tale of Peredur provided a middle stage for the transmission of an Irish Celtic myth through medieval Welsh tradition to the Breton poets who inspired the French Grail romances.

Sir John Rhŷs's *Studies in the Arthurian Legend* was published in 1891, only three years after Alfred Nutt's major study on the origins of the Grail texts. Rhŷs (1840–1915) was the first professor of Celtic at Jesus College, Oxford University and, like Nutt, interested in the comparatively new discipline of folklore studies.[9] Rhŷs's intention was to illuminate the ancient culture of Wales, both for the Welsh themselves and for a wider audience, and his book was based on lectures delivered under the aegis of the Hibbert Foundation, a body with a commitment to research of an improving nature. Although Rhŷs is better known for his linguistic studies, his work on folklore, Celtic religion and Arthurian literature influenced fellow Celtic scholars and folklorists. In this context he is part of the history of the Grail in Wales. He noted several prototypes for the Grail motif in Welsh narrative tradition, such as the cauldron of Diwrnach and Mwys Gwyddno in *Culhwch and Olwen*, and he compared the wasteland in the Grail romances with the enchantment of Dyfed in the *Manawydan* tale.[10] He also compared the bloody head and bleeding lance in *Peredur* with Bendigeidfran's spear wound and severed head, and noted parallels between the Grail procession and the otherworld feasts described in the *Four Branches of the Mabinogi*. Such prototypes and comparisons have become commonplaces in discussions of Celtic origins. In his Hibbert lectures, Rhŷs used the solar mythological theories of his Oxford colleague Max Müller, but by the time *Studies in the Arthurian Legend* appeared, Rhŷs acknowledged that these ideas were becoming obsolete.[11] He compared Celtic religion, Arthurian tradition and

Welsh mythology with that of other cultures and stressed their significance for the intellectual and spiritual evolution of the Welsh people. This, as the folklorist Sidney Hartland noted, was rather more important than his use of Max Müller's fading ideas on solar mythology.[12] Charles Squire quoted him extensively in his still popular retelling of Celtic legends, *Mythology of the British Isles*. Lewis Spence also used his ideas extensively.[13] Through writers like these, Rhŷs's work continues to influence popular scholarship.

If Rhŷs touched only lightly on the subject of Peredur and the Grail, Mary Williams looked at the sources for this romance and its relation to Chrétien's *Perceval* in depth. Mary Williams (1883–1977), a native Welsh speaker, lectured in French at King's College London and was President of the Folklore Society in the 1960s.[14] Her work focused on the idea that the Grail, despite its pagan links with an agricultural myth centred on the return of vegetation, was essentially a Christian Celtic symbol derived from a powerful religious talisman associated with an early Celtic saint.[15] Like her friend Jessie Weston, Williams edited and analysed medieval Grail romances and looked for meaning in ancient sources outside the romances themselves. Both Weston and Williams were influenced by Alfred Nutt's research in folklore and Celtic tradition and by the anthropological theories of James Frazer's *Golden Bough*. Like so many of her contemporaries, Williams attempted to apply a unifying theory of anthropology to the textual study of Arthurian literature and, at the same time, place it within the framework of mystical experience. She looked for evidence of agricultural ritual and the 'Dying God' myth in *Peredur,* and substantiated her theories about the ritual basis for this romance with Welsh literature and folklore.[16] She became interested later in life in Katherine Maltwood's ideas about a Glastonbury zodiac,[17] but she shares with the Anglo-Welsh writer, Arthur Machen, the assumption of a Celtic talisman behind the Grail.

The role of the *Peredur* romance in the development of the Grail legend can never be seen only in terms of Welsh academic criticism. Many scholars have examined the text[18] and have sought to clarify the relationship between the Welsh text and Chrétien's romance.[19] The seeming inconsistencies between the Welsh tale and its continental analogues have been explained as a failure on the part of successive redactors to understand the underlying myth.[20] More recently, however, attention has moved away from hypothetical reconstructions to focus on the rich storytelling milieu to which the redactors had access, or on cultural differences between the world of the Welsh *Peredur* and Chrétien's French *Perceval*.[21] As one critic points out, 'before postulating what the tale might have been, one must first determine what it actually is'.[22] The central character, Peredur, was a hero of the Old North, one of the historical and pseudo-historical figures who resisted the Saxon expansion during the sixth and seventh centuries and became legendary figures in medieval Welsh narrative. Although dating such material involves speculation, some traditions attached to Peredur, for example his contact with powerful female figures like the Empress of Christnogyl, may date from this early period. The name, Perceval, parallels Peredur, although they are not really cognate,[23] and despite the similarities between *Peredur* and Chrétien's Grail romance, the plot is handled differently.[24] The Welsh *Peredur* owes much to tales of marvels and wonders, and indeed to other tales in the *Mabinogion* such as *Owein, Gereint, Manawydan, Lludd, Macsen* and *Rhonabwy*. The action takes place on another plane, what is usually called the other world, and only once resolution is achieved does the action return to reality. This type of resolution is not characteristic of the other Grail romances.[25]

Some problems can be resolved by comparing the existing texts of *Peredur*.[26] Two end with Peredur at the court of the Empress of Constantinople and may represent a complete version of the tale. The longer version, copied as part of the *Mabinogion* in both *The White Book of Rydderch* and the *The Red Book of Hergest*, contains the hero's *enfance*, his arrival at Arthur's court, adventures such as the procession at the Castle of Wonders and a sojourn with the Empress of Constantinople. This longer version ends with the death of the witches after Peredur returns to the Castle of Wonders to learn the significance of the mysterious events he witnessed earlier. It is unclear which of these is the original, but if the return to the Castle of Wonders is integral to the logic of the story, then this has implications for the relationship between *Peredur* and Chrétien's text and its *Continuations* and for any speculation about the Grail as a Celtic myth.[27] Glenys Goetinck, for example, has interpreted the procession at the Castle of Wonders as the precursor of Chrétien's *graal*.[28] This retains the Celtic resonance of earlier commentaries by presenting the tale as the development of a myth concerned with kingship and agricultural fertility in which a ruler unites with a goddess of sovereignty who personifies his land. This reconstruction varies considerably from the existing texts. For her the original meaning behind the bloody head on its salver is Peredur's obligation to succeed to the sacred kingship by avenging his father, even though the texts identify the head as his cousin. Despite problems with the existence of a pagan sovereignty myth in so late a text, there may be some support for a sovereignty motif as a metaphor for kingship.[29] One possibility is the role of the Loathly Lady. Only the rightful heir recognizes her as desirable, and his acceptance transforms her. She in turn offers him liquid from a drinking vessel. This drinking vessel with its symbolic liquid is often identified with the Grail. Goetinck suggests that the *morwyn du* (black maiden) in *Peredur* represents sovereignty as 'Loathly Lady', while the empress represents her as goddess.[30] Professor Mary Williams also regarded the episodes involving the empress as the closest to Welsh/Celtic sources.[31]

It is hardly surprising that the interplay of French and Welsh elements in *Peredur* has attracted those interested in the Grail and its legends. While there is still no consensus on the exact relationship between this tale and medieval Grail romances composed elsewhere in Europe, translations and adaptations based on French sources provide evidence for interest in Grail literature in Wales. The Norman settlement of Wales forged close contacts between Wales and the Continent throughout the medieval period. The Glamorgan scribe Hywal Fychan undertook a Welsh translation of the Grail material for an important patron, Hopcyn ap Thomas, about 1400. Contemporary sources mention Hopcyn ap Thomas's copy of *Y Seint Greal*, so called because of a colophon which reads *ystoryaeu seint greal*.[32] The text combined two thirteenth-century French prose romances, *La Queste del Saint Graal* and *Perlesvaus*. The scribe identified himself clearly as a translator (*trossyawdyr*). He used Welsh forms for the names and adapted the romances for a Welsh audience. Consequently there is more emphasis on storytelling and less concern with concepts of *courtoisie* and chivalry.[33]

There are a handful of other references to the Grail in Welsh poetry. Dafydd Llwyd, a fifteenth-century poet, writes of wandering as if in search of the *Greal*.[34] Collections such as the *Triads of the Isle of Britain* (*Trioedd Ynys Prydein*) and *The Thirteen Treasures of the Island of Britain* indicate the way native and foreign, written and oral material came together in the narrative tradition of medieval Wales, and they were an important source for Welsh bards and storytellers. The anonymous compiler of one *Trioedd* manuscript evidently had a particular interest in ecclesiastical legend and incorporated several references to the Grail legend. One triad added the phrase '*Ystorya y Greal*' to the knights who won the Grail, while Joseph of Arimathea replaced an earlier figure as the third of the Kindred of Saints. According to the Welsh *Y Seint Greal*, Lancelot, Bors, Galahad and Perceval were descendants of Joseph, and thus part of his kindred.[35] Mention of Joseph points inevitably to Glastonbury where connections with the Grail were being strengthened in the late medieval period. Wales did not claim the Holy Grail among its relics until much later, and when it did other legends had replaced Arthur and his knights.

NANTEOS AND HAWKSTONE:
GRAILS AT THE MANOR HOUSE

The oldest of the Welsh Grails is a partially damaged wooden medieval bowl known as the Nanteos cup. This object was owned by the Powell family who lived on the Nanteos estate just outside Aberystwyth in Cardiganshire (Dyfed). Towards the end of the nineteenth century, it was exhibited at St David's College, Lampeter, at a meeting of the Cambrian Archaeological Society. About that time a drawing and a description of the cup appeared in the journal *Archaeologia Cambrensis*. It already had a reputation for healing, especially as a cure for post-partum bleeding. Borrowers left a pledge to be redeemed when the cup was returned. The Holy Grail legend was added only at the beginning of the twentieth century. Nanteos was sold in 1968 and has changed hands several times since, but the descendants of the original family continued to make the cup available to those who request it.

Early evidence for a relic at Nanteos is lacking. Samuel Rush Meyrick does not mention it among the antiquities of Cardiganshire in his early nineteenth-century survey of that county.[36] According to later legend, the relic was smuggled out of Glastonbury by seven monks at the moment Thomas Cromwell, Henry VIII's minister, and his men attacked the abbey. Further traditions claimed that the monks secretly carried the precious relic to Strata Florida Abbey in Cardiganshire. Each monk passed on the cup, until the last survivor gave it into the keeping of the new owners of the abbey, the Stedman family. They were to guard it, 'until the Church should claim its own'. Through marriage, the custody of the cup passed into the hands of the Powells and was taken to Nanteos, their new house. However, there is no mention of the cup in any will or inventory of Stedman or Powell possessions.

By the beginning of the twentieth century, a synthesis of popular legends linked the Nanteos cup to the Holy Grail. The Tudor historian John Stow documented the changing ecclesiastical world at the time of Henry VIII. His account contains more than a hint of nostalgia for the past, and the references to despoiled monasteries, fleeing monks and the fate of famous relics furnish an ideal background for the creation of a legend about a mysterious object.[37] The monks who narrowly escaped just as the king's henchmen entered the monastery are appropriate as legendary survivors of a disaster that disrupted the calm of monastic life and accord well with the popular idea of Henry VIII as a despoiler of monasteries. The drama is underscored as each monk hands on responsibility to a companion, until the last monk entrusts the relic into the keeping of a secular protector. A few monks *were* evidently pensioned off and continued to live at Strata Florida after the Dissolution, and such details provide apparent historical validation for legendary events. Survivors of disasters are part of 'epic of defeat' stories as different as Noah's Ark and King Arthur's final battle. They derive their impact from the pathos of tragedy and loss transformed by the expectation of renewal.[38] Although the Stedman family cannot be placed at Strata Florida until some time after the Dissolution, traditions quickly became associated with ruined or deserted monastic sites. The guardian monks in the Nanteos legend who pass on the secret story may have been adapted from a Glastonbury source about two monks guarding the secret of St Dunstan's burial place.

A more localized version of the Nanteos cup legend suggests that, in an attempt to exploit the lucrative pilgrim trade, the monks of the Cistercian Abbey at Strata Florida acquired a '*phiol*' (vial) known as the *Cwpan Nanteos*. This version transforms Bedd Taliesin, a Bronze Age tumulus associated with a Welsh poet/magician figure, into a shelter for pilgrims. In another variant, a monk was out visiting the sick when the king's men descended on Glastonbury and brought the Grail to Strata Florida. Unfortunately, there are no historical records of pilgrims or of a relic at Strata Florida, despite a romantic account, which declares that the Nanteos cup had its primary 'sphere of influence' in Cardiganshire.[39] The Nanteos story tells us little about actual history, but it creates an intense and emotional view of the past localized in Cardiganshire.

Traditions about cures in this area (comprising part of Cardiganshire and Carmarthenshire, now Dyfed) also reflect the social and economic interplay between local people and dominant gentry families during the nineteenth and twentieth centuries. The circumstances by which the Stedman family acquired Strata Florida are embellished with a charming story that claims the first Stedman was the son of the Duke of Arabia, a friend to Richard the Lionheart, and a crusader who was banished to Wales.[40] The murky period of the Crusades provides an ideal setting for the transfer of relics to Europe. Local historians, keen to give their local worthies the right pedigree, turned the most tenuous traditions into elaborate crusader histories. This dramatic cliché is a mainstay of the modern Grail legend, and there is still an echo of this in Nanteos traditions about a lathe-turned, olivewood cup made in Syria at the dawn of the Christian era. Many legends about the relics of the Shroud of Turin, and the spear of Longinus, also involve the Crusades. Interest in such relics was fostered by archaeological investigation during the 1930s. This was partly due to the popularity of alternative religion and partly to a scholarly interest in possible links between Christian sacraments and pagan rituals. The Nanteos cup material touches on other Grail candidates, but a correspondent assured Mrs Powell that hers is the real 'National Treasure'.[41]

George Powell of Nanteos exhibited the object for the first time at a Cambrian Archaeological Society meeting held at St David's College, Lampeter, in 1878. The description in *Archaeologia Cambrensis* combined tradition with archaeological speculation. Academic journals played an important role in the development of legends. The cup, allegedly made from the wood of the True Cross, was already known for its healing powers 'over a wide district of Carmarthenshire and Cardiganshire'.[42] John Worthington Smith's drawing shows a damaged object with two metal staples holding it together and no metal rim. He also drew the sketches for the earliest Strata Florida excavations, which suggests that the cup was among the excavation finds.[43] The damaged state of the cup has been explained by yet another traditional motif, namely that pilgrims bit off pieces as personal relics. Even before the Grail motif was introduced, legend elements were already established. A local writer recalled an occasion when the cup was placed on the site of the high altar at Strata Florida Abbey. Mysteriously, the rain stopped and a shaft of sunlight illuminated the cup. The bad weather returned as soon as the object was put away.[44]

The person most closely associated with the Nanteos Grail legend was Mrs Margaret Powell, who presided over a declining estate after the deaths of her son, in 1918, and her husband, in 1930. Mrs Powell encouraged the tradition, but was reluctant for specific claims to appear in print. The earliest and most elaborate description of the Nanteos cup as Holy Grail, with thinly disguised references to the owner and the house, appeared in a 1905 pamphlet entitled *Sought and Found*.[45] Letters among the Powell family papers in the National Library of Wales, Aberystwyth, illustrate in detail how the Nanteos cup absorbed traditions about the Holy Grail. On one occasion, the family solicitor expressed his concern that interest in the cup might affect the family's parlous financial state. Mrs Powell took the line that the family were custodians not owners of the cup, which is why it never appeared in any will or property inventory. A local vicar wrote a very poignant letter requesting permission for a mother and her epileptic child to visit Nanteos. The letter did not express belief in the cup's efficacy, so much as the feeling that the mother would derive comfort from the visit. The longest and most colourful exchange of letters occurred in 1938–40 between Mrs Powell and the Reverend Lionel Smithett Lewis, Vicar of Glastonbury. Lewis believed passionately in the legend of St Joseph and tried to establish Glastonbury as the site of a 'National Church' in Britain. He seems genuinely to have believed that the Nanteos cup was the

Holy Grail, and he recommended both the work of Archbishop James Ussher, a writer who was central to Lewis's own views, and A. E. Waite's *Hidden Church of the Holy Grail* to Mrs Powell. He was so horrified by the story about pilgrims biting off souvenirs that he urged her never to lend out so precious a relic again. He too contributed to the growing legend. He suggested that the monks escaped at the behest of Abbot Whiting, the last abbot of Glastonbury, who refused to accept Henry's decrees and was executed. He also noted that a little cupboard in the church at Ozleworth near Wootton housed the Grail when monks out visiting the sick could not get back to Glastonbury before dark. Lewis adopted an intensely flattering tone throughout, but the correspondence with Mrs Powell ceased abruptly after he requested the return of the object to Glastonbury.[46]

By the 1970s the descendants of the Powell family had left Nanteos, although a postcard with a photograph was still on sale in Aberystwyth shops. The legend is as much about the Powell family as it is about the cures, and it reinforced a sense of local identity. Three Anglicized Welsh families dominated economic, social and political life in this area of mid-Wales. Their manor houses, including Nanteos, stood within a few miles of one another. In contrast, the smaller landowners, merchants and craftsmen were a predominantly Welsh-speaking community. The folklore, with all its variations and contradictions, reflects the dynamic tension between a gentry family and its neighbours and social inferiors. Until recently, the Nanteos cup was little known in other parts of Wales, much less outside it. As a localized tradition in a relatively restricted area, it was less a relic of early Christianity than a symbol of social identity and power sharing. As protectors rather than despoilers of the monks, the Stedman and Powell families bridged the gap between the old and the new. They were custodians of an object saved during a time of dramatic change. In most local accounts, even those that are sceptical about the Nanteos cup's authenticity, the behaviour of the Powell family is an integral part of the experience. Many Cardiganshire informants visited the house on school or family outings. They recalled seeing the cup, together with testimonials recording borrowings, pledges and cures. The earliest testimonial is dated 1857 and records that a local man left money as a pledge when he borrowed it for his wife. On its return, the slip was marked 'cured'.

Local guidebooks also reflected growing interest in the legend. The *Aberystwyth Guide* of 1816 quoted references to Strata Florida by Tudor historians like Leland and Dugdale. W. E. Powell of Nanteos was among the subscribers to the publication, but there is no mention of a relic.[47] A century later, however, Nanteos was said to possess 'the Tregaron Healing Cup, which resembled the Holy Grail', and by 1934 the town guide confidently informed visitors that Nanteos 'preserved the precious medieval relic called the Cup of Healing, the surviving portion of a wooden bowl, a large part of which has been taken by believers in its magical properties'. Medieval pilgrimage to Strata Florida was taken as fact, and local villages with ecclesiastical names, like Ysbytty Ystwyth and Penrhydfendigaid, were transformed into hospices and way-stops for pilgrims.[48] Traditions, such as ghosts, secret passages, and anecdotes about family fortunes and family eccentrics, help create a feeling that visiting a country house is a special experience. The delights of Nanteos included a blackened window from which someone saw a fatal accident, a white lady who foretells death, and a heart-shaped table presented by Admiral Nelson to his mistress. The *pièce de résistance*, however, was 'Little more than a fragment of blackening wood, this is reputed to be the Cup used by Christ at the Last Supper . . . In 1538 came the Dissolution of the monasteries and the community at Glastonbury fled to Strata Florida . . . The Cup then passed into the hands of the ancestors of the Powells of Nanteos . . . for 200 years the Cup has been here, and the story of its healing power has become known all over the world. The present owner herself has received requests for water from every continent. At one time over-zealous pilgrims bit pieces out of the cup as relics, that is why it is so sadly diminished.'[49] Another tradition became attached to a picture of Richard Wagner. George Powell, who first exhibited the Nanteos cup, hung the picture in homage to a composer he admired. However, according to legend, the composer saw the Nanteos cup on a visit to the house, and it inspired his opera *Parsifal*.

According to the present owners, a local craftsman made a copy because the original was in such poor condition. Ordinary visitors were shown the copy, but the original cup was made available to those seeking cures. One report described it as a 'small shred of crumbling wood enshrined in a glass case' used as a drinking vessel in Strata Florida where cures were effected by taking food and medicine from it.[50] The copy has attracted traditions of its own, namely, that the real cup had been sold to a rich American because the family was short of cash and the copy was a replacement intended to save face in the community. In 1888, a harpist, not named, scoffed at the cup, but later repented and noted, 'Mind completely at ease.'[51] There were reports of monks' graves in the cellar and of a secret passage leading to Aberystwyth Castle. These traditions have been repeated in recent newspaper articles such as the Welsh-American newspaper *Y Drych*.[52] Printed accounts contain fewer local details, and the most dramatic ones are usually outside the Cardiganshire area. A priest from Herefordshire, who was miraculously cured of rheumatism, preached sermons about the history of the relic, although none of the local informants could recall the incident.[53]

Experts who examined the cup when it was exhibited at the National Library in Aberystwyth in the 1970s reached the consensus that it is a fourteenth-century example of a domestic vessel known as a mazer bowl made of wychelm, not olivewood. Mazer bowls were not usually ecclesiastical vessels, but they were valuable objects, and a number of them survive. Many are inscribed with pious sentiments or fitted with protective metal rims. The Nanteos example was probably found when archaeological investigations were undertaken at Strata Florida during the nineteenth century.[54] The lack of a metal rim may account for its poor condition, and this has encouraged the belief that pilgrims bit off relics. Some accounts suggest that a metal rim was fitted later to protect it, but this had to be removed since it destroyed the cup's effectiveness.[55] Varying, even contradictory, traditions identify the Nanteos cup with the Holy Grail and locate it either at Glastonbury or Strata Florida during the medieval period or in the aftermath of the Crusades. One correspondent described it as 'the most cherished treasure of the abbey of Strata Florida' and remarked on the fact that a sick child was taken all the way to Nanteos.[56] Other sources call it a curing cup, perhaps made from the True Cross.[57] During the first decade of the twentieth century, the Nanteos legend developed from being merely a healing cup to the much more elaborate Holy Grail form. The story of the fleeing monks and the prophecy share many features with antiquarian traditions associated with Glastonbury itself, and it is probable that antiquarian, rather than oral sources, lie behind it. Elements recall accounts, like that of John Stow, on the fate of the Catholic Church under the Tudor monarchs, and the statement about the church 'claiming its own' echoes Archbishop Ussher's prophecies.[58] Ancillary traditions about pilgrims, crusaders, and the destruction of monasteries support such accounts. They are typical of legend narratives about the survival of an ancient object. Dramatic and miraculous events, like Joseph's legendary journey to Glastonbury and the subsequent flight of the monks, explain the appearance of the object in an unexpected place. A perceived catastrophe, the Dissolution, threatens the existence of the sacred object, the Nanteos cup, but someone recognizes its true worth, rescues it, and preserves it in secret. Finally the object reappears, carrying with it, and transmitting to those who accept its reality, some of the beneficial qualities of the past.

This object was, and continues to be, a focus for local interest. Even sceptical informants are prepared to discuss the cup and its history, and this too strengthens the legend. The fortunes of the family, especially George Powell, aesthete and friend of Swinburne, or Mrs Powell, who fostered the Holy Grail story, are an integral part of this legend.[59] Accounts which involve the family are more likely to be sceptical. George Powell's role in the first description and exhibition of the cup, Mrs Powell's contribution to the development of the Grail stories, the selling of the house in 1968 and its subsequent chequered fortunes provide contexts in which amusement, sympathy and even criticism can be expressed through re-telling a familiar narrative. Such legends become an integral part of local history, and the mazer bowl becomes a relic, the focus for colourful anecdotes about a gentry family whose economic fortunes were in decline. Personal or familial luck has been linked to the possession of this object, a feature reflected in the story of a child who suffered a dreadful accident, but survived because of the power of the Nanteos cup. A late 1990s television piece filmed the current owner in silhouette and withheld details about her present residence.[60] These variations offer different points of reference from which to understand the legend, but such legendary narratives link both narrators and audience with the past and create a shared sense of identity.

Another persistent tradition is that the cup became damaged because pilgrims took pieces as relics. The souvenir-hunting pilgrims are just as fictional as the links with the Grail, but they too serve a function. Comments about the state of the cup emphasize the importance of 'rationalizing' motifs in the development of these legends.[61] For believers, the damaged condition adds credibility to its age and authenticity. For sceptics, the suggestion that pilgrims took pieces for souvenirs provides an apparently non-speculative element. Radiocarbon dating has been suggested as a scientific means of authenticating the Nanteos cup, but the family has declined, using the pilgrims as the reason. The earliest drawing in *Archaeolgia Cambrensis* depicts an already damaged object, and subsequent pictures do not indicate any further damage. Some contemporary commentators regret that, as the cup has been the focus of genuine belief, its authenticity should be questioned at all. In this context too, the damage caused by those who used the cup is seen as evidence of its important role in maintaining faith.

In so far as folk legends reflect the nature of belief rather than historical reality, the existence of such traditions helps clarify the process of legend formation. How exactly it came to be used for cures is not clear, but there is no credible reference to the Nanteos cup prior to the end of the nineteenth century and no mention of possible connections to the Grail until 1905. The pattern of traditions associated with the Nanteos cup indicates a manufactured legend lacking convincing links with the Holy Land, Crusades or Glastonbury. The Holy Grail motif may reflect a revival of interest in relics and in the meaning of the Grail at the turn of the last century when mystics like Wellesley Tudor Pole helped create a modern spiritual Glastonbury, and Lionel Smithett Lewis was active in reviving a 'national' British Church. Descriptions in late nineteenth-century archaeological journals provided a means for stabilizing and transmitting the details of the legend and disseminated local beliefs to a wider audience. Printed accounts, especially in newspapers, emphasized the mystery surrounding the object and the cures effected by its power. In many ways, the details of the story fulfil the criteria for synthetic and manufactured traditions for which the folklorist Richard Dorson coined the term 'fakelore'.[62] However, this overlooks a very real belief in its authenticity. Believers take great care to explain its existence, using a mixture of romantic history and notions of enduring folk memory. One member in the audience at a talk in Aberystwyth echoed Lionel Smithett Lewis's aspiration for a native British Church and announced that the Nanteos cup had been the rightful possession of the Welsh 'since the time of Christ' and should be returned to public display in Wales.

The lack of specific context for the discovery of objects like this one invites speculative explanations. Crusaders and Templars are essential to the modern Grail industry, and the Dissolution of the monasteries in Britain provided a similar context for disruption and mysterious continuity. For example, the belief that the cup was made from olivewood in first-century Palestine serves as positive indication of genuineness, despite expert opinion which identified it as a typical medieval mazer bowl. Like so many treasure trove legends, a mysterious history adds an aura of importance to discovery.[63] *Archaeologia Cambrensis* contains descriptions of other objects with mysterious qualities: a 'Gnostic object' called the 'Caernarfon Talisman'[64] anticipates alternative Grail theories involving 'Celtic Gnosticism', for which there is no credible evidence. Such speculations are not about the historical reality of such objects, but a means of attributing cultural importance to them. Motifs crystallize into a standard episode about the violent disruption of an old order, and the preservation of some secret passed on by an elite group of guardians who carry the message into another age. The Nanteos cup is only one example of objects given into the hands of sympathetic believers only to appear mysteriously generations later. Much the same story of peril, preservation and miracle was told about other objects, such as the *santo caliz* in Valencia, or the *sacro catino* in Genoa. The mystery confirms or casts doubt depending on the perspective of the narrator, and questions about origins and ownership reinforce both sceptical and sympathetic accounts of the legends.

New forms of mass media, such as the Internet and television documentary, provide news ways of disseminating legends like the Nanteos cup, but the mechanism of transmission remains much the same. Initially accounts adopt a sceptical, or at least questioning, attitude to some feature of the legend, and then use this moderate and rational stance to validate more imaginative aspects. A typical account begins with 'antiquarian opinion' linking the cup to Strata Florida, plus references to the Grail or Joseph of Arimathea. A few cures are cited leading to the suggestion that this must be a healing cup used by the abbey during the medieval period. History and tradition are ostensibly distinguished, but then conflated, as there is no documentary evidence for the cup being at Strata Florida at all, much less used to effect cures there.[65] Another account of the cup 'reputed to be the Grail' used pilgrims and their souvenir hunting to rationalize and perpetuate the legend, claiming that the family had to protect the lip with a silver mount to prevent further destruction.[66] Dramatic cures for rheumatism, epilepsy and deafness can be traced to a variety of sources.[67] An incident about a rheumatic priest cited a 'confidential' journal, and there is a request for an epileptic boy to visit in the Powell family correspondence. Cures for blindness and deafness are not characteristic of the Nanteos cup but they are mentioned in a short story by Arthur Machen. Requests for the cup's return recall Lionel Smithett Lewis's attempts to induce Mrs Powell to present it to Glastonbury. The effect of this narrative patterning is to create a seemingly neutral position, appropriate to a factual source, but one which actually invites the reader's belief in the legend.

American newspaper accounts place greater emphasis on the Arthurian aspect of the story. In Wales the Nanteos cup is not part of Arthurian legend, but a relic associated with a specific area and family. Although there are comparatively few printed accounts in Welsh, one is contemporary with the earliest archaeological accounts. It contains details found in other printed sources, but the emphasis is on local use and local importance.[68] An article about Strata Florida printed in the Welsh-language magazine *Cymru* described Ethelwyn Amery's booklet, published two years previously, as a 'charming novel'. It also mentioned the Last Supper, Joseph of Arimathea and the fleeing monks, and published a photograph that shows the damage very clearly.[69]

In Arthur Machen's story 'The Great Return', three relics, St Teilo's Bell, a miraculous altar and the Grail return to a fictional village called Llantrisant which Machen locates somewhere on the Welsh coast.[70] A sceptical journalist hears rumours about the appearance of shimmering lights during a Christian revival meeting. His investigation reveals a series of mysterious events: a dying girl who suddenly recovers, the smell of incense in a Protestant church, three mysterious 'Fishermen', a deaf woman cured by the sound of a saintly bell and a rose of fire out at sea which later appears as a jewelled object in the chancel of the church. The dying girl has a vision of three men holding a bell, a glowing portable altar, and a cup respectively. Machen creates this sense of seemingly real journalistic reportage by mixing tradition and fiction. The appearance of strange lights at religious meetings was a topic much discussed in such journals as *The Occult Review* at the time. The Welsh saints, David, Teilo and Beuno, and their holy talismans are the 'Fishermen' commemorated here in Machen's fictional church of the three saints (Llantrisant). The journalist-narrator drops hints about a 'Healing Cup of Nant Eos and Tregaron', which, like printed media accounts, adds an air of authenticity. A repentant harpist in this fictional montage appears in later newspaper accounts of the Nanteos cup, seemingly transforming the fictional journalism in Machen's story into history.

Machen's friend the occultist A. E. Waite visited Nanteos just before his death.[71] Both men were deeply interested in mysticism, although Machen believed that the Grail originated as a religious object belonging to one of the early Celtic saints. This touches on another popular modern theme, namely that the Grail was originally a holy relic of the Celtic Church. The Grail for Machen represented the real and ecstatic Celtic Christianity prior to the advent of the Latin Church.[72] A. E. Waite, on the other hand, favoured a complex mixture of early Celtic Christianity and a secret wisdom tradition. He argued that the Grail was essentially a mystical experience, not a physical object. This fin-de-siècle fascination with the Grail, in which academic and quasi-academic approaches intertwine, is important for understanding legends about the Nanteos cup. For the most part, traditions about the Nanteos cup are not linked to Arthur or Celtic Christianity. It is most frequently explained as a relic of the True Cross or the Last Supper, a source for miraculous cures not millennial transformation. The first account to identify it with the Grail combined a romantic view of the past with unabashed sentimentality. The author of this account, Ethelwyn Amery, was a member of the British Chatauquan Movement, which had its origins in the search for spiritual well-being. This highlights an important aspect of these legends, the belief that their survival has consequences for contemporary society. Wellesley Tudor Pole's attitude to the glass bowl at Glastonbury reflected a millennial tone,[73] while Amery's book linked the Nanteos cup to an ambiguous and evocative prophecy about the future. Lionel Smithett Lewis emphasized a revival of the British Church and there is evidence that he tried to incorporate the Nanteos cup into this project.

The legend of the Nanteos cup is ongoing. The pattern that emerges from traditions linked to this mazer bowl mirrors other relic legends involving an ambiguous history and at least one miraculous escape. These legends are typically associated with a saint or famous person, and the sphere of influence is likely to be co-extensive with that of the custodian. Originally the Nanteos legend was localized in west Wales, and only comparatively recently has it become absorbed into more general Grail legends. The

Arthurian past and the Welsh past both validate the legend, even though much of this is romantic rather than historical. Accounts in influential journals such as *Archaeologia Cambrensis* reflect both revival of interest in the Grail romances and in the archaeology of Wales. Specific individuals, such as George Powell and Mrs Margaret Powell, have also influenced its development. Throughout, it has maintained a connection to the family and the estate, and its local dimension continues to introduce fresh information and new traditions, while newspapers, mass media and the Internet have given it an international dimension.

The finding of an alabaster cup in the fantasy gardens of Hawkstone Hall in Shropshire on the Welsh Border provides some interesting parallels with the folklore surrounding the Nanteos cup. Both discoveries took place in mysterious circumstances, and both have links to once prominent local families. There is, however, a major difference between these two legends. The Nanteos cup was known locally as a healing object before becoming attached to the Holy Grail legend. In contrast, the small stone cup supposedly found in a garden statue at Hawkstone had no particular traditions associated with it until it was identified as the Grail or 'Marian chalice' in the 1990s. The Nanteos cup was, and still is, rooted in local tradition while the Hawkstone Grail is part of the modern genre of conspiracy history. Such theories have been influenced by mass media phenomena like *The Holy Blood and the Holy Grail* and *The Da Vinci Code* and are full of conspiracies, codes, sacred geography and eccentric sources.

The cup found at Hawkstone Park was identified as a Grail in a few recently published books on alternative history and on related Internet sites.[74] The story of this object begins with the historian, Olympiodorus, who supposedly recorded that the Holy Grail was brought to Britain in the fifth century. The Fitz Warine family of Whittington Castle guarded it and passed it to their descendants. In the nineteenth century, Thomas Wright, an antiquary supposedly related to the family, concealed the object in a statue in an ornamental grotto at Hawkstone Park. At the end of the First World War, statues in the gardens were disturbed, revealing a small alabaster object, which remained in the possession of a local family. A secret numerical code, supposedly concealed in one of Wright's books, leads to Victorian stained-glass windows in the medieval church in Hodnot, Shropshire, and eventually to the object and its secret. The links between the alabaster cup and its connection with Mary Magdalene and an alternative Christianity was revealed with suitably dramatic prose, but the history presented here is typical of the chimerical arguments that crop up regularly in popular Grail studies in which sources and crucial details are mysteriously missing from library catalogues and published works. Unfortunately for the argument, the writings of Olympiodorus contain no references to the Holy Grail, nor is there anything among Thomas Wright's publications to link him to Hodnot Church or Hawkstone Park.

The pagan historian Olympiodorus of Thebes described events in the western empire at the beginning of the fifth century such as the sack of Rome by the Visigoths and the political manoeuvres of Honorius and his devoutly Christian sister, Galla Placidia. The work was dedicated to Emperor Theodosius II, who had strong Christian sympathies. Although it is now lost, substantial sections were quoted by other historians,[75] and it is possible to give a reasonably clear idea of the original content and, more relevant for our purposes, its position in the modern Grail legend. The division of the Roman Empire was a significant factor in the emergence of Latin Christianity with consequences for the history of medieval Europe. However, it is significant only in retrospect. Olympiodorus' immediate theme was the decline of the empire. He was openly pagan in sympathy, adopting the position of many pagan intellectuals of his time, namely that pagan ritual had protected the Roman Empire from barbarian invaders.[76] There is no mention of either the Grail or St Helena in the passages quoted by other historians, and attempts to find authentication for the Olympiodorus Grail reference lead nowhere.[77] Despite this, the suggestion about the Grail has found favour with some Internet sites as 'a secure historical fact'.[78] It is a good illustration of how readily pronouncements of this type are accepted in popular Grail mythology.

Similar difficulties beset the attempts to link Hodnot Church and Hawkstone Hall. Thomas Wright, a well-known Shropshire antiquary who lived from 1810 to 1877, has been identified as the man who supposedly created the code and hid the Hawkstone cup. However, there is little apparent connection between Wright and the descendants of the Fitz Warines. Wright's family came originally from Bradford in Yorkshire. His wife was French, and they had no surviving children. Wright's grandfather, also called Thomas Wright, was a staunch Wesleyan Methodist,[79] who established a moderately successful printing business near Ludlow in Shropshire. Interest in antiquarian research began with Wright's father, another Thomas Wright, who compiled the volume *The History and Antiquities of Ludlow*.[80] Young Thomas, thanks to the patronage of a wealthy friend, went to Trinity College, Cambridge, where he developed an interest in the Anglo-Saxon heritage of the English people and formed a lifelong friendship with another pioneering editor and antiquarian scholar, James Orchard Halliwell-Phillips. He frequently collaborated with his friend on publications for the new literary societies such as the Warton Club. Wright's numerous publications on medieval literature, philology, archaeology, the history of science, geographical exploration, folklore and what would now be called cultural studies, provided a foundation for the use of vernacular sources as a way of understanding the lifestyle of earlier cultures. He is a significant figure, but not in regard of any codes or secrets.

Identifying details in romances with real places and hidden events is a technique with a long history in Grail studies, especially popular works. It is fraught with problems, not the least of which is that here it relies on Wright's early and rather inadequate translation of the Fitz Warine romance.[81] This romance concerns the adventures of a local outlaw hero, Fulk, and the Grail material is introduced only in the final episodes. Fulk's home, Wittington Castle, is called 'the white land' in the text and linked to the geography of the Grail romances. However, the implausibility of any attempt to link Wittington and the Grail is made clear in Wright's own notes to the Fitz Warine romance. Far from identifying Wittington Castle as the White Castle of the Grail romance, Wright derived it from the name of a Saxon family.[82] He was by no means the only Shropshire antiquarian to regard the link between Wittington and 'white launde' as nothing more than a poetic allusion found only in romance.[83] In an article on the local legends of Shropshire, Wright noted that the history of the Fitz Warine family combined real historical matter modified and greatly enlarged by stories and legends taken from medieval romances. 'These become family legends and as family legends they quickly become local legends ... It is surprising how much of this class of legendary matter has crept into history itself and how difficult it is to eradicate it ... The practice of localizing legends seems so inseparable from the popular mind that we actually find it going on at the present day; and it is quite remarkable how rapidly a legend is sometimes formed.'[84] Wright is describing the exact process by which Grail legends are being created in connection with such places as Hawkstone Hall and Hodnot Church today.

There is nothing in any of Wright's publications to support a numerical code linking the statues at Hawkstone with the windows of Hodnot Church. The code is assigned to a poem, 'Sir Gawain and the Red Knight', edited by Wright in 1855. The only two books recorded in Wright's publication list for 1855 are *Christianity in Arabia* and *The Romance of Fulk le Fitzwarine*.[85] The final page of this mysterious edition as it appears on the Hawkstone Grail websites gives the place and date of publication as 'George Lewis at Oswestry in 1855'. However, the only book listed for this publisher in 1855 is a history of Oswestry by William Cathrall and contains nothing about Arthurian poems or codes.[86] The confusion seems to have arisen in that the volume published by the Warton Club in 1855 bound together two works by different editors. One was Wright's edition of the Anglo-Norman romance, *The History of Fulk-fitz Warine*, while the second was an edition of *Early English Miscellanies* by Wright's friend, James Halliwell-Phillips.[87] It is also difficult to see how Wright, coming from a Methodist background and whose life was lived in genteel poverty, could have been the donor/ designer of windows in an Anglican church. The restoration carried out at Hodnot Church in the nineteenth century has been attributed to the Heber-Percy family whose ancestor, a well-known hymn writer, had been the incumbent.[88] There is no clear reference to an alabaster cup at Hawkstone Park before 1917, when it was being used as a military hospital and a local man found it. The suggestion that Wright concealed something may be the result of confusing Thomas with a later writer, Arthur Wright, who described how soldiers billeted at Hawkstone damaged the statues at the end of the First World War.

Although the Grail does not feature among Wright's substantial list of publications, he touched on a fruitful source for the Grail myth, namely the connection between the Order of the Knights Templar and a pre-Christian wisdom tradition. An ardent francophile, Wright drew on the revisionist views of the Templar trial put forward by the French historian Jules Michelet. This new approach, not easily available to an English reading public at that time, stressed the use of falsified evidence and torture as a means of achieving the political agenda of the French king, Philip Le Bel. Wright regarded the trials as a 'use which might be made of popular superstition as a means of oppression and vengeance',[89] and included relevant English manuscript material to bolster his opinion. He was critical of the highly speculative suggestions about Templar beliefs in the work of the German orientalist scholar Hammer Purgstall, who proposed that medieval monuments revealed the heretical Gnostic beliefs held by the Templars. Despite his interest in controversies surrounding the nature of Christ in early Christian theology,[90] Wright is unambiguous in his dismissal. 'Von Hammer Purgstall ... attempted to show from medieval monuments that the order of the Templars was infested with Gnosticism ... In fact, Von Hammer totally misunderstood the character of the monuments on which he built his theory.'[91] This is hardly the language of a man guarding a Templar secret relating to a Gnostic belief in a marriage between Christ and Mary Magdelene. However, in his commentary on Richard Payne Knight's treatise on Priapus, he did consider the idea of a phallic cult among the medieval Templars. 'Whatever degree of truth there may have been in this story [regarding the Templars], it must have been greatly exaggerated; but the conviction of the existence of secret societies of this character during the middle ages appears to have been so strong and so generally held, that we must hesitate in rejecting it.'[92] This is not a high-minded pagan philosophy or liberal alternative to Christianity, it was an ancient superstition, but, influenced no doubt by Jules Michelet, he felt that the medieval (i.e., 'romish') Church had exploited such practices in order to discredit opposing factions, such as the Templars.

Another approach to this Shropshire Grail uses dreams and visions to discover hidden artefacts and uncover mysteries of the past.[93] The use of psychic vision to illuminate the past echoes the work of the Glastonbury archaeologist Frederick Bligh Bond. However, it seems an unlikely scenario in regard to Thomas Wright, who adopted a critical rather than a nostalgic view of superstition and rejected the notion of mystical Templars. He had a brief correspondence with Lord Bulwer-Lytton, but the latter, despite an interest in Masonic and Rosicrucian philosophy, never visited Hawkstone. There are no credible traditions about neo-pagan rites at Hawkstone Hall in the nineteenth century, nor any substantial references to Grails or Templars in the considerable antiquarian writing on Shropshire by Wright's contemporaries. Hawkstone Hall does not feature among Wright's archaeological or historical interests, and only one source, a modern one, connects him to the place.[94] Wright published very little during the last decade of his life since dementia and diabetes took hold. His longtime friend and collaborator James Halliwell-Phillips helped support him and his ailing wife. He died in 1877 and was buried in Brompton Cemetery. When his wife died five years later, she was buried near him. The story of the alabaster cup in the grotto in the folly gardens at Hawkstone does not really fit events in the life of this fascinating antiquary. His notes to the Fitz Warine romance actually contradict the idea that Wittington Castle had any associations with a Grail tradition. However, in his comments about the Templars and the pagan cults, Wright touches on important sources in the development of the modern myth of the Templars as a secret society. As such he is an undervalued historian of the reassessment of the order in the nineteenth century,[95] and one who was able to speak, even if only in a tentative way, on the importance of folklore and legend formation in this matter.

Comparisons between the Hawkstone and Nanteos cup traditions illustrate the way in which modern Grail traditions develop both as popular legend and as a response to new intellectual paradigms. The first published reference to the Nanteos cup coincided with finding a curious glass bowl at Glastonbury and the growth of that city as a modern spiritual centre. The Nanteos cup already had an established reputation for healing, at least locally in Cardiganshire. The Glastonbury and Nanteos objects were not rivals as such, but some commentators were aware of the existence of two alternatives to the legend. A similar situation occurred when the Hawkstone cup was first reported in the media. The leader of an Italian

Templar organization claimed that he had the Grail and that this was proof that his group were the real descendants of the order suppressed at the beginning of the fourteenth century. His 'Grail', too, attracted media coverage.[96] Unlike the Nanteos legend, there are few, if any, local traditions, and the theory linking the alabaster cup with a secret 'Marian chalice' remains within the context of alternative publishing and the Internet. However, the Glastonbury, Nanteos and Hawkstone legends share a number of motifs. The present owners acquired their 'Grails' under unusual circumstances. The Glastonbury and Hawkstone objects were deliberately concealed by one owner and found much later, while the custodianship of the Italian Grail and the Nanteos cup was acquired through the offices of a 'last survivor' figure.

WELSH LITERARY HISTORY AND THE GRAIL

A Welsh-language periodical entitled *Y Greal* appeared briefly at the beginning of the nineteenth century,[97] but it has no direct references to Arthurian material. William Owen Pughe's eclectic *Dictionary of the Welsh Language*[98] defined *Grëal* as the 'celebrated book of Welsh stories'. Although Pughe was knowledgeable about medieval literature, he was influenced by the bardic fantasies of Iolo Morganwg and by outmoded speculations about the nature of language. There are comparatively few Welsh-language treatments of the Grail from the beginning of the twentieth century, when it was becoming a potent force in spiritual and esoteric revivals elsewhere. However, Welsh-language sources did not miss out entirely on the Grail revival. Professor Thomas Parry retold the story of the *Saint Greal*.[99] Much like Alfred's Nutt's series on popular mythology, it endowed a retelling of the legend with the authority of an important scholar in the field. Edward Tegla Davies (1880–1967), a well-known Wesleyan Methodist minister, produced a charming curiosity called *Y Greal Sanctaidd*.[100] This booklet for young readers traced the history of the Grail legend with the emphasis on its relevance for Wales. Tegla summarized the medieval Grail texts, pointed out parallels with early 'pagan' Welsh literature, such as Ceridwen's cauldron, and presented a short exposition on how three writers, Alfred Lord Tennyson, George MacDonald and Edward Arlington Robinson, used the motif in their work. The focus was on the spiritual meaning of the Grail and its continued relevance to Welsh life, but the distinctiveness of Tegla's book lies in the fact that it is aimed at a young audience. At the beginning of the twentieth century, John Dyfnallt Owen's poem on the Holy Grail won the prize for free meter poetry at the National Eisteddfod.[101]

Dyfnallt was minister of Sardis chapel, Pontypridd, and he knew the druidic bards, Morien and Myfywyr Morganwg, and their very different attitudes to the meaning of the Grail for Welsh culture.[102]

These neo-druids drew inspiration as to the meaning of the Grail from spiritual as well as historical sources. Their concern with the origins of Christianity in Britain anticipated some of the attitudes of new age spirituality, and their sphere of influence was by no means limited to Wales. However, Wales, with its ancient British traditions, was central to reconstructing their so-called heritage. The work of Owen Morgan, who adopted the bardic name 'Morien', provides one of the most curious settings for speculation on the meaning of the Grail in Wales. Born in the Rhondda, South Wales, Morien spent most of his life working as a journalist for a Welsh newspaper. He charted the industrial development of the South Wales valleys in the nineteenth century, but his connection with the history of the Grail stems from his interest in more controversial attempts to create a druidic history for Wales. Building on the earlier work of the famous creator of Welsh druidism, Iolo Morganwg, he was influential in shaping a local druidic revival in South Wales at the turn of the twentieth century. For Morien, the Glamorgan area of South Wales was not just an Anglicized centre for modern industrial exploitation; it was the focus for an unbroken tradition of druidic religious practice. He succeeded his friend and mentor Evan Davies (Myfyr Morganwg) as arch druid of the chair of Morganwg and wrote extensively on folklore, which he invariably interpreted as the living survival of an ancient druidic astronomical religion.[103]

Morien's project was vast. Not only did he enact neo-druidic rituals, most famously near the rocking stone on Pontypridd common, but he reinterpreted Welsh history and world mythology as a hidden bardic heritage. For him, all mythologies were linked to the Welsh druids through their Hyperborean ancestors from Atlantis. He sought the origin of religion in an understanding of the natural world rather than in divine revelation from an all-knowing deity. This mixture of mysticism and deism is prevalent in modern revivals of druidism, and Morien was a late flowering of a long-standing tradition, with a few unique features. His chapter on 'The Holy Grail discovered in Wales' in *The Winged Son* illustrates this uniqueness, although this tantalizing title does not lead to a specific Grail object at a specific location. Morien's Grail is part of the symbolic world of ancient druidic religion, which for him was expressed in the sexual union of sky-god and earth goddess. The Grail was a Christianized image of the great womb of goddess earth.[104]

Such comprehensive, if rather naive, attempts to recover a pre-Christian fertility religion are familiar in Grail scholarship, particularly through the work of Jessie Weston. They share many influences, such as the belief that modern folklore is a survival of ancient practice and the notion that ancient religion was rooted in rituals aimed at maintaining the fertility of the natural cycle. Morien died in 1921 at the beginning of the decade when Weston's work became popular, and his speculations, although in the same vein as hers, have a more metaphysical tone. They are closer to Max Müller's idea that the origins of religion were to be sought in a literal interpretation of symbolic language meant to convey philosophical truth. For Morien, true Christianity was not antagonistic to druidic religion, in fact it was essentially the same thing, and symbols such as the Grail embodied the wisdom of ancient druidry in the context of Christianity. He claimed to elucidate not only the mysteries of ancient British druidism and determine whether Jesus was a druid, but also to reveal the secrets of the court of King Arthur, the creed of the Stone Age and the discovery of the Holy Grail in Wales.[105] His arguments were founded in a neo-druidic philosophy that linked all megalithic monuments with druidic worship. Stone circles reflected the 'druidic' symbols of the sun and the sacred apple, and of course the Grail. Since Morien considered that druidism was at its strongest in Wales, then Wales itself he argued was the Holy Grail. As one commentator expresses it, he 'discovered, or so he believed, the true religion of the ancient Druids which was also the true and undistorted Christianity of Jesus; he presented that teaching to the world at large for its enlightenment, and he celebrated the rites and mysteries of phallic Christian druidism beside Pontypridd's rocking stone until the end of his life.'[106]

Another important source for Morien was a treatise published in 1796 by Richard Payne Knight, entitled *A discourse on the worship of Priapus and its connection with the mystic theology of the Ancients*. This analysed the sexual symbolism in myth at a time when the sexually charged symbolism it discussed was extremely controversial.[107] Thomas Wright also commented on Richard Payne Knight's treatise, drawing in Templars, Gnostics and briefly druids. His comments illustrate important elements of the modern Templar myth. Wright referred to Hammer Purgstall's suggestion that the Templars were secret followers of an ancient phallic cult and to Jules Michelet's thesis that ancient priapic rites were a form of social protest for the peasant class. Richard Payne Knight's study on the worship of Priapus allowed Wright, and subsequent writers, to bridge the gap between folk customs and the beliefs of the rural peasantry. These could now be seen as survivals of an ancient religion and, in a more philosophical form, as beliefs preserved by a sophisticated (i.e., upper-class) secret society. This model could be developed into a Celtic myth about a sacred 'Grail', a Gnostic myth about Christianity based on the union of masculine and feminine principles, or an Indo-European myth about the rebirth of a vegetation god. The Celtic, Gnostic and myth-ritual analyses of the Grail legend overlap. They are at once esoteric in that the 'real' meaning is conserved by a secret society of initiates, popular in that the beliefs and rituals are accessible to all, and, invariably, a target for the prevailing orthodoxy.

As part of an idealized view of the Dissolution of the monasteries in sixteenth-century Britain, the Nanteos cup created a link back to an authentic native British Church as envisaged by Archbishop Ussher and Lionel Smithett Lewis. Morien's speculations presented druidism as the paradigm for a theosophical view of mythology, and the Hawkstone cup localized a Gnostic alternative to orthodox Christianity within the geography of the Welsh Border. The very different versions of the Grail in Wales treated in this chapter cannot be fitted into a clear linear history, but the traditions attached to the Nanteos and Hawkstone cups and Morien's druidic speculations are compelling images of how imagination can alter the past as an attempt to transform the present. The idea of a pre-Christian wisdom tradition preserved by a secret society underpins all these legends. It also demonstrates how intellectual developments become popularized. As metaphors for the origin of religion or the development of social institutions they represent a way of understanding culture. As romantic fantasies they are a way to remedy perceived failures in contemporary culture by the transformative value of the past. However, as the distinction between cultural metaphor and romantic fantasy becomes blurred, ideas about druids, Celtic Christianity, Celtic paganism, Templars, Cathars, and Gnostics begin to coalesce.

These elements come together in the fiction of Arthur Machen. Born the son of the Anglican vicar of the village of Llandewi, near Caerleon in Gwent, in 1863, Arthur Llewellyn Jones adopted his mother's family name as a writer. He was affected by the surrounding landscape of his childhood – the Black Mountains, the ancient forest of Wentwood, and of course, Caerleon itself. His writings evoked these places as a prescient, ambiguous world in which his characters experience wonder, terror and transformation. The haunted landscape and the ancient history of places like Caerleon merged in his writing to produce both the dark pagan forces of his horror fiction and the mystical esotericism of his writing about the Grail. The materialism of society profoundly disturbed Machen, and he was critical of both rationalism, which denied the spiritual, and spiritualism, which sought to explain it scientifically.[108] In a pamphlet written at the end of the First World War he wrote that human life should be a journey of personal spiritual experience which he described as 'sailing the great deep of god'.[109] To deny this was to court the darker aspects of spirituality, and in his early horror tales, ancient and terrible powers surface into the modern world. Works, like 'The Great God Pan', embodied the tradition of 'decadent' aestheticism. It fictionalized assumptions about ancient, but still powerful, priapic cults as described by writers like Richard Payne Knight. Machen's fiction encouraged the reader to enjoy the rise of these powers with the frisson of a voyeur, but to be assured that those who transgressed were always punished. Like the medieval exempla, which Machen admired, supernatural experiences had a didactic function. Whether through the imagery of dark paganism or of mystical regeneration, Machen's fiction has a spiritual dimension, and both his fiction and non-fiction critique secular and materialistic visions of the world.

The use of mysticism and spirituality as a counter-balance to economic and scientific materialism became more prominent in his writing after 1900. Ancient paganism in Machen's work acquired a regenerative quality through its connection with a mystic ecstasy that was both life-enhancing and a foundation for aesthetic experience. Several factors influenced this. Decadent aestheticism was less fashionable, and certainly less marketable, after the Oscar Wilde trials. Also, Machen's wife had died, and a devastated Machen teetered on the edge of breakdown. In a sketch of despair and depression called *The Holy Things* (1897), a man walking down Holborn in London experienced the everyday bells, lamplight and traffic of a city street as incense, church bells and a choir of angels who 'sang in the tongue of his boyhood "Sant. Sant. Sant."'. Such experiences, in which the spiritual, the physical and the aesthetic are intermingled, paralleled his own mental state as described in his autobiography.[110] His wanderings through London, and his psychological recovery were couched in the same terms of spiritual and sensory experience that he used to such good effect in his writing and which recall motifs familiar from traditional supernatural visitations. It is also, although Machen does not say so specifically, a vision of the Holy Grail. The author described his early years in South Wales in rosy terms. The stability, the order, and the ceremony of life were what he remembered. This attraction to stability in the social world was in dramatic contrast to the intense emotional and supernatural presence with which he endowed his landscapes. His Anglican sympathies seemed to follow from this as well, and it is not surprising that he was interested in the importance of ritual, the meaning of the Holy Grail legends, and in the imaginative power of religion.[111]

This comes through clearly in *The Secret Glory*, whose main character despises materialism and finds salvation through Celtic Christianity. Through the experience of 'red' (that is, physical) martyrdom, he 'achieved the most glorious Quest and Adventure of the Sangraal'.[112] The alienated central character, the schoolboy Ambrose Meyrick, experiences this in circumstances that recall the Grail procession of medieval romance. He also 'speaks of a Celtic cup which had been preserved in one family for many hundreds of years. On the death of the last keeper this cup was placed in Meyrick's hands.' This Welsh relic, kept by a Welsh guardian, echoed legends about early Welsh saints as well as later traditions about the Nanteos cup.[113] The mystic experience of the Grail imbues the atmosphere of another short story, 'The Great Return'.[114] It is embodied in the three sacred relics, cup, bell and altar, of three saints commemorated in the fictional church of Llantrisant. This is the interpretation of the Grail Machen himself favoured, and his cleverly oblique references to traditions about the Nanteos cup create a history for the Grail in Wales. Critical reaction to his Grail fictions was mixed. Machen noted 'that in my book the Holy Grail was manifested to the common people, to common modern people, to Welsh tradesmen and farmers. He [an unnamed reviewer] seemed to think this very low. It may be low, but perhaps things happen in this way sometimes; and so with me: I, by no manner of means a knight, received joy and knew wonders while the trams clanged along the Clerkenwell Road in the grey winter afternoon.'[115]

Machen's enthusiasm for the Grail and its meaning was shared by his friend and onetime associate A. E. Waite.[116] Like many of the intellectuals, artists and writers interested in occultism at the time, Machen and Waite sought to counter the growing secular materialism in modern life with a revival of mystical and spiritual values. They collaborated on several projects and were both members of the occult order of the Golden Dawn. Although Waite did not accept that Celtic Christian mysticism was the ultimate source for the Grail, his affection for his friend and his respect for Machen's ideas was real. Machen's view of mystical Christianity depended on ecstatic contacts with the Christianity of the early Welsh saints. It is worth noting, in this context, the Welsh aspect of Machen's vision in 'the Great Return' and his account of a personal experience on Holborn Street in London. Too often Celtic Christianity is treated as a monolithic phenomenon. A Celtic Christian Grail meant one thing for the Anglo-Welsh writer Arthur Machen, another for the Anglo-Irishman W. B. Yeats, and yet another for the Scotsman Lewis Spence. A form of mystical paganism influenced the views of Yeats and Spence, while Machen's concept was more distinctly Christian. He saw parallels between the lives of the Welsh saint David and Joseph of Arimathea, and believed that Grail romances were based on the wanderings of Welsh saints.[117] For Machen, the origin of the Grail lay in a religious object belonging to one of the early Celtic saints, and it represented the real and ecstatic Celtic Christianity prior to the advent of the Latin Church.

The most widely known modern Welsh writer to use the Grail in any significant way is the poet and artist David Jones. Although born in England and not a Welsh speaker, Jones always retained a sense of his Welsh heritage and numbered many Welsh intellectuals among his correspondents and friends. His striking and original work abounds in complex, personal images, many of them drawn from Arthurian or Welsh sources. Jones's experiences during the First World War, as with so many modernist poets of his generation, deeply affected his art and poetry. His conversion to Roman Catholicism also provided a rich seam of images for his art. These collective experiences were voiced in poems such as *In Parenthesis* (1937), *The Anathemata* (1952) and *The Sleeping Lord* (1974).[118] The elegiac tone, the sense of alienation from a cultural wellspring and the search for a way to regain this through myth are characteristics of modernist writing and bring to mind T. S. Eliot's comparable treatment of the Grail myth in *The Waste Land*. Jones identified closely with the Arthurian legend both as the native myth of Wales, and as the common intellectual heritage of all Britons. Mankind could regain this heritage only by returning to its beginnings, and for Jones this meant rediscovering, and more importantly re-enacting, the myth of Arthur and the Grail. His war poem, *In Parenthesis*, described the Western Front in terms which evoked both the wasteland and the journey to the Chapel Perilous in the Grail romances. Empty and threatening though it is, this wasteland, like that in the Grail myth, can be transformed through the restoration of the Grail king. Here Jones, like Eliot, turned to the mystic Grail theories of Jessie Weston to provide a bridge to understanding the meaning of the Grail in the twentieth century. The anthropological nature of this archetype had relevance for Jones's concern with the creation and destruction of civilization, while the ritual nature of Weston's theory resonated with another prominent theme in his poetry, the dilemma of a religious artist living in a secular Britain.[119] The all-important Christian aspect is filtered through the theme of an ancient initiation ritual with the power to reunite the maimed king with the land through the actions of a hero. The Grail quest was the supreme achievement of the Arthurian world, but it was quintessentially an ideal of Christian asceticism and purity. In the complex multi-layered world of Jones's poetic imaging the Grail hero who heals the king merges with the figure of the Maimed King and ultimately with Christ the Redeemer.

In *The Sleeping Lord*, Jones evokes the candles and the spear of the romance Grail procession in order to identify Arthur, the sleeping cult-hero, with the Maimed King of the Grail myth. The fragment is dated winter 1966 and 1967, the time when the 'dying god' was traditionally inactive and awaiting resurrection. This identification is made even more strongly at the end when the poet asks whether the land awaits the sleeping lord or whether the lord is the land itself. Similar references to ritual myth and medieval romance appear in the 'Rite and Fore-time' section of *The Anathemata*. The 'cult-man' who stands alone in 'Pellam's land', the waste-land of Malory's *Morte Darthur*, relocates prehistoric man in a medieval wasteland. It also identifies the Grail castle with the institution of the Eucharist, 'the holy dysshe wherein I ete the lamb on sherthyrsdaye'.[120] Ancient ritual reinforces Christian theology in a seamless cultural conti-nuity; something expressed later in the poem in the juxtaposition of 'Sherethyrsdaye', that is Holy Thursday, which commemorates the first appearance of the Grail at the Last Supper, and 'Venus-Day' an evocation of the pagan ceremonies which foreshadowed this.

David Jones's belief in Arthurian tradition as the common heritage of Britain is reflected in his art as well.[121] Although the elements of the Grail myth are not often depicted directly, the eucharistic chalice as a kind of Grail overflowing with flowers does appear, sometimes on its own and sometimes as part of a mystic mass.[122] His essays on the nature of Arthurian literature articulated his understanding of the relationship between ancient ritual, eucharistic mass and the role of the cult-hero. In an extended review of Charles Williams's book about the Grail for the Roman Catholic journal *The Tablet*, Jones characterized the Arthurian legend as 'nothing less than genuine Myth and epic as fused in a medieval crucible and as interpreted or developed or used by individuals of a later date'.[123] 'The Myth of Arthur' described the creation of the cult-hero as a 'meander' woven of 'myth, plus legend, plus history'. For him, interest in pagan origins was an appropriate way to reconnect with the ancient past, but 'nothing of all this invalidates the identification of the Grail with the Horn of Plenty, Calix sanguinum mei ... mysterium fidei'.[124]

David Jones's poetic and artistic interpretations of the Grail legend were based on his personal response to Welsh tradition, modulated by his expe-riences in the First World War. Only a decade before that war, the first published account identifying the Nanteos cup with the Grail appeared. Despite it romantic sentimentality, the account localized the legend in a Welsh context. The predominant scholarly trend at that time focused on Celtic connections and pagan origins. While critical and fictional responses to the Grail in Wales need to be seen in this wider context, interpretations have moved in unexpected directions, and the most passionate advocates of Celtic Grails, especially of the pagan variety, are not necessarily those most deeply involved in Welsh culture. The publication of the medieval Welsh text *Peredur vab Efrawg* in Charlotte Guest's *Mabinogion* sparked off discussions about the relationship between Welsh and continental literature. If the comprehensive and grandly inclusive statements about Celtic sources were as compelling as some of the popular literature suggests, the Grail should be a prominent legend in Welsh tradition. That this is not so, is, in itself, interesting.

This fascination with the Grail in which academic and quasi-academic approaches intertwine is important for understanding the many facets of the Grail legend in Wales, but even more so perhaps for an understanding of the modern Grail legend. A link between the Grail and Christianity runs through almost all interpretations of the Grail in Wales. For writers like Dyfnallt and Tegla, conversion to Christianity dramatically changed the pagan worldview of the early Welsh. For writers like Arthur Machen and Mary Williams, there was a degree of harmony between pagan and Christian ideas, and for oddities like Morien Welsh Christianity was a thinly disguised veneer on an ancient druidic heritage. Even the existence of so-called physical Grails, whether in the heart of Welsh Wales at Nanteos or on the Border at Hawkstone in Shropshire, incorporates Wales as part of a British or alternative Christian vision. The variety of ways in which the Grail has been used to reconstruct history is exactly what keeps this legend dynamic and alive.

CHAPTER 4

Celtic Origins and the Grail Romances

'the sense of a great loss which lies at the root of all the Celtic magic, the Celtic mysticism, the Celtic wonder ... the same message is delivered in ... the great mystery of the Sangraal, the holy thing that healed all hurts and doles'

Celtic Magic, Arthur Machen

MANY OF THE novels and short stories by the writer, Arthur Machen, are set in a fictionalized version of Caerleon and its environs, the area in South Wales where he grew up. Caerleon, the 'city of the legions' and an important base for Roman forces, embodied for him the lost order of the Roman world, while the surrounding countryside was imbued with an ancient Celtic magic which threatened to break through into the modern world. The Sangraal connects these two worlds. In the essay quoted above, Machen articulates the nature of the connection between the medieval Sangraal and the traditions of ancient Celtic magic. It was a view shared by many of his contemporaries, and *Celtic Magic* expresses a common perception that the Grail story originated as an ancient Celtic myth whose meaning formed the essence of Celtic religion. That the medieval romances preserved that secret meaning clothed in symbolic language remains a fundamental assumption in many contemporary treatments of the Grail and still makes use of assumptions rooted in the academic discourse of the nineteenth century. Scholarly interest at that time focused on whether the episodes of the Grail quest constituted a single narrative, and if so, what was its original meaning and purpose. A consensus favoured a myth about a pagan Celtic talisman associated with abundance, and the newly edited texts of Irish and Welsh tales came to be regarded as the sources of the Grail romances. The existence of a rich oral folk heritage, whose narrative themes and motifs closely resembled those in medieval literary texts, was also discovered in Celtic countries and in non-urban environments. This is where scholars believed that the sources of romances like those attached to the Grail were to be found.

A renewed appreciation of Celtic myth was further strengthened by developments in the fields of anthropology and archaeology as well as the new discipline of folklore. They provided a mechanism by which intellectual innovations, like the theory of evolution, could be applied to medieval texts. The study of religion and mythology by the Scottish classical scholar Sir James Frazer (1854–1941) is undoubtedly one of the most influential books ever written on the subject. Frazer's study, *The Golden Bough,* treated the origin and development of religion as a cultural phenomenon. It sought the common elements in all belief systems and examined their influence on organized religions like Christianity.[1] According to his theory, all religions originated as fertility cults aimed at maintaining the stability of the vegetation cycle and, subsequently, evolved into more rational forms of belief. At the earliest stage of culture, a sacred king embodied the solar god, who died with the harvest and was reborn annually in the spring, while his consort embodied the eternal earth goddess. To ensure the continued repetition of this cycle, the sacred king, or a substitute, was sacrificed periodically and a younger more vigorous successor put in his place.

The concepts of rationality and cultural survival were important for Frazer's theory. His comparative and historical analysis as a way of demystifying religion followed from Enlightenment thinking. Linear progressive evolution was a given for Frazer, as was the universality of human nature. The concept of cultural survival provided a link between primitive and modern, and the religious beliefs of primitive (i.e., less technologically advanced) peoples could be seen as distant reflections of modern society. As the mythic world of primitive man gave way to increasing rationality, remnants of earlier rituals and practices lingered on to become modern folk beliefs and customs still practised among the rural peasantry of modern-day Europe. This enabled Frazer and his contemporaries to see folk practices as remnants of fertility rituals. Although contemporary anthropologists point out that Frazer's dying gods were the results of carefully selective and over-interpreted sources, his universal system harmonized with the late Victorian worldview. What seemed more shocking at that time was that Frazer applied his theory to Christianity, seeing the death and resurrection of Jesus Christ in terms of his dying god hypothesis and implying that Christianity itself was the remnant of a pagan religion.[2] Frazer's approach has been revived in the context of traditionalist contemporary alternative writing. In works such as these, the primitive aspects of nature worship and fertility ritual are presented as the essential elements of true religion, and the process of change, which Frazer regarded as the inevitable effect of social evolution, becomes a sinister conspiracy of repression. None of the scholars who searched for the Celtic origins of the Holy Grail in the late nineteenth and early twentieth centuries even went this far, but the work of Jessie Weston and Arthur Edward Waite took the subject in the direction of esotericism and laid the groundwork for further speculation.

The integration of extensive collections of oral material from Celtic areas with ideas about ancient myth, and the evolutionary development of culture comes together in the work of Alfred Nutt, publisher and founding member of the Folklore Society. *Studies in the Legend of the Holy Grail: With Especial Reference to the Hypothesis of Its Celtic Origin* was published in 1888, only two years before the first edition of *The Golden Bough,* under the aegis of the Folklore Society, an institution devoted to the study of traditional culture.[3] This detailed study is a seminal work in Grail scholarship and an important step in the process which transformed a medieval literary theme into a search for secret knowledge, a search that is now part of a public discourse embracing modern mass publishing and an ever-expanding Internet. A point of contact between the literary Grail romances and popular speculation is Nutt's thesis that a Grail myth existed in early Celtic culture and was transmitted in a Christianized form in medieval romance. These ideas were expanded and refined by later medievalists like R. S. Loomis, who attempted a detailed examination of the stages by which the myth was transformed. They were also adapted to more esoteric uses. Jessie Weston suggested that the Grail romances concealed a sacred initiation rite, and Lewis Spence advocated a revival of Celtic religion based on mystery cults, while for A. E. Waite the Grail embodied a Christian mysticism. Among those influential in shaping Glastonbury into a modern spiritual centre, Dr Goodchild and Lionel Smithett Lewis both believed that the Grail originated in a Celtic context. Indeed, it is in the area of esoteric interpretation that Nutt's academic theories continue to have their strongest impact.

The American Arthurian scholar and folklorist Jessie Weston summed up Nutt's contributions to Celtic studies. 'The great value of Mr Nutt's work has been his appreciation of the fact that the progress of Arthurian romance has been along the road of evolution, that direct literary invention has played but a secondary part in the growth of this wonderful body of romance ... he pointed out the part which specifically Celtic tradition had played in this evolutionary process.'[4] Weston's assessment stressed that the origins of romances written largely in French, English or German should be rooted in Celtic folk tradition and that the methodology for demonstrating this should be derived from scientific theory. The link between mythic origins and evolutionary progress she perceived still remains central to the search for a Celtic Grail.

FINDING A CELTIC MYTH

Alfred Trübner Nutt (1856–1910) was born into a publishing family. He spent several years learning the publishing business in Europe, and after his father's death, took over as head of the publishing house, David Nutt and Co. Through his writing on folklore and the Grail material, his publishing ventures, and his contact with other scholars, he helped extend new approaches to traditional narrative into the study of medieval romance and Celtic tradition. Neither the evolutionary approach to narrative analysis nor its specific application to Celtic material originated with Nutt, and his attitudes to folklore, Celtic culture and the origins of the Grail need to be seen in the context of wider cultural trends. However, as scholar and publisher he was in a position to influence the direction of research. The output of the David Nutt firm under his leadership synthesized earlier scholarly work. This included a series for the general public, *Popular Studies in Mythology, Romance and Folklore*, with several volumes devoted to Arthurian romances.[5]

The principles that guided Nutt and his contemporaries combined the techniques of the geologist in using fossils with those of the archaeologist in using material culture. He challenged the prevailing assumption that European folklore was merely a faded remnant of an ancient Aryan mythology and advocated a more scientific classification of material so that folklore could take its place with disciplines that depended on accurate classification of data.[6] Evolution and progress, not philological corruption and dispersion, were now the underlying principles in the development of culture.[7] An important consequence of this method was that early man could be compared to modern so-called primitives like the Celts. Nutt's interest in theory was complemented by an interest in collecting and classification.[8] Collectors such as Douglas Hyde, John Campbell of Islay, Sir John Rhŷs and Paul Sébillot began scouring areas in which Celtic languages were still spoken. The abundance of Celtic folktale texts provided data comparable to the abundance of species in biology and undoubtedly contributed to the notion that Celtic peoples had preserved their ancient heritage in contemporary oral tradition.[9] Nutt also recognized the importance of accurate texts and good translations in order to make Celtic literature available to the Celt himself and to the non-Celtic peoples of Europe.

He published translations by distinguished scholars such as Jessie Weston[10] and Eleanor Hull, whose work on pagan and Christian Irish history drew heavily on the assumptions of evolutionary archaeology and previous work by Nutt himself.[11] The Irish scholar Kuno Meyer was another close collaborator. Meyer had called attention to the value of Irish literature in the evolution of western European thought and suggested that modern Irish, far from being a degenerate form of Old Irish, was a natural development of it. These ideas echoed Nutt's objections to the mythological school with its emphasis on folklore as the detritus of early mythology and reinforced his belief in the importance of collecting existing folklore.[12]

A significant aspect of Nutt's work was his use of folk narrative to present a coherent argument for the continued existence of myths and beliefs over the centuries. In his study of the Celtic origin of the Grail legend, Alfred Nutt examined Irish, Welsh and Scots Gaelic folk narratives in order to find the ultimate source for the Grail episode in medieval romance. According to him, the real meaning of the Grail narrative lay in the original Celtic myths still preserved in contemporary Celtic folktales, while the retellings in medieval romance preserved these meanings to a lesser, somewhat confused, degree.[13] His assumption that meaning existed outside a romance narrative and in the distant past was not unique, but he substantiated his claims with the full panoply of nineteenth-century folklore theory. The idea that a sacrificial ritual intended to renew the fertility of the agricultural cycle was common to all ancient societies formed the centrepiece of James Frazer's *The Golden Bough*.[14] Initially Nutt accepted Frazer's theories about a myth concerning the death and rebirth of this vegetation god. He argued that such a myth had been central to Celtic mythology and was present with special vividness in Celtic folklore.[15] This helped put the idea of a sacrificial ritual at the root of Celtic belief on an academic footing. He subsequently altered his view about the function of this agricultural cult, but he continued to use the newly collected wealth of Celtic narrative to support the idea that beliefs in contemporary Celtic societies were survivals of ancient strata of culture.

For him, as for so many of his contemporaries, human intellect, while progressive, never left the past entirely behind but always retained 'distinct marks of the ruder simpler stage out of which (it) emerged'.[16] The Celts seemed the ideal embodiment of this. Their lively 'pagan' imagination was fashionable thanks to such writers as Matthew Arnold and was about to become more so under the spur of romantic ideas about Celtic culture, led by such figures as the Irish poet W. B. Yeats. The prevailing view about contact between the Celts and Christianity provided a mechanism for the transformation, and inevitable distortion, of myth. Thus the often quite dramatic inconsistencies between early Celtic tradition and the Grail episodes in medieval romances could be resolved in terms of the distorting effects of oral transmission or the adaptation of pagan myths to the context of Christian doctrine. This process of transmission might be compared to a game of Chinese whispers. As the myth was passed on it changed; the more it was passed on the more it changed until the original meaning became lost or reinterpreted as something quite different. Important elements of the original myth, which survived in later romances, included supernatural vessels with magic properties, vengeance plots, and stories of heroes seeking supernatural brides. These seemed to confirm belief in the antiquity of Celtic tradition and in the effect of Christianity, which had provided a force for preserving ancient pagan Celtic myths while introducing significant transformations and adaptations.

Ideas about Celtic culture and nationhood undoubtedly influenced Nutt's thinking. Interest in the moral universe of the Celts and a feeling that, whatever the political conditions, Celtic poets attempted to preserve their special inheritance, revealed a predisposition towards the imaginative and poetic nature of Celtic folklore. However, his brand of 'sophisticated nationalism', like the notion of Britishness suggested by Matthew Arnold, included all of medieval Britain.[17] In an essay on why the Matter of Britain (i.e., Celtic narrative) was taken up by the Anglo-Normans, he suggested that, this new elite shed the old mythology of the Charlemagne cycle (the Matter of France) and the classical stories (the Matter of Rome) and sought myths appropriate for their new social and political circumstances. They found them in the stories of the Celts which, and Nutt was very perceptive here, could be used to create a new national identity and express the aspirations of a powerful feudal elite by a return to the moral structure of ancient times.[18]

Nutt was not the first to explore Celtic food-producing vessels as a source for the Grail, or the first to look to the Celts for an origin myth. The noted French scholar Theodore de la Villemarqué proposed some tentative links between Breton tales and a Welsh poem, *The Spoils of Annwn* (*Preiddeu Annwn*), about an otherworldly raid to bring back a cauldron.[19] This idea was taken up by another influential French critic, Ernest Renan, whose writings did much to create the idea of the Celts as an imaginative, poetic race. Renan suggested that Bendigeidfran's *peir dadeni* ('cauldron of plenty'), as described in the *Mabinogion,* was the pagan source for the Grail and that it represented an initiation rite for 'a kind of freemasonry'. Renan's essay appeared in the same year as Darwin's *Origin of Species* (1859), but already the elements of myth, initiation and Freemasonry intertwined with the conservative nature of Celtic tradition had been established as a viable approach to their heritage.[20] Welsh neo-druid writers from the early nineteenth century had been among the first to notice similarities between objects belonging to traditional Welsh heroes like Arthur that provided abundant food and drink and the Grail of later romances.[21]

The Reverend Sabine Baring-Gould (1834–1924) also realized the importance of Celtic tradition in relation to the Grail story. A man of wide interests and a noted collector of folklore, he explored the sources for the Holy Grail and its meaning in his popular and influential compendium *Curious Myths of the Middle Ages*. These included episodes from Villemarqué's translation of the *Mabinogion*, Archbishop Ussher's book on the future of British Christianity, and the *Myvyrian Archaiology* edited by the Welsh antiquarian Iolo Morganwg.[22] Baring-Gould believed that the medieval Welsh tale of *Peredur* was the earliest text, even though it appeared in comparatively late manuscripts, certainly later than Chrétien's *Conte du Graal*. It seemed to him to bear evidence of a 'higher' antiquity, despite the fact that the incidents had been 'modified and softened' and 'various points indicative of barbarism and paganism omitted'. His work reveals a growing confidence in the reliability of scholarly reconstruction, and he assured his readers that 'a practised eye will be able to restore what is disintegrated and will know to detect antiquity, though disguised under the newest robe'.[23] He saw parallels for the *disgyl* seen by Peredur at his uncle's castle in lists of magic objects from Welsh and Irish literature, and therefore had no trouble assuming that the Welsh text had simply Christianized an ancient myth. The neo-druidic overtones of Iolo Morganwg's *Myvyrian Archaiology* already pointed in that direction. 'The Sangreal' was for Baring-Gould 'a mysterious relic of a past heathen rite', a Christian version of the cauldron of Ceridwen associated with human sacrifice that formed part of the druidic initiation. He also discussed possible connections between the accusations against the Templars and the Grail. Although he dismissed the idea that Gnostic beliefs lay behind the Templar heresy, he did connect the head supposedly worshipped by them with the head on the platter in the Welsh romance *Peredur*. This he believed was part of an ancient druid initiation rite that 'lingered on and gained consistency again among the Templars'.[24]

A number of interesting studies made significant contributions to the idea of a Celtic myth as the origin of the Grail. Arthur C. L. Brown, for example, traced the Grail back to Irish mythological texts and folktales about heroic journeys in which the hero meets a 'hospitable host' whom he saves from enchantment. Brown also compared the Grail to the cauldron of the Irish god Dagda, which gave abundant food.[25] Most influential of all, however, was the work of the American Arthurian scholar Roger

Sherman Loomis, whose study of the origins of Arthurian romance was a landmark in its time. Loomis has been called the 'archetypal Celtic enthusiast',[26] and he traced the origin of the Grail to a series of motifs from the mythological sources of the Irish adventure tales. These mythological motifs were transmitted through medieval Welsh tales to the French *contes* by way of Breton *jongleurs*. In this way he accounted for the movement of material from Celtic to French sources and then into the Grail romances. 'What is not available in the scanty remains of Welsh can be discovered in Irish sagas and folktale ... To reach Chrétien they must have followed the usual route through Wales.'[27] The motifs he identified as sources for the Grail story included meat and drink magically produced from a golden cup, a woman who was transformed from ugly to beautiful, a test in which the king and the castle disappear if a question is asked incorrectly, a hospitable king wounded in the thigh, a magically blighted land and finally heroes who inhabit an ageless other world. In the context of medieval romance these became the Grail quest, the twin aspects of Grail maiden and loathly damsel, the Fisher King in his castle, the wasteland and the Grail knights.[28]

Loomis's work focused on the idea of linguistic misunderstanding as a factor in the development of the text, and less on parallels in folklore that underpinned so much of Alfred Nutt's thinking.[29] Nevertheless, his conclusions were markedly similar. Loomis too saw the Grail myth as a remnant of druidic esoteric lore, a seasonal myth in which the change from winter to spring was expressed in terms of the god's sexual relations with a goddess who embodied the land. He compared the Grail with Irish talismans and with the vessel presented to the hero by a sovereignty goddess. After the original Irish myth had been transmitted to Wales, it became the sacred vessel of Bran the Blessed, one of the heroes in the Welsh *Mabinogion*. In this context, it was misinterpreted as the body of Christ, thus conflating a pagan myth with the Christian Mass.[30] Loomis's theories, especially his linguistic speculations, have been heavily criticized, but his idea that an ostensibly Christian image in a medieval romance could be traced back by apparently sound academic arguments to a pagan past remains very popular.[31]

Not everyone was convinced that the origin of the Grail was to be found in folklore, and specifically Celtic folklore at that, or that Christian development was a later feature of the story. The American scholar William Wells Newell was sceptical of the idea that the Holy Grail was a gradual transformation of old Celtic folktales into a poem drenched in Celtic symbolism and mysticism. He recognized that 'Celtic symbolism and mysticism' was just as likely to be the result of individual imagination as folk belief, and he focused on the literary context of the manuscripts and the conscious artistry of the poets. His critique, published at the end of the nineteenth century, offered a rigorous rebuttal of the Celtic hypothesis.[32] Newell was not the only commentator who offered an alternative to what was rapidly becoming the prevailing view. Adolf Birch-Hirschfeld held that the Grail was a Christian narrative and only subsequently acquired folklore characteristics.[33] Lisette Andrews Fisher offered a Eucharistic interpretation superimposed on a fusion of pagan legend and the Joseph of Arimathea story.[34] The Grail was identified with the Eucharist cup, and the Fisher King became a metaphor for the crucified Christ. The possibility of a Christian origin for the Grail has had more adherents than has perhaps been recognized,[35] although scholars had different ideas about what this Christianity was like. The Eucharistic rites of the Eastern Christian Church, in which a cup is used for the wine and a lance-like knife is used to cut the bread, have been put forward as a possible source. The Grail procession as a whole bears little resemblance to these rites,[36] and others located the origins of the Grail in a primitive and pure form of Christianity described in the biblical Apocrypha.[37] The idea that it derived from a specifically Celtic form of Christianity underpins the work of several Welsh scholars and those who advocate the link between St Joseph, Glastonbury and the Grail. But in recent years, the idea of a Gnostic Christian origin for the Grail has outstripped other explanations.

Whether Christian or pagan, the aim was to find a common origin for the Grail romances that 'would explain its diversity and make of it a unity'. The work of scholars like Alfred Nutt established a strong theoretical basis for origin studies grounded in source evaluation and careful textual analysis. However, this type of criticism focused on reconstructed originals rather than the actual extant texts.[38] Another problem is that origin theories rely heavily on the timeless universality of oral tradition. If a tradition could be described as 'oral', it was automatically considered to pre-date any written versions. The significance of parallels was often exaggerated in the search for origins, and many of the complicated linguistic arguments have not held up to scrutiny.[39] A further theoretical difficulty was the assumption that the development from oral to literary is a one-way process. This overlooked the possibility of mutual influence between oral and literary forms, and the fact that many oral folktales collected during the nineteenth-century collecting surge had their origins in manuscripts.[40] Nutt called the Grail romances 'the happy hunting ground of mystical enthusiasts',[41] and his own rigorous studies were an attempt to redress this. The treatment of the oldest stratum of material moderated the rather harsh view that the primitive world was a savage one and presented a more sympathetic picture, but it paved the way for a romantic view of the Celts as a culture that preserved imaginative, and even moral, faculties which had been lost. Despite these very real theoretical problems, Celtic tradition is still recognized as important to the background of the Grail texts.

THE ESOTERIC GRAIL

The search for a Celtic myth produced a relatively coherent interpretation of the Grail story, whatever the theoretical problems. Those who sought origins in Celtic mythology often viewed the Grail in medieval romances as a confused or misunderstood version of an ancient myth. An alternative approach regarded romance writers as members of an elite who utilized the genre to conceal some cosmic secret. Special groups whose task was to guard the secret message carried this information beyond the romance narratives. Writers like Archbishop James Ussher looked to medieval religious groups, like the Waldensians, for guardians of the true message of Christianity.[42] The Reverend Sabine Baring-Gould linked the Templars with the secrets of the Grail, although he believed that they acquired their wisdom from the Celtic West, not the mystic East. These early, and somewhat tentative suggestions, helped pave the way for one of the most prevalent assumptions in the modern Grail legends, namely that the authors of medieval romance were privy to some cosmic insight, and that they used the romance genre to conceal that information from all but a chosen few initiates. The mechanisms behind secret tradition theories, however, are very different. Origin theories look for a single principle that will unify everything, while secret tradition theories seek out unrelated scraps that can be welded into a whole. Secret tradition theories resemble nothing so much as a scavenger hunt in which a series of clues lead to a hidden treasure, and the proponents of such theories often look beyond the Celts to ever more ancient rituals in their search for the origin of the Grail.

Much has been written about the ways in which science and an increasingly sceptical attitude to religion shaped the intellectual outlook of the nineteenth century. Darwin's theory of evolution provided not just a model for understanding the diversity of species, but one that could also explain the origin and development of social institutions. This evolutionary view was adapted to the history of religion. An increasingly sceptical attitude to the literal truth of the Bible and the application of the theory of evolution to anthropological studies also encouraged this interest in the origin of religion. Writers sought to identify the most primitive myths and rituals and to demonstrate how they changed over time, evolving into the rational worldview of contemporary society. No one epitomized this better than James G. Frazer's monumental work *The Golden Bough*, revised over several decades and which attempted to trace the history of religious belief for the entire human race. For Frazer rationality was associated with modernity and progress. Primitive people looked to non-rational forces to explain critical aspects of existence, such as human fertility and the repetition of the seasonal cycles. As culture evolved, increasing rationality brought about changes in outlook. Earlier beliefs, like customs and myths that once formed a coherent worldview at a more primitive level of culture, became the quaint 'survivals' of folklore.

The centrepiece of Frazer's work was a myth about a vegetation god who died with the passing of the growing season and was reborn each spring. At a very early stage of culture, the group's leader, or a substitute scapegoat, was literally sacrificed in order to maintain the cycle of fertility. Over time, the ritual gave way to a narrative reflex, namely a myth about a dying god who revived each spring. The myth sustained the fertility-giving agricultural cycle without an actual sacrificial ritual. This shifted the emphasis from myth as a primitive explanation of natural phenomena to the notion that myth provided a magical maintenance of worldview. The emergence of modern anthropological theories and literary criticism from these early roots has been well documented,[43] but Frazer's dying god myth influenced more esoteric interpretations of culture. What folklorists regarded as the fossils of primitive rituals relating to agriculture, others came to regard as evidence for the continued existence of a secret tradition, a mystery cult, associated with seasonal renewal. The theory of cultural evolution, which used contemporary folklore as evidence for past cultural forms, was transferred to the context of a secret tradition where it provided evidence for the continuation of belief. Where folklorists and anthropologists saw mere remnants resulting from an inevitable progressive evolution in culture, other writers asserted the continued existence of an agricultural fertility cult driven underground by a rival belief system, usually Christianity. In this way, cultural theory was transformed into mystic belief.

From this evolutionary perspective, Grail motifs could be derived from ancient Celtic mythic tradition, and the similarities between Christianized Grail romances and existing Celtic folktales provided apparent support for the evolutionary character of tradition. Initially Alfred Nutt accepted the relevance of Frazer's proposed vegetation god for Celtic mythology. He helped define the parameters of the pagan Celtic versus Christian debate by focusing on what he considered the central condition, namely the harmonization of Celtic agricultural ritualism and mythology with alien Christian rituals and romance.[44] It would be simplistic to consider Nutt the only source for this, and other writers developed these ideas further in the direction of esoteric theory. For Arthurian scholars like Jessie Weston, Celtic revivalists such as Lewis Spence, poets like W. B. Yeats, and occultists such as A. E. Waite and G. R. S. Mead, the rituals of the primitive agricultural world were not fragmentary survivals, but a coherent worldview supported by a ritual mechanism, which had continued in secret. Weston saw these rituals as the esoteric explanation for the Grail and Spence saw them as a way to renew national consciousness; but they found their most imaginative synthesis in Waite's writings on the tarot.

Theories that sought the origin of the Grail in ancient rituals often looked beyond even Celtic pagans or Christians. Ancient Greek mystery cults were presented as a source for the Grail legend, although even here Celtic tradition formed an important intermediate stage. Such theories assumed that a higher purpose lay behind the purely physical fertility rite. Jessie Laidley Weston's somewhat eccentric ideas about 'mystery rituals' are an excellent example of the anthropological approach to folktale and ancient myth.[45] Her insistence on an ancient secret fertility ritual caused her to reject concrete objects like the Nanteos cup.[46] Her ideas are typical of the esoteric search for something more fundamental than Celtic paganism as a source for the Grail legend.[47] 'Celtic fairy-tales,' she wrote, 'charming as they are, can never afford a satisfactory or abiding resting place . . . a path that leads but into a Celtic Twilight can only be a by-path'.[48] The wasteland theme was the essential feature of the Grail myth according to Weston's interpretation, despite the fact that it is not prominent in all the Grail romances. For her, the romances described the sexual initiation of the knights. The wasteland motif represented the dormant phase of the lifecycle of the dying god and could be broken only by the suitably initiated young hero. According to Weston, medieval texts preserved the rituals of an ancient mystery religion, which had to be disguised to escape the notice of Christianity. Before publishing her thoughts on the development of the Grail tradition, she submitted them 'to a mystic of experience' who assured her, 'this is the story of an Initiation told from the outside'.[49] The mystic was probably her mentor, G. R. S. Mead, or just possibly Annie Besant, as both were cited in her bibliography.[50] Mead's book, *Fragments of a Faith Forgotten*,[51] used exactly this anthological approach to symbolism in literature in order to reconstruct, not an ancient lost original, but a living secret esoteric tradition.

Some of the most influential texts for the contemporary revival of Celtic mysticism are to be found among the writings of the Scottish journalist and folklorist Lewis Spence. Born James Lewis Chalmers Spence in 1874, he received his education at Edinburgh University before choosing a career in journalism. He was an active supporter of Scottish independence, and his romantic brand of nationalism emphasized the 'Celtic' history of Scotland as a way to explain the differences between the Scots and the English, or more romantically, the Celts and the Saxons. In his view, Scottish history was a struggle between a democratic and progressive Celtic culture and an authoritarian, imperialistic Saxon conqueror. For Spence, Celtic language and culture were quintessentially Scottish, and he advocated the idea that Scottish national Celticism would act as a regenerative force to transform and save the British nation.[52] This well-meaning, if naive, political philosophy informed his approach to Celtic culture. His numerous books, articles and pamphlets are devoted to mythology and occult philosophy and what he believed they revealed about the ancient past and the workings of the human mind.[53]

Lewis Spence combined a suggestion made, although later rejected, by Alfred Nutt about a mythic food-producing vessel at the centre of a Celtic agricultural myth with his own interest in shamanism and ancestor cults. This led him back to the neo-druidic speculations of the eighteenth century about druidism as proto-Christianity. The result was a Celtic Christian mystery religion centred on the mystic experience of the Grail. It was a heady mix, created out of a magpie collection of Scottish folklore, snippets of Celtic texts, theoretical fragments from Alfred Nutt and James Frazer, hints of Nietzsche's Dionysian aesthetics and oddments of occult lore. Like many of his contemporaries, Spence believed that the occult impulse was a psychic power inherent in human nature, but one that was particularly strong among the Celts.[54] His version of ancient Celtic religion was centred on a complex system of beliefs about the seasonal and vegetative cycle of growth, decay and regeneration, expressed in a myth about a fertility deity who died annually, but was reborn with the spring vegetation. In primitive society, this myth was embodied in a ritual surrounding a divine king whose 'death' through sacrifice brought about the continued fertility of the vegetative cycle and, by extension, of the kingdom. Initially the king was physically sacrificed, although later substitute took his place, and eventually the physical ritual gave way to a symbolic and metaphorical act. Ordinary men, and women, could participate in this journey of death and regeneration through personal initiation into an ancient system of wisdom whose secret had been preserved in some disguised or hidden form. This idea permeated several books on mystery religion, which Spence considered a positive manifestation of the occult impulses of ancient cultures like the Celts.[55] The conservators of this mystery were not a cabal of intellectuals, the 'mystery' that would save mankind was preserved in the untainted Celtic peasant world of folk beliefs.

The occult wisdom enshrined in mystery religions could be abused, and Spence attributed the demise of Atlantis to the misuse of occult knowledge.[56] In doing so, he followed in the footsteps of other writers who used the concept of a failed utopia to draw attention to the shortcomings of their own civilizations. Crucially, for Spence, the Grail myth was the means of renewal. He combined A. E. Waite's speculation on the Grail as the non-corporeal endpoint in a mystical search with Alfred Nutt's suggestion that it was a cult object in Celtic religion. Mystical Celtic religion and the occult came together in two millennial tracts written during the world wars. These wartime tracts cast European history and its future prospects in terms of the fate of Atlantis, whose destruction had been brought about by the misuse of the occult arts. Spence linked the rise of Nazism in Germany with a similar misuse of occult power, and he argued that only the revival of Celtic religion would stem the tide of the 'dark Germanic *cultus*' and save Europe.[57] The seemingly bizarre combination of psychic power, Atlantis and the Grail was based on an alternative view of history that looked west instead of east for cultural origins.[58] The Grail had become an occult experience of the divine accessible for ordinary men and women.

By mixing occult ideas with speculations about folklore, Spence created a Celtic mystery religion based on the concepts of a traditional cult vessel and a divine king. It also reflected the notion that the occult (i.e., mystic) impulse in man was a protest against the manipulations of orthodox religion.[59] His idealized image of divine kingship linked to the cycle of nature took the form of an Arthurian cult whose purpose was to preserve the sacred isle of Britain from destruction by invading barbarians. 'Arthur was one of the central figures of the great British cult of the dead, the British Osiris, who was associated with the drama and ritual of agriculture and of war and who "died" ritually with each succeeding Winter'.[60] This 'military and arcane *cultus*' was charged with 'the conservation of British ideals and civilization and the cherishing of that Secret British Celtic Tradition which had flourished in our island from time immemorial. Central to that cult was an arcane initiation in the underworld preserved in poems such as the *Spoils of Annwn* (*Preiddeu Annwn*), the motif of the Cauldron of Inspiration owned by the mythological Welsh figure, Ceridwen, and eventually in the context of Christian chivalry, the Holy Grail.'[61] This legacy was not lost, but went underground after the invasion of the Anglo-Saxons and the Normans. It encapsulated, first in a Scottish, then in a European and ultimately in a global context, all the qualities of a liberal and tolerant society, and the revival of Celtic religion would somehow magically make things right.

The writings of Arthur Edward Waite (1857–1942), especially his idio-syncratic *Key to the Tarot*, brought together ideas associated with modern occultism and assumptions about the nature of culture. The history of the Holy Grail and the people who have become involved with it is full of striking personalities, but even among these, Waite is one of the most unusual. Among his many Grail-related activities, he examined the Glastonbury Grail and visited Nanteos.[62] After the death of his American father, Waite's English mother returned to Britain and converted to Roman Catholicism. Although he received minimal formal education, he pursued a career in journalism and writing. His output was prodigious, although his impenetrable and florid writing style can be off-putting. His intensely curious mind embraced the whole range of subjects covered by what has become known as the occult revival in the late nineteenth and early twen-tieth centuries. These included theosophy, alchemy, mysticism, Freemasonry, Gnosticism, ceremonial magic and, of course, the medieval Grail romances. He was involved in the reform of the Order of the Golden Dawn which saw members like Aleister Crowley ousted and shifted the focus towards more mystical practice. In line with these reforms, Waite oversaw the produc-tion of a new pack of tarot cards and wrote an accompanying book, the *Pictorial Key to the Tarot* which expatiated, at length, on his personal interpretation of its symbolism and its relation to the Grail.

THE CELTIC TAROT AND THE HOLY GRAIL

Tarot cards made their first appearance as a means of fortune telling and esoteric investigation in France at the end of the eighteenth century, although they had already been used for non-occult card games for several centuries.[63] A widespread revival of interest in the occult from the late 1880s to the 1930s affected the development of the tarot in Britain and transformed it into a vibrant manifestation of popular culture. It was in the context of this occult revival that tarot cards became irrevocably linked with the Grail. During this period, ideas about the origin and meaning of Arthurian tradi-tion and ideas about the nature of culture drawn from folklore and anthro-pological theory were combined to create an esoteric, pseudo-academic legend about the tarot as a secret tradition. The occult revival in Britain challenged what it perceived as the stultifying effects of social conventions, and tarot imagery became a way of projecting this.

Waite was both a Freemason and a member of the Order of the Golden Dawn. His interest in the Holy Grail stemmed from his conviction that a 'secret tradition' had been preserved through the ages and that it could regenerate mankind and allow individuals to attain union with the divine. He shared this interest with his friend and fellow writer Arthur Machen.[64] Waite popularized the existence of such a tradition in western esotericism, although for him the 'secret doctrine' was more mystical than occult. The Anglo-Welsh Machen, on the other hand, saw the Grail in terms of the Eucharist and Celtic Christian relics.[65] The two friends collaborated on a verse 'mystery play' about the Grail and discussed it in their correspondence.[66] There was a strong vein of populism in Waite, despite his involvement with esoteric orders such as the Golden Dawn, and his writings suggest that this secret wisdom was accessible to all individuals through personal mystical experience. His ideas about the availability of mystical experience anticipate the spirit of new age religion, and are at odds with the elitism which lies at the heart of many secret tradition theories.[67] Waite's esoteric ideas seem rather naive and quaint now, but his commitment to what he believed was vital work in the spiritual and intellectual redemption of mankind cannot be doubted.

The images for Waite's tarot pack were realized by Pamela Coleman Smith, a fellow member of the Golden Dawn, and first published by Rider Press in 1910.[68] Unlike earlier packs, in which only the court cards and the trumps had pictures, every card is lavishly illustrated. Waite created the 'rectified' tarot from an eclectic collection of influences, and the way in which he departed from these sources is both interesting and revealing. Personal ritual books kept by members of the Order of the Golden Dawn illustrate the imaginative, but often idiosyncratic, nature of the imagery they used. It can be difficult to sort out exact sources where mutual influence was so common, but the Rider pack undoubtedly reflects the spirit of this esoteric institution. The cabalistic ideas of the French occultist Eliphas Levi (Alphonse Louis Constant), whose works Waite translated, also influenced the imagery on some of the cards.[69] Levi's illustration for the Devil trump in the tarot depicts an enthroned figure with a goat's head. It holds a flaming torch, like the one used in the classical rites of Dionysus. Levi implied that this figure presided over the rituals of the 'old religions' driven underground by Christianity who had transformed this prototype fertility deity, so important in ritual interpretations of the Grail legend, into a demonic being.[70] The figure turns up again as a face inscribed on Levi's five-pointed pentagram talisman. Waite's somewhat uncertain French seems to have rendered this as 'pentacle' or 'pentangle', thereby introducing these terms into the vocabulary of modern tarot. Waite equated the 'pentacle/pentangle' symbol with the suit of coins/spades in his tarot deck, and then proceeded to claim that the pentangle was actually the ancient source of the modern coin suit.

Some imagery reflects earlier tarot decks.[71] The twenty-two trumps of the Rider pack are called 'Major Arcana'. The term was adopted from the vocabulary of French occultism when mystical interpretations of what had been a card game became popular. One of the most important cards according to Waite is the Hanged Man. The imagery may have been influenced by Renaissance depictions of public shaming for criminal behaviour, or it may have entered the tarot by accident as a misprint of an image of Prudence.[72] Esoteric and ritual interpretations of the Grail story associate it with the dying god of J. G. Frazer's mythic reconstructions.[73] Another possible source for images on Waite's tarot cards may relate directly to esoteric beliefs about the nature of the Grail. The esoteric scholar Howard Bayley claimed that certain early watermarks depicted a 'Cathar Grail' and provided what he believed was a cogent emblematic link to the mystic traditions of the Cathars.[74] His book *New Light on the Renaissance,* in which he examined the 'hidden' Cathar symbolism to be found in emblems and watermarks in early printed books, appeared in the same year as Waite's *The Hidden Church of the Holy Grail.* The two writers approached the subject of secret tradition in a similar way, even when their conclusions differed.[75] Some cards in Waite's suit of cups, such as the Ace and the Queen, resemble early illustrations of watermarks printed by Bayley.[76] A rather quirky book, *The Medieval Manichee,* by the distinguished historian Sir Steven Runciman, suggested that the Trumps, or Major Arcana, of the tarot pack contained symbolic references to dualist heresies, but the theory was not taken up by the academic community as a whole.[77]

Existing research on Celtic myth and folklore as a source for Arthurian Grail literature offered Waite a 'Celtic' interpretation for the four tarot suits.[78] In Waite's own phrase he called them the 'Four Grail Hallows'. The most likely source for this idea was the suggestion put forward by none other than Alfred Nutt, that the objects in the Grail procession in medieval romance could be identified with four supernatural objects belonging to the Tuatha Dé Danann.[79] Waite, and later esoteric writers, added the idea that these were Celtic talismans held in trust by a secret fellowship.[80] In this way, mystical interpretations of tarot cards were linked to speculations about Irish mythology and medieval romance. Although he was never as committed to the pagan Celtic idea behind the tarot as W. B. Yeats or Jessie Weston, Waite insisted that the Celtic Church practised true Christianity, untainted by later distortions. The identification of talismans and tarot suits glossed over the fact that the number of objects in the Grail procession varied in the Grail romances and in the Welsh or Irish lists of supernatural treasures. The fact that Waite failed to establish a compelling connection with Celtic culture has not hindered his popularity. Two explanatory volumes accompanied his 'rectified' tarot. In a short volume entitled a *Key to the Tarot* with the subtitle 'Being Fragments of a Secret Tradition under the Veil of Divination', Waite described a divinatory layout he claimed was 'used privately in England, Scotland and Ireland' to read the meaning of the cards.[81] A year later in a more comprehensive elaboration of his theories, *The Pictorial Key to the Tarot*, he called this layout the 'Celtic Cross'. The reason for the change is not clear. The credit for linking Irish myth with the tarot is often given to W. B. Yeats, but Waite had formed his own opinions about Celtic tradition and was somewhat resentful when others received credit for his suggestions.[82] Whatever the source, the 'Celtic Spread' has entered tarot mythology.[83]

G. R. S. Mead, theosophist and member of the Golden Dawn, hoped to encourage the academic study of esoteric subjects, and he invited Waite to lecture to his Quest Society on the esoteric links between the tarot and Arthurian literature.[84] Mead also influenced Jessie Weston in her search for the ultimate meaning of the Grail. She too equated the four treasures of the Tuatha Dé Danann with motifs found in the Grail romances and with the tarot suits, although she does not credit Waite for this.[85] She acknowledged the lack of direct connection between the supernatural treasures, the Grail story, the tarot cards and fertility rituals, but she looked to 'fragmentary survivals which would give evidence of the fertility ritual'. She sought, and found, such evidence in descriptions of traditional folk performances, like sword and Morris dances. These depended almost wholly on the writings of other scholars with an interest in the ritualistic explanation of modern folklore. Weston, rather coyly, queried in a footnote whether the pentangle could have been a sword dance figure.[86] A few pages later, she transformed her own query into an affirmative, and identified the pentangle tarot suit created by Waite at the beginning of the twentieth century with a device on Gawain's shield in a fourteenth-century poem *Gawain and the Green Knight*. In effect, this created a sense of antiquity by altering the symbolism in the desired direction and then cited the alterations as proof. Having demonstrated to her own satisfaction that tarot suits, Grail objects and ritual dances were derived from fertility rituals, she went one step further and equated the Green Knight in the medieval romance with a fertility deity analogous to Eliphas Levi's esoteric Devil. The initiation ritual, which, rightly or wrongly, had been associated with esotericism, was thus projected into a medieval romance using folk dance customs and ideas about ancient agricultural myths as proof.

Speculations about the Grail and the tarot weave in and out of occult, academic, and fictional writing. Arthur Machen used the image of the Grail in his writings, while Lewis Spence hoped the revival of the mystical

Grail religion of the Celts would provide a buffer against the evils of fascism. W. B. Yeats incorporated tarot images, derived in part from his personal understanding of the esoteric philosophy of the Golden Dawn, into *Red Hanrahan*.[87] Charles Williams's novel *The Greater Trumps* made use of tarot imagery,[88] while Eliot incorporated tarot images from the Waite/Coleman pack, although not their esoteric meaning, into *The Waste Land*.[89] They present a very attractive and imaginative vision of an alternative reality onto which it is possible to project a multitude of meanings, and they illustrate the process by which a cultural theory and its methodology can be transformed into belief.[90] There is, however, a fundamental difficulty in using arguments that assign meanings to tarot cards and their history where these are exactly the things that require independent proof. Such interpretations assume that material from different contexts and different periods can be linked, and that one can be used to explain the other without concern for external validation.

When ancient myths are suggested as sources for the Grail romances, episodes within the romances can easily be interpreted as fragmentary remains of these myths. The tradition that the king's virility is reflected in the health of the land is often used to explain the figure of the Fisher King. His injury is interpreted as an emasculation that causes his land to become wasted and barren. In parallel to the wounded king, his consort, the land over which he rules, is embodied in the form of goddess, beautiful and ugly by turns according to the health of the land itself. When a hero asks the right question the king is healed, the land is restored, and the hero assumes the kingship. The key to this process is a sacred object known as the Grail.

None of the Grail romances preserves this pattern intact, and the 'source' can be reconstructed only by rearranging elements from several romances and by interpolating material not actually in the texts. A loathly lady tells Perceval that his question would have healed the king and the land, and since the wounded king is his uncle, this might imply that Perceval is the rightful heir. However, the actual Grail-bearer serving the wounded king is beautiful, and it is not clear whether she and the loathly lady are the same. It was left to Chrétien's continuators to suggest solutions to this intriguing situation. In the *First Continuation* Gawain partially restores a wasteland, but there is a dead warrior rather than a sick king. *Parzival* heals a crippled king and takes his place, but without a wasteland. *Perlesvaus* contains the elements of sick king and wasted land, but no healing. The romance that comes closest to this supposed mythic pattern is the comparatively late *Suite de Merlin*. This raises a number of questions about the relationship of the romance writers and their sources. How aware were they of these supposedly pagan themes? How conscious were they of transforming them into a Christian format? These questions might be easier to answer if the Irish, Welsh, Breton and Cornish sources, which constituted the Matter of Britain, contained a text which preserved a cohesive version of this supposed myth of Celtic kingship. But they do not, and the myth itself has to be reconstructed and then used to make sense of references in romance texts.

The search for origins was part of intellectual life in the nineteenth century, and explanations for the Grail were sought in pagan Celtic myths, Celtic Christianity, or an ancient wisdom tradition. Early critics drew on newly collected folk narratives and recent editions of medieval texts to demonstrate that both the Grail romances and modern Celtic folklore descended from Celtic myth and existed in the same 'moral universe'. Celtic tradition was regarded as relatively independent of both classical and mainstream Christian civilization, and therefore provided a clear field for testing theories about origins. Having presented Celtic culture in this way, it is hardly surprising that early critics readily discovered a pagan Celtic origin beneath a subsequent Christian overlay. Writers who favoured a secret wisdom tradition as the origin for the Grail used a similar methodology, although they relied more heavily on texts associated with Renaissance philosophy and ritual magic. Western paganism was thus credited with possessing a profound sense of oneness with nature and with the rejection of pietistic religion. Once Christianity was presented as a factor in the transformation of a pagan Grail myth, it became easy to see it as distorting a preferred reality lying hidden just beneath the surface.

The idea of occult procedures as practical embodiments of esoteric ideas gained prominence with the popularity of Rosicrucianism and Freemasonry and the transformation of the old chivalric military orders into esoteric ones. Together with a growing interest in ritual techniques and in complex systems of symbol and metaphor, various movements sought, through esoteric knowledge, to achieve an ultimate integration of human culture, which would resolve religious differences and better the lot of mankind.[91] This kind of hermetic thinking may not have been as influential as some cultural historians suggest, but it helps to understand and evaluate the development of the modern tarot in the context of the nineteenth-century occult revival, and the emergence of an idea that a coterie of individuals possessed secret esoteric wisdom that could transform society. Categories identifiable at a philosophical level were redefined as history. This process, in part, underlies the esoteric tarot whose meanings were projected backwards onto the Renaissance and beyond. Many writers of the occult revival viewed the secret meanings of the tarot as a lost tradition that could be rediscovered only once the code was understood. The Grail encapsulated that secret, and writers like A. E. Waite believed that a continuous esoteric tradition had been handed on in secret by a coterie of initiates. For him, tarot cards were the conduits by which the secret tradition was transmitted, and his writings are important in popularizing the idea of a secret tradition within this kind of esoteric thinking.

It matters for our understanding of the Grail romances whether they are the result of an existing story or whether they develop by drawing on a wide fund of motifs. There are without doubt some very striking parallels outside these romances, such as Lugh's spear bubbling in the cauldron, or the wounded Bendigeidfran who owns the 'cauldron of regeneration'. There are problems even when the parallels are striking. The existing texts are too late to reflect myths directly. The story of Bendigeidfran from *Pedeir Keinc Y Mabinogi* is as much a product of conscious authorship as Chrétien's romance. Re-creating mythic material from these literary sources presents many of the same problems as re-creating myths from the romances. All too often popular attempts to recover supposed ancient wisdom from cultures removed in terms of historical time and with a very different world-view have been founded on a romanticized view of history and human nature. The search for the origin of the Grail romances was influenced by nineteenth-century assumptions about the evolution of culture, the march of progress from savagery to civilization, the advantages of the industrial over the rural world, and the importance of rational analysis. However, it also embodied the opposites of these qualities, seeking a harmony with all that was natural and unspoiled. Thus it distanced itself from the foreign and the rural as belonging to a more primitive stage of culture and, at the same time, it romanticized them, and through them sought to reclaim a spiritual wholeness which had seemingly been abandoned.

Theories that focused on a conjectured original often failed to appreciate the extant texts, and the assumption that the original meaning of these romances was rooted in the distant past was not without its critics. Many pointed to the subjectivity of arguments explaining original unity and subsequent diversity by what was essentially a process of corruption in which elements suited to a pre-conceived model confirmed continuity, and those which did not confirmed deterioration. Despite these reservations, theories about Grail origins, whether they concerned pagan Celts, unorthodox Christians or the followers of a secret wisdom tradition, have fired the public imagination, and the assumptions at the root of this approach continue to be refined and adapted.

CHAPTER 5

Secret Relics and
Hidden Codes

IN UMBERTO ECO'S sprawling satirical novel *Foucault's Pendulum*, a group of writers join forces to create a fictional conspiracy organized around a series of rules.[1] The central principle is that 'the Templars are involved in absolutely everything.' Ironically, but perhaps not surprisingly in a post-modernist novel, they become engulfed by their own creation. Truth and fiction become inextricably tangled, leaving only the weird shadows of a conspiratorial world. Eco's novel appeared before the publication of conspiracy thrillers like *The Da Vinci Code* and the frenzied interest they inspired, but Eco based his satire on the plethora of books already available about alternative history in which notions of Templar secrets and world conspiracies were advanced as serious, albeit speculative, revisions of history.

Earlier scholarship regarded the Grail romances as the survivals of a far older tradition combining both history and mythology. The historical material constituted a genuine core of information, while the confused and fragmented mythology reflected the myths and rituals of a remote age. Much speculation focused on Celtic myths about a pagan Grail, and the pre-Christian fertility ritual that it embodied. Even more grandiose claims appeared outside the scholarly field. The idea that the pagan world survived into the Christian Middle Ages, in secret, is a nostalgic and romantic view, while the belief that modern readers can understand and recapture it provides a flattering view of the present. Glastonbury became a focal point for many of these ideas, but it was not the only place where revelations about a mystical meaning rooted in a historical reality were sought. Semi-historical events, like the building of Solomon's temple in Jerusalem many centuries before the Christian era, also provided a context for speculations about the founding of secret societies. Historical conflicts like the Crusades became a conduit for passing on secrets and, behind them, even more obscure cosmological events were enshrined in ancient sites and in real or imagined features of landscape. The Templars soon began to rival the Celts as a popular source for the Grail story, and the current revival of interest in the Grail abounds with theories about Templars, Cathars, divine marriages, mysterious treasure and secret codes. These alternative theories are expansive, but surprisingly vague. A unified plot emerges only in fictional works like mass-market conspiracy novels, but the individual elements that make up these conspiracy legends have a unique and separate history of their own.

Attitudes to the Templars, the most popular source for conspiracy legends, started to shift when writers began to suggest that magic, rather than just idolatry and sodomy, had been part of their secret practices. The Templars were not immediately rehabilitated, however. Early in the sixteenth century, one of the most famous Renaissance writers on ritual magic, Cornelius Agrippa von Nettlesheim, included Gnostic magicians, pagan worshippers of Priapus and Pan, and the Templars in his discussion of the misuse of magical knowledge. The standard fantasies of sexual perversion and corruption, so essential to descriptions of otherness, were applied to the Templars, and the charges of sodomy were embroidered with tales of night orgies in dark caves and baby killing.[2] By the time Agrippa's work on magic was translated into French as part of a nineteenth-century revival of interest in the occult, the Templars were not only rehabilitated, but also endowed with elaborate doctrines and a complex and secretive internal structure. The south of France provided scope for geographical and historical speculations about the Grail. This area was the stronghold of a medieval religious sect known as the Cathars and a place where the Templars had also been powerful. Throughout the eighteenth and nineteenth centuries, both were reinterpreted in a more favourable light. Today Cathars and Templars, or rather the mysterious secrets they were supposed to guard, have become linked to popular interpretations of the Grail. Claims about occult geometrical patterns in baroque paintings have been invoked to reveal hidden doctrines or applied to the landscapes of France, Scotland, Scandinavia and Canada. The Cathars, the Templars, and, to a lesser extent, the evangelical Waldensians have been absorbed into modern Grail theories. These groups have become linked to one another, as they never were historically, by loose notions of gnostic dualism. The very fact of persecution allowed the members of these movements to be seen as martyrs. The added fact that their organizations no longer exist enabled them to be re-created as secret societies. Stated thus, it seems a very naive project, but the idea of a secret gnostic system that manifested itself in the beliefs of Cathars, Templars and Waldensians has become a powerful tool of alternative history. To understand how they came to be entangled in modern Grail fantasies it is necessary to look briefly at the history of these organizations and at how that history has been refocused.

CATHARS

On 14 January 1208, someone in the entourage of Raymond VI, Count of Toulouse, murdered the papal legate. It is unclear whether Raymond had any active involvement in the murder, but he did little to apprehend the culprit. Tensions between the Catholic Church and the Cathars of southern France stretched back several decades, but this event brought matters to breaking point. The tensions were as much political as religious. Many aristocratic families in the Languedoc supported Catharism, and the powerful Counts of Toulouse were a constraint on the expanding influence of the Capetian kings of France. Count Raymond seems to have been a man of conventional and orthodox piety, despite the fact that his wife, Beatrice of Beziers, entered a Cathar community. Given the political situation in the Languedoc with its strong semi-autonomous towns, it is unlikely that Raymond could have crushed Catharism effectively had he tried. However, accusations about his alleged Cathar sympathies were made during and after the Cathar wars, and he was ultimately denied a Christian burial.

The Latin Christian Church engaged in open debate with the Cathars in the 1160s in an unsuccessful attempt to persuade them to abandon what were considered heretical views. During this time Cathars openly preached what it considered the true form of Christianity in many cities, especially in the Albi region of France (hence the alternative name Albigensians). Catharism was a public not a secret sect with a coherent doctrine and structure. There is evidence that the Cathar Church introduced reforms at this time to bring the French Cathars in line with their eastern brethren and to regularize the appointment of Cathar bishops. They lacked a sacramental priesthood, but a class of holy men and women provided a focus for Cathar life. These individuals, known as *perfecti,* received the Cathar sacrament of *consolatamentum* and acted as teachers. This important ritual took place in the presence of other believers and was administered by a *perfect. Perfecti* swore constancy to their beliefs and committed themselves to an ascetic lifestyle to purge the corruption of the flesh. Both men and women could become *perfecti,* and often lived in small ascetic communities. Ordinary believers, not yet ready to embrace this degree of asceticism, promised to receive the *consolatamentum* on their deathbed and sometimes met with the *perfecti* for a ritual meal. Many more, and this would include members of the nobility and the soldiers who defended Montségur during the final full-scale siege of the Albigensian Crusade, were probably sympathetic to the sect, but did not join formally.

Taken as a whole, records concerning the Cathars document the existence of a flourishing and dynamic cult with differing levels of religious and political influence in the areas where they existed. They were critical of the sacraments of the Church, which they considered corrupt, and many Cathars espoused a 'baptism of the spirit' instead of the Catholic 'baptism of the cross'. Many renounced luxuries and foods such as meat, eggs and milk, possibly because they were the result of sexual activity or because Cathars accepted some form of metempsychosis. A Cathar document known as the Ritual of Lyons, which came to light only in the nineteenth century, provides some information about the nature of the *consolatamentum* ceremony. In addition there are references in chronicles and accounts from those who recanted their beliefs. Several treatises described Cathar heresy from the point of view of contemporaries, and there are the records of the Inquisitors, although these present a stereotyped view of Cathars as heretics.[3] Although variations in belief existed, and there was a contrast between intellectual and popular understanding of the doctrines, common features do emerge. God and the material world were completely separate and matter itself was viewed as transitory and corrupt. Cathars believed, along with other dualist sects, that there were two divine principles, one a perfect and eternal god who created all things spiritual, the other a demonic principle who created the material world. This led them to reject the Old Testament with its capricious god and his creation of the world. Some Cathars explained the origin of matter in terms of the myth of Lucifer's fall. The angels of light who had fallen with Lucifer were trapped in material bodies, and the ascetic lives of Cathar *perfecti* were dedicated to release this light. Cathars were uncomfortable with the idea of an incarnate Christ, as this implied that God himself had become trapped in a material body. Many apparently adopted the position that the humanity of Christ and events like the Resurrection were an illusion.

In 1198, Lothaire de Segni was elected Pope Innocent III, and this shrewd canon lawyer was more than ready to deal with heresy in the Languedoc. He threatened the Count of Toulouse with a papal crusade and eventually excommunicated him. The belated attempts to negotiate ended when his legate was assassinated. The first battle in 1209 went in favour of the crusaders and resulted in a massacre at Beziers, whose population contained only a few Cathars. It was during this massacre, according to a hearsay anecdote recorded by a medieval chronicler, that the leader of the crusading army allegedly declared 'Kill them, god will recognize his own.' This utterance, recast in a slightly more emphatic form 'Kill them *all*, god will recognize his own' and minus the caveat that it was hearsay, has come to express a modern, and wholly contemporary, disapproval of this internecine European crusade.[4] On the whole, the war went well for the crusaders. The city of Carcassonne surrendered and Count Raymond's nephew, Roger Raymond of Trancavel, a hero in later romantic Cathar history, died in 1211, leaving the region even more vulnerable. By that time, Simon de Montfort had effectively become leader of the crusade and remained its great strategist (or its villain in the later myths). The papacy finally attempted to establish some stability by protecting the young son of the Count of Toulouse, later Raymond VII. Events turned against the crusaders. There was a resurgence of Catharism after Simon de Montfort was killed in 1218 at the siege of Toulouse. Matters were partially resolved after the French king, Louis VIII, led a further campaign against the region, and by 1229, the French kings finally brought the Languedoc into their sphere of influence. But even this did not immediately eradicate Catharism.

Heresy had become an increasing problem during the twelfth century. At a time when the Church was consolidating its power and unifying its practices, consistent legal procedures and a clear definition of the nature of heresy were needed.[5] The Inquisition clarified the definition of heresy as a denial of an article of truth of the Catholic faith and as a continued public persistence in that error. It also attempted to bring order to the process of dealing with heresy. Despite the fact that the Inquisition was strong in areas such as southern France, local interests, both secular and ecclesiastical, did not necessarily support it wholeheartedly. Issues of papal versus national power, and even powerful localized ecclesiastical interests hindered the Inquisition's ability to act effectively. In the wake of the Albigensian crusade in southern France, the Inquisition questioned suspected heretics, assessed the reliability of witnesses, collected and archived evidence. It was this sustained institutional pressure, more than inquisitional brutality, that eventually undermined Cathar influence. Montségur was not actually the last Cathar stronghold to fall, but by the end of the siege, the Cathars could no longer maintain an effective administrative structure in the region and support for them gradually dwindled away.

WALDENSIANS

The Papal Inquisition instituted by Pope Gregory IX in 1231 focused on curbing the influence of the Cathars, but it also turned its attention to another sect known as the Waldensians. There were Waldensian communities in the Languedoc at the same time as the Cathars, and, perhaps inevitably, the two became confused.[6] Peter Valdes, from whom the sect takes its name, was a rich merchant in the town of Lyons. According to tradition, he renounced his wealth and embraced a life of poverty and preaching and gathered a large following before he was excommunicated. The Waldensians were an evangelical sect, not so much heretical in their doctrines as critical of the privileges of the clergy and of a monolithic, increasingly wealthy and remote Church. They did not accept the sacraments or the need for a clergy, but, unlike the Cathars, they were not dualists. Nevertheless, the speed with which both the Cathar and the Waldensian movements spread reflects the fact that they struck a chord with people, at least in terms of their social criticisms. Later Protestants saw Waldensians as precursors of the Reformation because they encouraged ordinary people to read the Bible in the vernacular and not to rely on a priestly hierarchy to interpret scripture. They also became absorbed into the revival and romanticism which engulfed both the Cathars and the Templars in the nineteenth century. The Waldensians are not as important in modern Grail legends as the Templars and Cathars, but they do figure, at least tangentially, in some early speculations, notably those of Archbishop Ussher, Sabine Baring-Gould and Thomas Wright.

TEMPLARS

Pope Urban II's call to all Christians to free the Holy Land resulted in the First Crusade and the capture of Jerusalem in July 1099. In the wake of this initial victory, the crusaders and their allies set up four enclaves, known as Crusader States. These were the kingdom of Jerusalem, the county of Edessa, the county of Tripoli, and the principality of Antioch. The kingdom of Jerusalem had charge of civil administration, while two patriarchal seats, one at Antioch and one in Jerusalem, plus a network of bishops and archbishops, administered to spiritual needs. Their hold on this 'reconquered' territory was to prove insecure. There were a number of factions among the crusaders as well as among the people they governed, which included

Sunni and Sh'ite Muslims, plus Armenian, Nestorian, Syrian and Maronite Christians. Pilgrims, however, began to return to the Holy Land at the beginning of the twelfth century, despite the fact that Muslims, pirates and bandits continued to harass the long and difficult journey. Local campaigns were mounted by groups of knights, some of whom had come on pilgrimage themselves, to control the unrest. It was in this context that 'the Poor Knights of Christ of the Temple which is in Jerusalem', a military order commonly referred to as the Templars, was founded.

Among these knight/pilgrims was a man from north-east France, Hugh, Count of Champagne, who joined the newly formed Order of the Temple at the beginning of the twelfth century. At the time, the order was still struggling to attract members and to build up a reputation as effective protectors of the Holy Land. Perhaps because of this uncertain start, the circumstances of its founding were not recorded until some time later, and the details in the sources differ. Orderic Vitalis, an Anglo-Norman monk, reported that Count Fulk of Anjou joined *venerandi milites* (worthy knights) in Jerusalem in 1120 and continued to support them after his return to France. Orderic does not describe these knights as a religious or even a military order. More than a decade later, however, another monk, Simon of St Bertin (a town in north-east France), claimed that the Templars were crusaders who remained in the Holy Land to devote themselves to a godly life. Again there is no mention of official Church recognition. The most elaborate account occurs in Archbishop William of Tyre's *Deeds beyond the Sea*, written between 1165 and 1184. By then the order was well established and William's account stressed the close links between it and the Church at the time of its founding, which he places in 1118 or 1119. William characterized the first Templars as a band of noble, religious knights, led by Hugh de Payns and Godfrey of St Omer, who put themselves under the guidance of the patriarch of Jerusalem. They lived communally and followed a religious rule. Their initial mission was to safeguard the pilgrim routes, although small numbers and restricted funds made this difficult. The King of Jerusalem, Baldwin II, gave them living space in his own palace, now the Al Aqsa Mosque, known to the Christians as Solomon's Temple. Another even later account written after the fall of Jerusalem in 1187 characterized the first Templars as a group of pilgrim knights coming together in the wake of the First Crusade. According to this account the order was based initially at the church of the Holy Sepulchre but moved, with the approval of the king and the patriarch, to the site of the Holy Temple. This explains how they acquired their name and why the domed church of the Holy Sepulchre appeared in their iconography.

The accounts are clearly trying to make sense of fragmented, and some-times inconsistent, material relating to the uncertain start of what became a major institution in the Holy Land. Later details, which may or may not be true, were introduced to explain aspects of an established military order. This process of retrospective rationalization is a common narrative technique in both written and oral history. It implies that the importance the order achieved later was foreshadowed in its early history. In the case of the Templars, where so many popular writers have combed the sources for minutiae to use as clues to a secret, this narrative technique is often over-interpreted to imply a level of secrecy and conspiracy that is more romantic than accurate. A number of excellent histories of the order are now available. They present a detailed and authoritative picture of its origin, development and legacy, and they discuss the way in which sources and events have been misinterpreted to create a modern mythology of the Templars.[7] The purpose of the following survey is to highlight the process of legend formation as it affects the image of the Holy Grail, not to present counter-arguments to the enormous number of popular Templar books.[8]

According to the testimony of Orderic Vitalis, the order was visible enough in 1120 to attract the attention of Fulk, Count of Anjou. When Hugh, Count of Champagne returned to the Holy Land in 1125 and joined the order, he may have brought it to the attention of the leading churchman of the day, Bernard of Clairvaux. St Bernard was not just a leading theologian, he was also a member of a powerful Burgundian family and a Cistercian, a movement of reformed monasticism named after its motherhouse in Cîteaux in Burgundy. The Cistercian monks wore white habits, lived simply, and allowed non-noblemen to become 'lay brothers'. Their devotion to the work ethic of monastic life, as well as its contemplative side, made them a powerful force in the changing medieval economy. Cistercian monasteries were organized into a network centred on the abbey at Cîteaux, a departure from the essentially autonomous pattern of monastic life elsewhere, and this gave them singleness of purpose and a supranational strength within the power structures of the medieval world. Baldwin II, King of Jerusalem, another aristocratic supporter of the fledgling order of knights, allegedly sent two Templars with a letter to Bernard requesting his support. One of the Templar emissaries, Andrew, may have been Bernard's uncle. Whatever the reason, Bernard produced a kind of open letter portraying the order as a 'new knighthood', a community fighting for God. It would be devoted not to personal honour and glory but to the honour and glory of Christendom. As propaganda for the Templars, Bernard's supportive letter, written some time in the 1130s, made an enormous difference.[9]

Walter Map, an advisor to King Henry II of England, included anecdotes about the Templars in his *De Nugis Curialium*, a collection of medieval folktales, marvels and elegant moral conceits. According to his account, Hugh de Payns (called here Paganus) defended a watering hole against the Saracens and then went on to found the Order of the Knights of the Temple.[10] His name suggests that he came from Payns, a small town near Troyes, but little is known about Hugh's background. He may have accompanied the Count of Champagne and stayed in the East to become a member of the Order of the Knights of the Temple. Calling himself Hugh Peccator (i.e., sinner), he addressed a letter to the Templars in the early formative years before their status became official. He painted a picture of a poor order with few recruits and a disheartened membership, but assured them that their task, fighting the enemies of the Church rather than contemplation and prayer, was a worthy one. Hugh lacked the theological and rhetorical sophistication of St Bernard, and may therefore better reflect the views of ordinary Templars. His sincerity and dedication are obvious, even if the piety is conventional. For Hugh, God allotted a task to each person, and salvation could be achieved by performing this task.[11] In 1129, the Council of Troyes established a Rule for the Order of the Temple and authorized the wearing of white robes like the Cistercians. As Christ's warriors and as a symbol of martyrdom, they added a red cross to their white mantles. Hugh gave his account of the order openly before the Council delegates. The Rule was a public document, and St Bernard himself may have drawn up some of the details. There was certainly no secrecy. Membership and donations began to increase, although not everyone felt that an order committed to violence was consistent with the monastic way of life. The order was answerable only to the pope, and a papal bull, *Milites templi* (1144), called them the new Maccabees, referring to the Jewish warrior priests, brothers in fact as well as brothers in arms, who defended the Jewish Temple before the birth of Christ.[12] However, accusations of pride, mismanagement and cupidity were levelled against them as the thirteenth century progressed.

From its eastern headquarters, located in Jerusalem until 1187, then Acre and finally in Cyprus, the Order of the Temple flourished. The Master and a number of officials were based at their headquarters, and the European lands were divided into provinces under the charge of a provincial commander. A system of chapter meetings kept Templar officials and Templar foundations in touch with one another. The role of the foundations in the West was to raise money for the defence of the Holy Land. The order administered large grants of land at a time when agriculture and trade were on the rise. Inevitably, managing land, trade and money drew the Templars into politics. The commandery was the basic unit and would have contained Knight Brothers, who were fully professed members of the order, as well as sergeants, chaplains, associates, pensioners and servants. Although the chaplains were priests, fully professed Templars were not monks, but took vows of poverty, chastity and obedience. Women were permitted to join the order as associates in certain circumstances; some were widows or became associates when their husbands joined. The Templars were responsible for at least one nunnery in Germany, and there were a number of women who described themselves as Sisters in Catalonia. Only men could become fully professed Knight Brothers, but the position of associates varied from a commitment to join the order and endow it with property and income, to regular donations in return for care in sickness or old age and the promise of Christian burial. Such associations were common in medieval religious life. Sometimes they were organized into 'confraternities' of lay people, which provided members with a link to the religious life and security that their physical as well as spiritual needs would be met.

An important aspect of the Templar way of life was to defend pilgrims and protect the Holy Land. They commanded a number of fortifications, but the main one was at Acre, overlooking the harbour. These fortresses represented a huge investment of money, manpower and prestige and their loss, culminating in the fall of Acre in May 1291, was a crushing financial as well as psychological blow. Many Templars, including the Master, William de Beaujeu, died in the siege, and the remnant eventually relocated to Cyprus, the same island to which the Hospitallers had retreated. When James of Molay was elected Master of the Order of the Temple in 1293, he immediately travelled to the West to see the pope, Boniface VIII, and the kings of England and France to garner support for a crusade to reconquer the Holy Land. Unfortunately, the situation in Europe did not favour such a venture. Although Edward I was keen to go on another crusade, the French invasion of his holdings in France and later the revolt of Robert the Bruce (1307) kept him occupied defending his own kingdom. Pope Boniface was fighting with his family's hereditary enemies, the Colonna, and was in dispute with Philip IV (Philip the Fair) of France. King Philip's ancestors had been on crusade and Philip wished to follow in their footsteps, but only if France took the lead in any expedition. In any case, his problems with the pope over the conflicting rights of king and clergy were reaching crisis point. With the help of his advisor, William de Nogaret, Philip accused the pope of heresy and simony, the serious offence of trading in Church offices, plus sodomy and sorcery for good measure. In 1303 the Colonna family and William de Nogaret briefly imprisoned the pope. Boniface was rescued but died shortly after. After a brief interim papacy,

The *santo caliz* in Valencia Cathedral is one of the chalices reputed to be the Holy
Grail. (Photograph courtesy of Consellaria de Turisme, Valencia)

2. In Terry Gilliam's *The Fisher King*, Jeff Bridges is a modern urban quest knight who brings the Holy Grail to cure an equally modern Fisher King in the person of Robin Williams. (Distributed by TriStar pictures. Reproduced with the sole purpose of enhancing the discussion of film.)

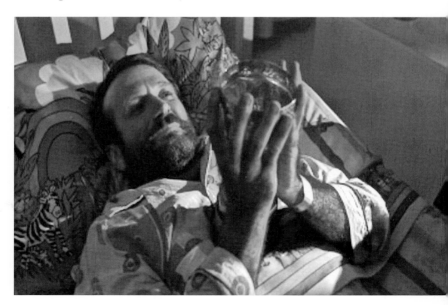

3. A sports trophy becomes the Holy Grail and cures the lost and disturbed Parry, played by Robin Williams in a modern version of an Arthurian romance. (*The Fisher King* directed by Terry Gilliam. Distributed by TriStar pictures. Reproduced with the sole purpose of enhancing the discussion of film.)

In John Boorman's *Excalibur* Perceval sees the Holy Grail, displayed and illuminated e a precious archaeological object. (Distributed by Orion Pictures. Reproduced with sole purpose of enhancing the discussion of film.)

Perceval (Paul Geoffrey) brings the Holy Grail to Arthur (Nigel Terry), who, in John orman's *Excalibur*, is equated with the wounded Fisher King. (Distributed by Orion tures. Reproduced with the sole purpose of enhancing the discussion of film.)

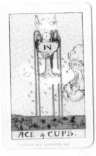

6. This miniature version of the most influential set of modern tarot cards was designed by A. E. Waite and drawn by Pamela Colman Smith at the beginning of the twentieth century. The four knights represent the four suits, cups, wands, pentangles and swords, which Waite associated with the sacred 'Grail Hallows'. The images in the four cards on the right recall descriptions of the mysterious hand which holds the Grail in the medieval romances and book watermarks linked to a lost language of Cathar symbolism. (Author's collection)

7. The image of the Holy Grail is now used widely in other arenas such as satire and advertising. (*Herald of Wales*, Thursday, 14 July 1994)

The Temple Church in London has been associated with a number of alternative Grail theories. A modern statue depicting the Templar seal of two knights riding the same horse adorns the square. (Photograph courtesy of Nigel Nicholson)

9. 'Perceval and Galahad: the Vision of the Grail', one of a series of decorative plates depicting scenes from Arthurian legend. (Used with kind permission of Royal Doulton (UK) Ltd)

Above: 10. The gardens of Shugborough Hall, Staffordshire, embodied eighteenth-century visions of a pastoral Arcadia. Today they have become the setting for modern fantasies of Templars and the Holy Grail. (Courtesy of Staffordshire County Council Museum Service)

Left: 11. The Shepherd's Monument. The Latin inscription from the bas-relief of Poussin's painting and the series of letters have been linked to the location of the Holy Grail. (Courtesy of Staffordshire County Council Museum Service)

Right: 12. This stone commemorates the spot known as St Bride's Well, where Dr Goodchild placed a glass bowl which become associated with the Holy Grail legend at Glastonbury at the beginning of the twentieth century. (By kind permission of C. & N. Pollinrake Ltd)

Below: 13. The Chalice Well decorated for Beltane. The cover was designed by Frederick Bligh Bond to represent the fusion of religious beliefs at Glastonbury. (By kind permission of the Chalice Well Trust)

Above: 14. Each of the Grail knights visits the Chapel Perilous and has a different experience of the Holy Grail. Tessa Mackenzie illustrates one of the knights approaching the chapel.

Above: 15. The Kirkwall Scroll is covered with eighteenth-century Masonic symbols, but it has been interpreted as a Templar map leading the way to the Holy Grail.
(© Robert L. D. Cooper)

Left: 16. In this illustration from *The Stories of King Arthur and the Round Table* by Beatrice Clay, the Knights depart from Camelot to seek the Holy Grail.
(The Orion Publishing Group)

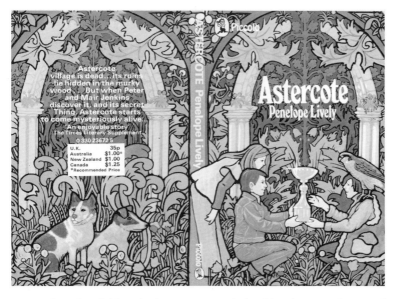

17. Modern-day children find a mysterious chalice-like object on the site of a lost medieval village in Penelope Lively's reworking of the Grail theme. (This edition published 1973 in paperback by Piccolo Books (Pan Books))

Was Hitler a Satanist? No actual proof that he was has yet emerged but there is ample evidence that he regularly consulted occultists. On their advice he took many of his decisions. Those decisions resulted in appalling physical suffering, prolonged agony of mind and gruesome death for many millions of human beings. In June 1943, while on a mission to penetrate the secrets of Hitler's V weapons Gregory Sallust became unwillingly involved with a Jewish Black Magician. Sixteen months later they met again and decided to use occult forces in an attempt to destroy Hitler.

By combining ESPIONAGE, BLACK MAGIC and LOVE against a background of FACT Dennis Wheatley has produced what may well be acclaimed the greatest of all his splendid stories.

THIS EDITION ISSUED BY
THE BOOK CLUB

Originally published
by Hutchinson
at 21s. 0d.

18. Dennis Wheatley's thriller *They Used Dark Forces* uses traditions about black magic and occultism in Nazi Germany. This has become a popular alternative Grail legend. (With kind permission of Random House)

19. In the Welsh romance, Peredur sees the bleeding lance and the head carried on a bloody platter at the Castle of Wonders. (Courtesy of Cardiff University Library)

" Bearing a spear of mighty size, with three streams of blood flowing from the point to the ground. "

Below: 20. The archway into the main church at Strata Florida as it appeared in the nineteenth century, at the time of the first archaeological excavation. (Courtesy of Cardiff University Library)

WEST FRONT
STRATA FLORIDA ABBEY

Whittington Castle is associated with the Grail quest in the medieval romance about outlaw hero Fulk Fitz Warine. (Courtesy of Cardiff University Library)

THE WEST VIEW OF STRATFLOUR ABBY, IN THE COUNTY OF CARDIGAN.

This seventeenth-century drawing shows the house originally built by the Stedman ily in the grounds of Strata Florida Abbey. Archaeological excavation in the eteenth century uncovered the Nanteos cup among the abbey ruins. (Courtesy of diff University Library)

23. Perceval on quest. This image evokes the darkness and isolation associated with the wasteland in Grail romances. (Courtesy of Cardiff University Library)

Below: 24. Sir Lancelot sees only a partial visio of the Holy Grail. Dora Curtis's illustration from *The Stories of King Arthur and the Round Table* by Beatrice Clay evokes the strangeness Lancelot's vision in mar Grail romances. (The Orion Publishing Group

Adventures of Sir Launcelot and End of the Quest

25. An illustration of 'Perceval's Dream' from an 1816 edition of Malory's *Morte Darthur*. (Courtesy of Cardiff University Library)

26. Hodnot Church in Shropshire became linked to modern legends about secret codes and hidden objects. (Courtesy of Cardiff University Library)

27. The medieval Welsh castle of Dinas Bran in Denbighshire and the river that winds through the Dee Valley have been associated with the Fisher King in the Grail romances. (Courtesy of Cardiff University Library)

28. An image of Gawain on a quest adorns the cover of one of Jessie Weston's translations. Her theories helped establish the ritual interpretation of the Grail legend. (Courtesy of Cardiff University Library)

The area known as Beckery Island, where Dr Goodchild concealed a glass bowl associated with the Holy Grail at Glastonbury. (By kind permission of C. & N. Linrake Ltd)

The illustration is from a manuscript of 'The Story of the Grail' written in France in fourteenth century. It depicts the scene in which Perceval sees the Grail procession the first time at the castle of the Fisher King. (Image from Wikipedia Commons, viously made available under the GNU free documentation licence)

31. The crusader Guglielmo Embriaco holds the *sacro catino*, in the fresco from Palaz
San Giorgio, Genoa. (Image from Wikipedia Commons, graciously made available unc
the GNU free documentation licence)

Bertrand de Got was elected to the weakened papal see and took the name Clement V.

The French-born Pope Clement V features in modern Grail mythology as one of the architects of the destruction of the Order of the Knights Templar. Contemporary medieval sources hint at Clement's indebtedness to Philip IV of France even before his election to the papacy. The fact that the papal investiture took place at Lyons with Philip in attendance, rather than in Italy, could have done little to dispel the appearance that the King of France was the pope's puppet master. In addition, the papal court transferred to Avignon. Although not strictly part of France at the time, Avignon was well within the French sphere of influence, and this made the pope's eventual collapse inevitable. While Philip ordered the arrest of the French Templars in October 1307, Clement did not immediately support the move since Philip had pre-empted his right to investigate charges against a papal order. Nevertheless, in November of that year, the pope ordered the arrest and interrogation of the Templars in Catholic kingdoms under his jurisdiction.

The Templars were in a difficult position. The project to regain the Holy Land was considered a just war, but the fall of Acre attracted criticism that those responsible had failed morally as well as strategically. After his election as Master in 1293, James of Molay tried to regain some initiative in the East and set up a Templar base from which to launch further operations. He chose Arwad (Ruad Island) off the coast of Syria, but the island was too small to defend, and they were driven off. Another military order, the Hospitallers, chose a much better island base, Cyprus, and, as we have seen, eventually the Templars moved their headquarters there too.[13] It was even suggested that the two orders should merge for greater strength and better use of resources. In 1306, Pope Clement V called the Masters of the Temple and the Hospital to his papal court in France to consider this among other matters.

The suppression of the Templars at the beginning of the fourteenth century appears considerably less singular, and therefore less a subject for mystery, when it is seen in the context of this wider political and social world. The handsome appearance of the Capetian king, Philip IV, earned him the name of the Fair (*le Bel*). During his reign, from 1285 to 1314, he strengthened the monarchy and increased royal land holdings, primarily by his marriage to his beloved queen, Jeanne de Navarre. However, his policies of taxing the clergy led to clashes with Pope Boniface VIII. When a French archbishop was elected as Pope Clement V, Philip's influence increased, and it was further strengthened when the official seat of the papacy transferred to the enclave of Avignon, conveniently surrounded by French territories. On 13 October 1307 agents of the king arrested virtually all the Knights Templar in France. Philip had been attempting to undermine this group with charges of heresy and blasphemy for several years. Eventually, through his own political power, the agency of the Inquisition and his influence over the pope, he was instrumental in having the order disbanded at the Council of Vienne in 1311. Philip had money problems and powerful enemies on his borders, and, in addition, Christendom had lost the Holy Land. Philip had used the accusations of heresy and sorcery against other opponents. He accused the far from malleable Pope Boniface VIII of heresy and magic and orchestrated a posthumous trial. Other individuals, such as the female lay-preacher Marguerite of Poiret and a powerful prelate, Bishop Guiscard of Troyes, were also targets. Some of his contemporaries were convinced that Philip's reason for acting against the Templars was financial, but historians are divided on whether the king believed the charges. Hunting heretics would have increased his reputation as a devout Christian king, God's vicar in France, but equally, their considerable monetary holdings brought him financial gain.

The charges against the order were complex, but specific aspects have a bearing on the development of subsequent Templar myths. Heresy, although a serious charge, was not unusual at the time. However, defining heresy is not always easy. At the time of the Templar trial, it meant any non-orthodox belief condemned by the Church, but the exact nature of orthodox belief was itself a slippery category. Parallels might be made to the fear of communism in the 1950s and the fear of satanism in Britain in the 1990s.[14] The charge of heresy was, however, an effective weapon against a political enemy, even if the charge could not be finally proved. In the end, this is what happened to the Templars. The Council of Vienne did not accept the charges relating to heresy, but the level of defamation was deemed such that the Templars could no longer continue as an effective institution. Sorcery was a newer element in the mix. Folk magic, involving the use of talismans, curses, cures and a whole variety of ritual practices, was undoubtedly widely practised throughout Europe, and accusations of obscene kisses, black cats, secret night meetings, and worshipping demonic idols have become familiar as part of the witch trials of later European history. Accusations against the Templars involved formal magic, a type usually preserved in written Latin texts meant for individual study by educated practitioners. Contemplation and intellectual study were the aspects of religious life least relevant to the Templar lifestyle. Some members were literate, but knowledge of Latin was rare. Certain improving works were translated into the vernacular for Templar communities, and these were read aloud communally, but they were certainly not works of magic.

During the thirteenth century, accusations of sorcery were used increasingly to undermine political rivals. Charges were often combined to give them greater force, and eventually magic and sorcery came under the very elastic definition of heresy. At the time charges were brought against the Templars, King Philip le Bel had also initiated two other high-profile trials involving sorcery, one against a female preacher, the other against a former ally. The Templars were accused of homosexuality, of worshipping an idol shaped like a head called Bahomet, a variant of the name Mohammed, and of spitting on the cross. Activities involving idol worship and blasphemy also implied that, instead of defending Christendom, the Templars had adopted Muslim practice. Such accusations reflect stereotypes that demonized Muslims and were the fictions of prejudice, since Islam forbids both the worship of idols and homosexuality. Outside the French sphere of influence, there were doubts about the charges, and some contemporary commentators were aware that torture played a role in confessions. However the extreme charges were rooted to some extent in distortion of Templar practice, and this allowed the accusers to exploit weak points like any irregularities in religious practice or their lack of theological understanding.[15]

The nine-year period in Jerusalem before the official recognition of the military order at Troyes in 1228 has been the focus for a number of alternative theories about the purpose of the order and the nature of their beliefs. Instead of an interval during which the order struggled to establish itself, which is the explanation suggested by the existing records, alternative authors see a period of covert exploration during which a secret cabal looked for all manner of powerful talismans, among them the Holy Grail. A number of objects with romantic histories, but no clear context, were allegedly found then and are described in recent books. The Temple Mount was thought to be the site of Solomon's Temple at the time of the Crusades. This edifice, if it ever had been built, would have been long destroyed and the structures on the site are more recent. Today, only a small portion of the Second Temple, the one destroyed by the Romans, survives. Hugh de Payns's letter shows no trace of the subtle dualist philosophy which allegedly motivated the secret searches hinted at in later legends. For the Templars, education was not a priority; theirs was a straightforward and largely unquestioning faith. Indeed, one of the striking differences between the Templars and the non-military monastic orders like the Cistercians was the lack of theological education. Only by assuming that Hugh was being deliberately disingenuous and throwing up a smokescreen to hide secret activities can these early documents be made to look mysterious.[16]

The records relating to the trial of the Templars also present particular difficulties. Membership was drawn from a wide social spectrum, which could result in friction between knights from higher and lower social groups. Tensions within the order, even some administrative corruption, were exploited in the protracted examination of the order. Accusations of heresy were not unusual, but the Templars were not accused of heresy prior to the trial of 1307–12, and outside the accusations of sodomy made during the trial, the Order of the Temple was remarkably free of sexual scandal. They had, however, been accused of unfairly exploiting the financial advantages of their papal privileges, of excessive pride and, after the fall of Acre, of failure to defend the Holy Land. This failure was ascribed to moral turpitude of a non-specific nature. Charges of blasphemy, worshipping idols and strange rites, the basis for esoteric theories about the Templars were a useful and expedient political tool, and confessions extracted under torture are certainly suspect. In the trials conducted outside the reach of Philip's power, the Templars generally denied all charges.[17] Unfortunately, charges such as these have the force of gossip with its negative implications despite lack of obvious proof, and this makes them difficult to refute in a clear and absolute way.

Much has been made of hidden codes in Templar architecture and the possibility that escaping Templar ships conducted global exploration, despite the fact that neither architecture nor sailing were important activities for the order. The round naves of some Templar churches, which provided a visual link to the church of the Holy Sepulchre, have been a particular focus for speculation. The most famous example is undoubtedly the church in the New Temple in London, but there were others, like that at Garway in Herefordshire. Although not all Templars were fighting knights, there is no evidence for a specialized class of Templar masons or architects who could build churches with complex symbolic geometry. Increasingly, Templar funds depended on economic activities rather than donations. Produce needed to be shipped, money had to be transported to the East for the all-important purpose of fighting, and ships provided cheaper and safer transport for pilgrims whom the Templars had pledged to protect. After the fall of Acre in 1291, the pope ordered both Templars and Hospitallers to build up their fleet and continue attempts to recover the Holy Land. The period from the fall of Acre to the beginning of the fourteenth century was one of retrenchment for both orders and neither really had the resources for expensive naval operations. None of the surviving sources states clearly how many ships the Templars owned, but the type of ship would not have been suitable for oceangoing exploration. Records mention the transport of goods, money and pilgrims, even buying and hiring, but Templar shipping practices conformed to the general picture of maritime, economic and warfare activity in the period.[18]

The ceremony of initiation into the order was a focal point for accusation. The Templars were accused of worshipping an idol called Bahomet, of wearing a secret amulet, spitting or trampling the Cross and sodomizing one another. Carrying amulets that have touched some sacred object is a common religious practice, but the accusations claimed that the Templar amulets had touched the idol Bahomet. Some Templars did wear a cord tied under their tunic to remind them of their vows, but they testified to the papal commissioners that the cord had been first wrapped around a stone or church pillar associated with the Blessed Virgin, patroness of the order. The initiation ceremony was not a secret rite; it was laid down in the rule and statutes of the order. The details varied, but by the end of the thirteenth century, just before accusations were brought against them, the form was very similar to that for investing a new knight, namely a dawn ceremony after an all-night vigil. The ceremony was usually private, although family members and occasional outsiders might attend.[19] This did not stop the accusers claiming that a secret rite existed, even though they found no trace of it. This ploy of suggesting that lack of evidence is itself evidence of a conspiracy is still an essential part of the Templar myth and of modern Grail legends.

Although many documents have been lost, this does not indicate a deliberate attempt to destroy records that might contain hidden esoteric knowledge. When the Order of the Knights of the Temple was suppressed, the archives, along with most Templar property, became the possession of the Hospital of St John, and it presumably remained on Cyprus until the Ottoman Turks captured the island in 1571. Copies of the Rule for the Order still exist, as well as charters, known as cartularies, recording land grants. In addition English, French and Spanish and Portuguese archives preserve documents recording the order's relations with various governments, and the Vatican Library preserves the papal bulls relating to the Templars. These documents contribute to our understanding of the extent and distribution of Templar landholdings, the names of members of the order, their relationships with central authority and their wealth and influence.[20] Archaeological excavations of Templar commanderies provide additional information about daily life and economic activity. None of these sources, however, contains detailed personal information about individual members or whether their beliefs held any element of unorthodoxy, and these are what many modern readers, familiar with myths about Templar treasure and esotericism, wish to know. Pilgrim accounts sometimes refer to the Templar knights who protected them, while medieval chronicles and histories also preserve more personal views. Chronicles tended to record a wide range of events that interested the writer, like Orderic Vitalis's work, while histories focused on a single theme, like William of Tyre's account of the Crusader States. The personal comments of writers in both genres give a more intimate picture of the events from the point of view of contemporary or near-contemporary observers. Templars appeared in epic and romances as heroic defenders of Christendom, but they were also the targets of moral or satirical works.

In the light of new research into the history of the Order and the clear indications that they were not involved in unorthodox activities, alternative writers increasingly invoke the idea of plausibility.[21] They suggest that events *could* have happened even if there is no definite proof or, perhaps, the real proof was hidden or destroyed. This is not a strong argument at the best of times, but an added difficulty is that the so-called 'plausibility' does not so much offer an alternative as contradict what the sources do make clear. Walter Map's account of the knight Paganus is one of individual courage and sacrifice. It is not attested elsewhere. Significantly, considering this medieval account is closer to events, there is no hint of any magic or esoteric activity. Such anecdotes about the brave actions of Brother Knights might have formed part of the Templars' own narrative tradition. It is just the sort of heroic story that gathers about leaders and is a good indication of how quickly folk legends provide an alternative to the uncertain complexities of history.

Medieval documents contain different details about the origins of the Knights Templar, but none suggests that the founder members were anything other than pious orthodox men. They were not a learned order, indeed quite the reverse, and there is no evidence of a special knowledge of science, architecture or magic. They did not have an extensive naval fleet of the kind that could travel long distances and explore the world. Templars were not especially unpopular or secretive. Ceremonies and chapter meetings were not open to outsiders, but this was standard practice for religious Orders generally. Although the charges were not proved and they were not declared heretics, once papal support was withdrawn and the order's property seized, the Templars could no longer continue to function.

AFTERMATH

Modern Grail legends take the early history of the Templars in an entirely different direction despite the fact that many assumptions about them are actively contradicted by medieval evidence. There is no indication that the order was involved in intellectual or esoteric pursuits, and the idea that it went underground to pursue an esoteric project which was somehow its real function is part of the modern myth of revived Templar groups mixed with eighteenth-century speculative Masonic thinking. Ironically, in this odd looking-glass world of secrets and conspiracies, lack of evidence provides a powerful fuel for conspiracy thinking. The less evidence that actually exists, the more firmly convinced certain writers become that hidden evidence must exist somewhere. The Grail has had a varied history since its appearance in Chrétien de Troyes's twelfth-century verse romance. The ideas of the Reformation and Counter-Reformation weakened its impact as a religious image, and its importance as a literary motif diminished when other fashions eclipsed the romance genre. However, its fortunes rose once more in the context of romantic nineteenth-century reinterpretations of the past. Today the myth of the Templars and the Grail is one of the most productive contemporary legends, sustained by popular books, media coverage and an ever-expanding network of Internet sites.[22] In order to create a secret history, the Grail romances had to be reinterpreted as historical events, and linked to the present. The defeated Cathars and Templars were about to get a second chance.

References to both Cathars and Templars occur in the work of Walter Map, a priest from Hereford whose life spanned the end of the twelfth and the beginning of the thirteenth century. A famous wit and storyteller, Map was a courtier and friend of Henry II, King of England. He was even credited, at one time, with the authorship of the *Vulgate Grail Cycle.* Certainly he was contemporary with the writing of many of the romances, and Eleanor of Aquitaine, Henry's queen, was the mother of Chrétien's patroness, Marie de Champagne. Whole theories have been built on more tenuous connections in the world of Grail mythology. Map described a Cathar/Albigensian orgy complete with *osculum infamum,* cannibalism and promiscuity, and a demonic black cat that entered by climbing down a rope. Although he would have had very little, if any, contact with this sect, his story of a young man saved by the intervention of his uncle makes use of stock motifs of demonic otherness. By contrast, his anecdotes about the Templars sound very like legends that might be told within the order itself. One concerns the son of a Saracen emir who converted to Christianity and joined the order. The other is a typical medieval legend about the Virgin Mary in which she saves a devotee by taking his place. In Map's version, she enters a tournament in the guise of a knight who was delayed because he stopped to hear mass in her chapel. He also records a unique account about the founding of the Templars which casts Hugh de Payns in a heroic role. Map would undoubtedly have known real Templar Brothers, who could have been the direct sources for the legends he tells. Certainly he has no reservations about the Templars he knew. Peter Valdes and his followers, the Waldensians, also appear among Walter Map's anecdotes.[23] He does not link the three groups, and the traditions he records about them are different. The Cathars hold a demonic meeting, while the Templar legends are tales of heroic deeds, and those associated with the Waldensians are pietistic.

Despite the clear distinctions made by this astute observer, Cathars, Templars and Waldensians became absorbed into later theories which sought to establish the legitimacy for an alternative history by creating a continuity presenting all three groups as counter-cultural movements connected by a common thread, namely the Grail. Cathars and Templars are the main focus for these theories, but the Waldensians also became absorbed in the romantic revival that engulfed these groups. During the French wars of religion in the early part of the seventeenth century, Protestant polemicists began to use the Albigensian crusade as anti-Catholic propaganda. The influential *Histoire des Vaudois* (1618) linked Cathars and Waldensians as those who preserved 'true Christianity', which could be passed on to suitable 'rightful heirs' when the time was right. There is no mention of secret societies and nothing about the Grail, but the rhetoric of a true faith passed on to worthy descendants is an important part of the structure from which later fantasies were spun.[24] Comments about the origin of the Grail by men like Sabine Baring-Gould and early work on the Templar documents by Thomas Wright, considered possible Waldensian influence on these legends.[25] However, the really influential speculations about Grail mythology were those that linked the Cathars with the military order of the Knights Templar.

Certain events in the Albigensian crusade have become part of the paraphernalia of the modern Grail legend. The executions of Cathar *perfecti* and *perfectae* during the early years of the crusade presented a spectacle of committed men and women going willingly to be burned as heretics. Seemingly, at least in retrospect, they were victims of a repressive regime, and this is reinforced by the final siege at Montségur, whose destruction spawned later tales about Cathars escaping with secret treasure. Support for powerful Cathar sympathizers, like the Count of Toulouse, was on the wane, and Montségur had become a refuge for Languedoc's persecuted Cathar Church, although it was not actually the last citadel to fall. The fortress occupies a rocky prominence, and in 1243 it was besieged with approximately 500 people, most of them refugees from weakened Cathar communities, crammed inside. The garrison negotiated a period of grace before the surrender. Apparently many of the besieged received the *consolatamentum* at this time and eventually went to their deaths, although those who recanted, and this included most of the defending soldiers, were allowed to leave. Inquisitorial records are the main source for events inside the besieged town, and, while these need to be taken advisedly, they suggest that the garrison commander had been responsible for monetary resources belonging to the Cathars in Montségur. Just before the surrender, several Cathars escaped under cover of darkness, presumably to look for the treasure hidden in a nearby cave. The outcome of the venture is not known, but it has become the basis for several enduring myths, in particular that the treasure was the Holy Grail – although Cathar records make no mention of such an object. The Grail with its overtones of a eucharistic sacrament is not appropriate in the context of Cathar belief, which rejected the sacraments of the orthodox Christian faith. Sir Steven Runciman suggested that the Cathar Grail was associated with an unorthodox sacrament with a dualistic meaning, but he did not expand on this.[26] One theory links it to a sexual ritual of the type suggested by James Frazer and Jessie Weston,[27] while another popular interpretation sees the 'Grail' as a person.[28] None of these ideas fits very comfortably with the ascetic nature of Catharism or with the surviving records.[29]

However, while the mysteries about this sect are more apparent than real, they provide great potential for romantic reconstruction. Deodat Roché was among those who saw the Cathars as a vehicle for his personal spiritual and moral values and whose writings on the Cathars have influenced others. Born at Arques and fiercely loyal to his region, Roché was interested in the history and philosophy of the Cathars. He produced books and journal articles and eventually founded a society aimed at reviving Cathar doctrines. In the 1920s, he met Rudolph Steiner, whose philosophy sought to rediscover spiritual faculties lost or obscured by contemporary materialism by developing the intellect. This struck a chord with Roché's own spiritual interests. Although not the first to suggest this, Roché believed that Catharism was rooted in Gnosticism and the doctrines of speculative Freemasonry that had been popular since the eighteenth century. He was himself a mason, but was dismissed by the Vichy government because of his interest in what was termed 'spiritualism'. He survived the war to found the Societé du Souvenir et des Etudes Cathares in 1950, an organization not unlike the Priory of Sion founded about a decade later.[30] Both organizations focused on an incident recorded by the Inquisition after the siege of Montségur. According to one of the defenders, a treasure had been removed the night before the citadel fell. The account strongly suggested that the 'treasure' was monetary, but subsequent attempts to recast the Cathars as a secret organization have insisted that it was some deeply significant Cathar secret. Roché believed that the treasure was the secret Gnostic literature of the Cathar sect.

Nostalgia for a world of chivalry made it fashionable to theorize about deep philosophical roots in romances.[31] For Roché, and for many others, the culture of the Languedoc region embodied a spirit of independent resistance to outside pressure. Even when the defeated Cathars seemed to have been crushed by their opponents, the spirit of this culture lived on. Although none of the Grail romances can be linked directly with southern France, Wolfram von Eschenbach's romance, *Parzifal,* appeared soon after the Albigensian crusade, and one of his fictional sources, a writer called Kyot, has been identified with the real troubadour poet Guot de Provence. There is no evidence that this troubadour poet ever wrote verse romances. However, the speculations have allowed the Grail literature to be absorbed into the myth of the Cathars and their alleged ancient wisdom to be projected onto the medieval romances. The suggestion that Wolfram's masterpiece could be connected to historical events in southern France opened new possibilities for secret discoveries. At the beginning of the twentieth century, Joséphin Péladan identified the Cathar stronghold of Montségur with Montsalvache, the Grail castle in Wolfram's poem. Péladan, the novelist Maurice Magre[32] and Deodat Roché helped create the idea that Cathars and Templars were linked as custodians of an esoteric secret and that this secret was entwined in some mystical way with the national character of France. Their romantic ideas, rather than any ancient documents, formed the background to the creation of the Priory of Sion by Pierre Planchard in the 1950s, and by extension, to the further elaborations found in the later alternative histories.

The young Otto Rahn, a romantic German explorer born in Hesse in 1904, had taken up these ideas even earlier. His first book, *Kreuzzuge gegen den Graal (The Crusade Against the Grail),* was published in 1933, and a French translation appeared the next year.[33] The book identified connections between the Albigensian crusade and Wolfram's romance. The Grail maiden, Repanse de Shoye, was a real noblewoman, Esclarmonde of Foix, a supposed Cathar *perfecta* who presided over a court at Montségur. Anfortas, the Grail king, was equated with Esclarmonde's brother. Trevrizont, the hermit, became the Cathar Bishop of Toulouse, while Parsival's role was assigned to Raymond Roger Trencavel, who died in prison in 1209. Since the most likely date for the completion of Eschenbach's romance is 1210, the timescale is difficult to resolve, but the undaunted Rahn went even further, and equated the Templars with the Cathars. In Rahn's version the 'Grail maiden', Esclarmonde, presided over the sacred precinct of the Grail, Montségur, and just before it fell, Cathars, who were really Templars, escaped with the Grail. Cathar mythology was already well established by the time Rahn came on the scene.

According to Rahn, Catharism in the Languedoc dated from the time of the Celts and the Visigoths. They, in their turn, preserved the Persian wisdom of Zoroaster who first preached the dualist doctrine. The young German pictured a native Aryan cult free from any Middle Eastern influences. The Teutonic nationalism which lay behind this fantasy came through more strongly in his second book, *Luzifers Hofgesind (Lucifer's Courtiers)* in 1937. According to Cathar belief, Lucifer was the creator of matter who took angels of light with him when he fell from heaven. Rahn turned this into a cosmology in which Lucifer was the real deity at the centre of an ancient untainted religion pitted against the Judaic god of the Old Testament later exploited by a corrupt Roman Catholic Church. Rahn's association with the SS was undoubtedly a factor in the spin he puts on this 'Boy's Own' adventure leavened with a dash of Nietzsche,[34] but by this time, rumours of homosexuality had clouded his popularity. According to an unsubstantiated tradition, Rahn was sent back to the Languedoc to find the Grail and bring it to Germany. Eventually he was found frozen to death on a mountainside, an apparent suicide. Not surprisingly, his death has attracted conspiracy legends of its own. His story influenced alternative books and novels like *Nouveaux cathars pour Montségur,* and a stream of writing which seeks to explain Nazism as an occult aberration by seeing Hitler as part of a long tradition of dualism.[35] Himmler envisioned Wewelsburg Castle in Westphalia as an elaborate cultural centre for a new Aryan knighthood, but the grandiose alterations were never completed. What survives resembles the pseudo-pagan Germanic traditions so beloved of Nazi Aryanism, rather than Arthurian tradition. However, the lack of detail encourages speculations that the Nazis intended to house relics like the Grail and the lance there or that they organized expeditions, headed by men like Otto Rahn, to find these powerful talismans.[36]

The idea that limitless occult forces are embodied in biblical talismans belongs to a body of vague but persistent rumours that a secret occult society wielded the real power within the Nazi hierarchy. Nazi occultism and supposed interest in the Grail is a popular theme for novels, in which the gothic atmosphere of black magic is mixed with the excitement of a spy thriller.[37] One of the fountainheads for this gothic occultism was the fiction of Sir Edward Bulwer-Lytton, whose own novels incorporated esoteric ideas. A secret theocracy ensures the success of *The Coming Race* (1871), while rituals and secret powers abound in *Zanoni, a Rosicrucian Tale* (1861).[38] Both find their way into alternative works of history as a background to the Lance of Longinus or the Grail. The doyen of the occult thriller, Dennis Wheatley, incorporated these ideas into his novel *They Used Dark Forces* (1964), and Duncan Kyle set the climax of his novel *Black Camelot* (1979) in Wewelsburg Castle. For Rahn, the Grail embodied a rather vague Aryan Cathar dualist philosophy, and his fantasies were directed at Germanic supremacy. His contacts and sources, however, were French esoteric writers like Péladan. For example, the source of the rumour that a Nazi plane inscribed a Celtic cross above Montségur in 1944 can probably be traced to such a source – Antonin Gadal (d. 1966), an enterprising local, keen to glorify his little corner of France.[39] The belief that the Grail embodied the power of a pure national consciousness was eventually repatriated when ideas about Cathars, Grails and secrets were adapted to a new French setting by the creators of the Priory of Sion.[40]

A mixture of fiction and pseudo-science, ideology, popular culture and rumour characterizes conspiracy legends. Alleged Nazi occultism, and the fascination and revulsion it evokes, is ultimately if somewhat tortuously linked in a rational tradition going back to Enlightenment thinkers. They saw the suppression of groups like Templars and Cathars as an unjust and unnecessary cruelty on the part of corrupt government. The fact that these persecutions had taken place in enlightened, liberal France, rather than in some remote barbarian realm, suggested to some writers that dark forces must have been at work and conspiracy theories with satanic overtones became a propagandist weapon.[41] The Scottish folklorist Lewis Spence embodied this view of Nazism, creating a complex alternative history involving occult power, Atlantis, the Celts and the Grail.[42] Mysterious documents, unnameable sources and shadowy secret agents abound, and the ripple effect is dramatic. The founder of anthroposophy, Rudolf Steiner, has been drawn into this exceptionally elaborate network. Steiner did lecture on the Grail,[43] but his links to the theft of a relic from the Habsburg treasury in Vienna and the involvement of occultism at the heart of the Nazi hierarchy are more dubious. Even Spence's Atlantis makes a comeback as the mysterious land thought to lie under Antarctica where, for some inexplicable occult reason, the Nazis took their stolen talismans.[44]

The rise of Freemasonry in the eighteenth century was another factor that provided a context for nostalgic reconstruction, specifically that the obsolete institutions of chivalry were a repository of secret wisdom. Many professional men, members of a rising middle class whose influence was changing the political and social power structures of Europe, belonged to Masonic lodges. Freemasonry epitomized core values of the eighteenth-century Enlightenment. These include a strong work ethic, social tolerance and the application of rational principles to scientific study and the understanding of religion, as well as a contrasting interest in secret meanings, mystical speculation and elaborate ritual. One of the dominant attitudes to religion at this time, certainly the one most prominent among the intelligentsia, is summed up in the idea of deism, which insisted that individual reason was sufficient to observe and to understand the divine plan in the natural world. This approach stood in sharp contrast to the complex theology of revelation in which a priesthood controlled access to divine benefit. It was this attitude to science and religion that created a climate in which secret societies could be created. Not surprisingly, such social and intellectual innovation provoked a reaction, a desire to return to a stable past or to access an alternative knowledge capable of transforming the future. This counter-movement to the rationalism of the Enlightenment sought deeper realities behind the confusing array of experience and looked for hidden connections, apparent to the initiated, who would unify the world and transform society.[45]

Freemasonry adopted legends about the cosmic architecture of Solomon's Temple as metaphors for its origin and organization. A more speculative strain within Freemasonry historicized these motifs as a literal reflection of Masonic history, and, in the absence of substantial proof for such links, a secret history was created. The official name of the Templars, the Order of the Knights of the Temple, and the fact that they occupied a section of the Temple Mount in Jerusalem, the traditional location of Solomon's original temple, provided an opportunity for the mythic history of the two organizations to be combined. Writers began to speculate that Freemasonry, whose own foundation myth looked back to the building of Solomon's Temple, might somehow be much older than the medieval chivalric orders. Among the first to make such a connection was a Catholic convert, the Chevalier Andrew Michael Ramsay (c.1687–1743). He suggested a link between Freemasonry and the crusading orders. In order to appeal to potential aristocratic members of the French lodges, Ramsay stressed the Christian nature of the enterprise and differentiated it specifically from 'a revival of the Bacchanals'. In other words, it was not pagan and had nothing to do with the worshippers of Pan, one of the groups cited in Agrippa's critique of the misuse of magic. One of the long-term effects of Ramsay's ideas was to introduce the 'higher' grades into some aspects of Freemasonry based on an idea of knighthood as transmitting esoteric knowledge.[46] As a movement Freemasonry varied, often quite markedly, in different areas and at different times. The trend towards egalitarianism and rationalist principles took root with comparative ease in England and Scotland, while in France it had to accommodate a more aristocratic membership. In conservative, and politically fragmented, Germany the details of the myth were altered to serve the needs of local Masonic lodges.[47]

Nostalgia for a world of chivalry that never actually existed as expressed in fictional reworkings of chivalric adventures was another factor that would transform the Templars into romantic outsiders, carriers of secret doctrines. The Chevalier Ramsay also wrote a book in the spirit of the gothic novel. *The Travels of Cyrus* (1727) was full of secret chambers under Solomon's Temple and parchments in hollow pillars,[48] just exactly the motifs so crucial to later Grail legends like the ones associated with Rosslyn Chapel and Rennes-le-Château. Some revisions of Templar history focused on the rumour that Jacques de Molay organized the removal of the Templars' treasure before his execution and arranged for it to be concealed in hollow pillars at a Templar site. The idea that treasure was hidden from Philip le Bel has also proved a tenacious motif in Templar legend, including the one localized at Rennes-le-Château. Yet another revivalist, George Frederick Johnson, who claimed to be a Scottish nobleman, suggested that the escaping Templars had fled to Scotland.[49] The Masonic myth of the murdered architect of Solomon's temple, Hiram the first mason, became fused with the execution of de Molay, initializing yet another strand to the legend in, for example, traditions surrounding the Apprentice pillar in Rosslyn Chapel. In Germany the Templar revival was closely linked to the occult, to stories of lost treasure and to the idea that shadowy Grand Masters who succeeded de Molay were pulling the strings in European plots to overthrow heads of state.[50] Other suggestions linked the Templars to the disgraced Illuminati, a group of radical intellectuals based in Bohemia during the latter part of the eighteenth century, which gave the supposed conspiracy a sinister political as well as an occult dimension.[51]

Among the many writers who considered the Templars, several stand out both for the way they synthesized the various strands of the legend and for their subsequent influence. The anti-Jacobite writings of the Abbé Augustin Barruel (1797) depicted both Templars and Freemasons as negative forces out to destabilize the French monarchy and the Catholic Church by fomenting revolution. For Barruel, everything was connected in a vast historical conspiracy of evil beginning with Manichaeanism in the third century AD and embracing Cathars, the Assassins, Oliver Cromwell, the Templars, the Illuminati and the Freemasons. Although the Templars were not yet involved in 'absolutely everything', Barruel's worldview, supported by carefully chosen and translated quotations from a wide range of sources, fed elements of the Templar myth and the idea of a political Masonic plot into the general consciousness.[52] Templars are prominent in the work of Austrian-born scholar of oriental culture Joseph von Hammer-Purgstall. He too believed that everything in history was connected by conspiracy and secrets. In *The Mystery of Bahomet Revealed* (1818), Hammer-Purgstall linked Templars with Gnostic sects who, he believed, forced their members to denounce Christ and practised a form of phallus worship. Bahomet was an androgynous deity who presided over this phallic cult and here, finally, the Holy Grail becomes a Gnostic vessel with no Christian links. The Templar 'Grail' appears in all manner of ancient architectural monuments, many unrecorded outside the pages of Hammer-Purgstall's own work. These dubious archaeological finds and medieval objects transformed the account of the medieval heresy trials into a meditation on comparative religion, a topic of great interest in the early nineteenth century.[53] This set a precedent of reading secret meaning into iconography that would be taken up with enthusiasm by later Grail seekers.

Medieval romance writers did not directly equate the Templars with the Grail knights. At best Wolfram's reference to *templeisen* is ambiguous. The Grail knights act alone, while Templars were part of a community working together in the service of God, not seeking individual martyrdom and glory. However, as neo-templar and masonic organizations took root after the French Revolution, a more positive view of the order began to develop. For example in 1808 a group led by Bernard Raymond Fabré-Palaprat celebrated the anniversary of the death of Jacques de Molay with all the pomp of medieval re-enactment.[54] This was but one indication that what had been regarded as a conspiracy to undermine the forces of society by Gnostics, Cathars, Templars and Freemasons was about to be turned on its head. The position shifted to become a conspiracy against these groups, in other words, a conspiracy aimed at suppressing the secret knowledge passed on by a gallant force struggling against the oppression of the Church and the tyranny of repressive government. One of the symbols of this struggle became a secret Grail, the embodiment of an alternative world, sometimes Christian, sometimes pagan, but always suppressed by the forces of an orthodox clerical power.

ROSSLYN CHAPEL:
THE GRAIL AS ARCHITECTURE

Rosslyn Chapel entered into the media world of the Grail legend in the 1990s when the Scottish author Andrew Sinclair published the first of a series of books that put the structure at the centre of a theory involving Freemasons, Templars and the Holy Grail. Rosslyn was included among the 'Conspiracy through the Centuries' sites in the immensely successful book *The Holy Blood and the Holy Grail*.[55] These well-established themes of alternative history created a new and tenacious modern tradition for Rosslyn, and this in turn has spawned other works supporting and countering Sinclair's claims.[56] Rosslyn Chapel is located near the village of Roslin in Midlothian, Scotland. In the world of *The Da Vinci Code*, the name means 'Rose line', but this is an etymology created for plot purposes. The spelling, Roslin, is modern. Earlier citations use Roskelin (1185), Roskelyn (1245), Rosselyn (1336–7) or Ruslyn (1498). The meaning is sometimes explained as a Gaelic word for 'head of the waterfall', but even this may be part of its elaborate legend, here creating links with the Celtic heritage of Scotland. The meaning of the first element is not entirely clear, and, although the second refers to a water feature, this could be Old English, *hlyn*, or Welsh, *llyn*.[57]

William St Clair Earl of Orkney (c. 1404–84) originally built the chapel to serve as a family-owned church of a type common across Europe. Although never completed, it is, properly, the Collegiate Church of St Matthew. A collegiate church was a secular foundation, not associated with a religious order. It was serviced by canons, priests who lived with the precinct and followed a religious life, but were not monks. One of their duties was to ensure that the patrons of the church were given decent Christian burial and to say prayers for the souls of the departed. There were about forty such churches in Scotland and similar foundations throughout the Catholic world. Many became parish churches after the Reformation, but some, like Rosslyn, which was off the beaten track, continued in use, albeit somewhat restricted and subject to the control of Protestant clergy. The plan of the building followed the usual east–west axis of medieval churches and would have been a substantial cruciform structure. What exists today is an oblong choir, plus a Lady Chapel, dedicated to the Virgin Mary, another common feature in medieval churches. A flight of steps leads down from the Lady Chapel to a small room that has served a variety of purposes. The most striking feature of the building is the profusion of carving, and it is this which has been interpreted as Masonic, Templar, pagan, and/or Celtic.

The original building at Rosslyn dates from the fifteenth century, and the mystic associations coincide with a rise in the popularity of Freemasonry during the eighteenth century when the much-damaged chapel was repaired and reopened. These strikingly idiosyncratic interpretations apply to a relatively small percentage of the carving, and some may not be contemporary with William St Clair's earliest building since work continued after his death and periodic restorations were carried out subsequently.[58] Traditions associating it with the Grail are linked not with ancient history but with ever-widening interest in alternative theory. That ubiquitous recorder of mystical Scottish traditions, Lewis Spence, is one of the first to record folklore associated with Rosslyn and to suggest that it was built according to the plan of the Chapel Perilous in the Grail romances.[59]

Briefly, the secret history of Rosslyn started with a few knights who supposedly escaped before the mass arrests of the Templars in France. These knights fled in Templar ships with a vast treasure that included a secret talisman excavated while they were based at the site of Solomon's Temple in Jerusalem. Some of these escaping Templars sought shelter with Robert the Bruce and their timely intervention at the Battle of Bannockburn (1314) ensured Robert's victory and Scotland's independence from England. However, the grateful Scottish monarch could not support the Templars openly, since by this time the order had been suppressed. He therefore created the Order of Freemasons as a cover for the fugitive Templar Knights who had aided him in his decisive battle against the English king. A century later, the Sinclair family, who were, according to this secret history, the covert Grand Masters of the Templars and the Freemasons, built Rosslyn Chapel, supposedly to house the Templar treasure. The carvings provide a key to this secret history and to the treasure's hiding place. Other evidence for links between Templars and Masons are found in a document known as the Kirkwall Scroll and in various gravestones scattered in churchyards throughout Scotland.[60] Based on this alternative view of history, carvings in Rosslyn have been identified with historical figures, such as Robert the Bruce and Masonic heroes such as Hiram, King Solomon's master-builder.

Attempts have been made to find a 'key' to a secret meaning behind the carvings, and, documents like the Kirkwall Scroll have been used as 'coded maps' to locate the hiding place of the Holy Grail. Unfortunately for such theories, neither the Battle of Bannockburn, nor the Kirkwall Scroll is particularly mysterious. The key point for this alternative view of the Battle of Bannockburn is that a contingent of Templars arrived just in time to save the day. As a major Scottish victory, the details of the battle appear in many sources[61] and are not as is claimed 'sparse and fragmentary'.[62] The account in *The Holy Blood and the Holy Grail*, which started this hare running, states that 'a sizeable contingent [of Templars] is said to have fought' and that 'a spate of archaic legends has for centuries linked Bruce with the Templars'.[63] Another account claims that 'the evidence suggests that they had formidable help – in the form of a contingent of Knights Templar'.[64] Sources for these 'archaic legends' are not clearly documented and many spin-off books simply quote one of the secondary sources.[65] One can sympathize with more orthodox historians who become a bit testy when lack of evidence in historical sources is taken as indication that the Templars were really present at the Battle of Bannockburn but that everybody kept it a secret. A similar problem exists in connection with the

Kirkwall Scroll, which has been interpreted as a map indicating the hiding place of the treasure at Rosslyn. The earliest possible date for the cloth, on the basis of radiocarbon dating, is the fifteenth century, and it could be much later.[66] Critics have pointed out that the iconography is the important feature, and the argument hinges on when the scroll was painted rather than when the cloth was made. Since the biblical quotations come from the 1611 version of the King James Bible and the coat of arms depicted on the cloth was granted in the 1780s, a medieval date is unlikely.[67]

Repairs and alterations to the original decorations in Rosslyn Chapel also affect interpretations of the carvings. For example the 'wounds' on the supposed 'Apprentice' head appear to have been added later to enhance the legend.[68] Taken as a whole, the carvings conform to established conventions in medieval iconography. Such 'bibles in stone', as they have been called, were not unusual. Saints carried symbols reflecting the important accomplishments in their lives. Martyrs carried the palm of martyrdom and evangelists held an open book. Granted the system for depicting or interpreting religious symbolism was not always consistent, this introduces a note of ambiguity into the identification of some images. Similar images can be found in other medieval buildings where there is no question of esotericism. To assume that ambiguities indicate the existence of a secret key is problematic. Rosslyn's oddity lies in the fact that it remained largely intact, despite Reformation reaction against elaborate iconography which it considered distracting or even idolatrous, and the chapel stands out more today than it would have when it was built.[69]

The iconographic scheme at Rosslyn illustrates the salvation of humankind. The carved ceiling depicts the Creation. St Michael stands with his sword next to the Trinity, namely God the Father, Christ with his hand raised in blessing, and a dove, surrounded by the sun, moon and stars. The roof is also decorated with flowers associated with the Virgin Mary such as roses, lilies and marguerites. Series of figures at different locations illustrate important principles of Christian life. Other carvings illustrate the Works of Mercy and culminate with St Peter holding the keys to Heaven for all good Christians, while a companion series illustrates vices with Hellmouth waiting to swallow sinners. Skeletons lead figures from all walks of life in an elaborate *danse macabre* to remind the viewer that death comes for both high and low. Other carvings illustrate important Bible stories. The Fall of Man is represented on one of the pillars, elsewhere the star of Bethlehem shines on the familiar figures of the Nativity. These are balanced with scenes of Christ's Passion and Resurrection. There are representations from the Old Testament stories, such as the sacrifice of Abraham, Tobias wrestling with the angel, King David with his harp, King Darius's dream and the freeing of the Israelites. Other figures depict the Apostles and important saints, such as St Roc, protector from plague, and St Sebastian. On one of the corbels of the Lady Chapel, Moses, with the horns/rays of light that surrounded him on his descent from Mt Sinai, holds the Tablets of the Commandments. Numerous angels represent different orders of the Nine Choirs; some carry scrolls as messengers of God, while others play instruments as part of the heavenly host.[70]

A small number of carvings thought to represent Masonic or Templar images feature regularly in esoteric interpretations of Rosslyn, although these too fit into a schema of Christian iconography in contexts that have no esoteric, Masonic or Templar connections. A carved corbel, which appears to show a blindfolded figure led by another, has been linked to Masonic initiation. The use of the blindfold was not a feature of Masonic rituals until the eighteenth century, and this carving may simply illustrate the dictum of 'the blind leading the blind'.[71] Angels in 'Masonic' postures may represent another overly enthusiastic search for mystery, since there is no clear explanation as to why these postures are Masonic or how they feature in Masonic ceremonies.[72] Similar problems arise in connection with the so-called Templar seal and the *Agnus Dei* carvings. Two knights riding the same horse, a symbol of their close and supportive brotherhood, appear on the Templar seal. However the two figures in the Rosslyn carving do not ride the same horse, rather one is standing behind the mounted figure. The *Agnus Dei*, a lamb holding a banner, is a widely used symbol of Christ, but was not unique to the Templars.[73] Gnostic as well as Masonic interpretations of carvings are also popular. One of these involves St John the Evangelist who often holds a chalice from which a snake emerges to signify an unsuccessful attempt to poison him. This is not a 'rare device' of a 'gnostic snake appearing from the Grail',[74] but a typical attribute of St John in western art.

The idea that the Grail lies hidden at Rosslyn is the most recent layer of the myth. Lewis Spence suggested that the building's design mirrored the Perilous Chapel of the romances, and both Trevor Ravenscroft and Walter Johnnannes Stein believed that the Grail was somewhere at Rosslyn. However, Grail imagery as such is not prominent at Rosslyn and proponents have to work quite hard to find it. There are frequent references to 'The EnGrailed Cross' on the Sinclair arms. Although the use of upper case and the definite article seem to imply a connection between the arms and the Grail, the term 'enGrailed' is used in heraldry meaning scalloped and the Sinclair arms bear an enGrailed (scalloped) cross.[75] Seemingly more promising is the suggestion that Grail symbols, described as a 'chalice with a long stem inscribed with a floriated cross', were carved on gravestones.[76] These supposedly were covert markings for Templar graves after the order had been suppressed. The symbol on the graves is a stylized representation of a flowering rood cross, not a chalice. This common iconographic image combined the Tree of Life in the Garden of Eden with the cross of the crucified Christ into an image of salvation. Here, as so often, these arguments become forced and circular by reinterpreting an uncontested iconographic symbol as a secret Templar sign and then using the idiosyncratic reinterpretation to suggest that Rosslyn was a Templar stronghold.[77]

Several popular legend motifs have become localized at Rosslyn Chapel. These migrating legends become attached to many places, and, while they indicate the continued popularity of a site, they cannot be patched together to form a history. According to one tradition, Oliver Cromwell, or more specifically General Monk, stabled his horses in Rosslyn.[78] Since there was no wholesale destruction of the chapel, this is taken to mean that Cromwell himself might have been a Mason and therefore hesitated to destroy this important site.[79] Cromwell is a popular folk villain, and tales often characterize him as a rather wayward figure destroying or sparing human lives and religious sites at whim.[80] The intricately carved Apprentice Pillar is certainly one of the wonders of Rosslyn. Earlier sources call it the Prince's Pillar, and the story about the master mason and his apprentice appeared only later. The title 'Prince's Pillar' may reflect the power and influence of the original builder, William St Clair, the so-called 'prince' of Orkney. A later account of the mason story notes that the carved head now known as the apprentice has been altered. The source calls the apprentice story a legend,[81] and it is not unique to Rosslyn. The theme of the envious artisan murdering either a competitor or an apprentice is attached to a number of trades.[82] The addition of the Apprentice legend at the end of the eighteenth century may indicate, not the memory of an ancient secret, but the popularity of the Hiram story. The murder of Solomon's master-mason, Hiram, by his apprentices was an important metaphor in Freemasonry, and may be an instance where later Masonic lore affected Rosslyn rather than Rosslyn being a source for such lore.

Hints of Nazi occultism have also found their way into the Rosslyn legend. Rudolf Hess's trip to England has been linked to Rosslyn Chapel.[83] The attempt to create a credible historical case for Templar involvement at Rosslyn will always involve belief and supposition. The link between the Knights Templar and Scotland had its roots in romantic tradition, expanding, as we have seen elsewhere, eighteenth-century traditions about Freemasons with various esoteric talents. As a legend, it has something for everyone and illustrates how quickly legend motifs become attached to places and are disseminated by the mass media.

The sphere of influence for modern Grail seekers has expanded. New theories about the origins of the Grail allowed writers to transform the Grail quest in medieval romance into an image of personal and cultural transformation. Theories about alternative Grails have both adherents and detractors, and it would be impossible to review all the published books, much less the vast range of comment on the Internet. However, these sources share two assumptions, namely that the Grail legend contains a cosmic secret and that the guardians of the Grail are targeted by a sinister conspiracy. The secret and the conspiracy add the thrill of a detective story to the adventures of the Arthurian knights. As a result the audience participates in the adventures once assigned to medieval heroes and becomes personally involved in unscrambling the clues to discover a secret.

Signs of a shift in attitudes to groups such as the Templars appeared as early as the sixteenth century when Cornelius Agrippa von Nettlesheim listed Gnostic magicians, pagan worshippers of Priapus and Pan, and the Templars among those who misused magical knowledge. By the twentieth century, the Templars had been rehabilitated as defenders of freedom and possessors of wisdom beneficial to humanity. Visitors like Otto Rahn found a flourishing neo-Cathar myth in southern France and had little difficulty in identifying them with the Templars. All three groups mentioned by Agrippa, the Gnostics, the worshippers of Pan and Priapus, and the Templars, would eventually be absorbed into the Grail legend, not as examples of the misuse of magic but as the successive guardians of a secret religion.

The dualistic beliefs of these revived and restored Templars and Cathars add a mystic dimension to popular interpretations of history. On the one hand, they provide theosophy and other occult movements with links back to Gnosticism. On the other, they embody the liberal and secular values of republican France, despite that fact that Catharism was a religious sect. In the context of new age thinking, the avoidance of meat and eggs becomes active vegetarianism and respect for nature, while the fact that both sexes could become *perfecti* has been transformed into enlightened gender politics. Thus they can occupy seemingly conflicting spaces in popular discourse as precursors for a range of modern ideas. As such they have been embraced by the tourist industry, by both liberal and right-wing political movements, by new age pilgrimage and by modern conspiracy theory. There are a number of different agendas here, but with a common belief that groups like the Cathars and the Templars preserved secrets that transcended the historical and cultural circumstances of their origin, development and demise. Freed from the constraints of historical thinking, these modern perspectives exploit the dramatic potential of what they perceive as an attempt to conceal eternal truth.

The main thrust of the myth is always the transmission of secret wisdom. However, there is no clear indication of how specific elements originated. When the legend began to take shape during the eighteenth century, it combined the ideas of the wholeness and unity of creation, which had been prominent in Renaissance philosophy, and applied new techniques of historiography and ethnology to create a supposedly unbroken transmission from ancient to modern civilizations. In many popular books dealing with ancient links and conspiratorial theories, Freemasons have succeeded the medieval Cathars and Templars. They in their turn are typically regarded as a unified pan-national organization, although this, as with so much else in this mass of legends, is something of a simplification as Freemasonry existed, and still exists, in different forms. The metaphors and parables of Freemasonry began to be woven into a system, and where evidence of connections was lacking, or at best tenuous, secrecy was used to bridge the gaps.

CHAPTER 6

The Religion of the Grail

THE MOST INFLUENTIAL modern Grail legend began as a trio of documentaries on British television. They were presented, with considerable panache, by the writer and researcher Henry Lincoln.[1] The book that followed, *The Holy Blood and the Holy Grail* (published in America as *Holy Blood Holy Grail*), became an immediate bestseller. Several updates and sequels appeared,[2] and the book became news again when two of the authors brought an action for alleged copyright infringement.[3] The influence of *Holy Blood Holy Grail* on the historical conspiracy genre has been immense. Just as crucially it has influenced fiction, notably Dan Brown's *Da Vinci Code*, and the sophisticated satire of Umberto Eco's *Foucault's Pendulum*.

The main argument is that the Grail of the medieval romances, the *sangreal*, is in reality a misunderstanding of the phrase *sang real* or *royal (holy) blood*; and that therefore the Holy Grail is a person not a physical object. The heir to this sacred bloodline is a descendant of Jesus Christ and his wife, Mary Magdalene, who married into a noble family, the Merovingians, the first Christian dynasty to rule France. Mainstream Christianity attempted to suppress the hereditary cult represented by the descendants of Christ and the Magdalene in order to maintain the apostolic succession of St Peter. However, at the time of the Crusades, a secret organization known as the Priory of Sion was founded in order to protect the divine bloodline, and the Order of the Knights Templar was created as the military and financial wing of the Priory, and the medieval Cathars were also privy to this secret. Before the fall of the Cathar stronghold of Montségur, they smuggled out a mysterious treasure, variously described as the Grail, the Grail heir and/or the Gnostic Gospels. After the suppression of the Cathars and Templars, the Priory allied itself with Freemasons and Rosicrucians. Its aim is the restoration of the Merovingian descendants of Christ and the Magdalene to rule a utopian European superstate.

This was, to say the least, a startling thesis. The authors based their extraordinary claims on a local history story about a treasure found by a nineteenth-century French priest, Bérenger Saunière, at Rennes-le-Château, a small town in southern France. According to this story, the priest found documents in an ancient column in his church. The information they contained was so explosive that the authorities bought his silence. When the authors decoded this material, it led them to someone who claimed to be the last Merovingian heir. The thesis is considerably less shocking and original than it first seems, being an imaginative synthesis of popular ideas about conspiracy, a secret theocracy and the destiny of mankind. The ideas have been attached to groups as diverse as the Illuminati of eighteenth-century Bavaria and the theosophical movements that became so influential in Britain and America at the end of the nineteenth century.[4] The religion of the modern Grail legend is essentially a theosophical one in which events are never random; all that is lacking is the key to understanding their pattern, and, once the occult meaning of history is understood, the human race will be able to achieve its noble destiny. Various groups, such as the Templars, the Cathars and the troubadours of medieval Provence, practised this doctrine and were targeted by Church and State authorities. The beliefs of this secret religion always coincided to a marked degree with the fashionable anti-establishment attitudes of the day. By the middle of the twentieth century, these ideas had become entangled in Wagnerian fantasies with somewhat unfortunate Aryan overtones and with speculations about Atlantis and extraterrestrials. This was also the period when modern Wicca myths about the survival of Neolithic religion were developing.[5] At the core of *Holy Blood Holy Grail* is an institution called the Priory of Sion created in France in the middle of the twentieth, not the twelfth, century. What is interesting about this secret conspiracy legend is that it took speculative ideas about the alleged activities of Cathars, Templars and troubadours, which had originally been localized in France, and, in effect, repatriated them. This strong local context added considerably to the attractiveness of the core on which the *Holy Blood Holy Grail* books were built. Mary Magdalene and the children of Christ were not in the original Priory material, and here the authors incorporated modern research, much of it highly speculative, which questioned the historical accuracy of the Bible. The Mary Magdalene element has developed beyond the parameters of the original *Holy Blood Holy Grail* books and has been absorbed into a search for ancient goddesses, which is part of a wider movement to restore the sacred feminine aspect of religion.

The original English-language publication sparked a furore that still continues. Books, television documentaries and Internet sites abound giving both sides of the argument.[6] From a historical point of view, in the words of the most comprehensive published assessment of the sources for this theory, the 'evidence on the ground' does not hold up.[7] Nor is the mystery an ancient one. It began in France in the 1950s, and the first account of treasure and mystery at Rennes-le-Château appeared in a series of articles in a local paper not long after a new owner had turned Saunière's property into a hotel.[8] Rumours about local eccentrics, treasure, mysterious artefacts and secrets are a common, well-nigh universal, basis for local legends. The factual content for such legends, when it exists at all, is never as elaborate as the legend implies, but it adds colour and charm to familiar, even rather ordinary, sites. Enhancement is after all a function of legend, and in the case of Rennes-le-Château, enhancement considerably outstrips historical information. The story generated enough interest to get into the media, and, fortunately, it also attracted the attention of an excellent local historian.[9] This more sober account suggested that rumours about mysterious documents and vast treasure might have been occasioned by the finding of hidden coins and by documents relating to church repairs, not ancient parchments. The actions of Bérenger Saunière, the priest at the centre of the mystery, are also given a less occult explanation. Parishioners complained about the priest's cavalier treatment of the cemetery, his extended absences, something not consistent with his duty as a parish priest, and his excessive spending. Saunière avoided giving too many details of his income, thus incurring censure from the authorities. This account, based on local documents before the story of Rennes-le-Château escalated, also suggests that rumours of the priest's wealth were somewhat exaggerated.

Whether one is dealing with a man who failed to fulfil the obligations of his office or one who was part of a vast conspiracy, the mystery of Rennes-le-Château, a small town in the Languedoc in southern France, began when Bérenger Saunière was appointed to the parish church in 1885. The appointment was not without problems since the young priest's royalist sympathies for the ousted French monarchy brought him into conflict with his government paymasters. In the course of restoring the dilapidated church, he apparently found some strange documents, either inside a Visigothic pillar or near the staircase of the church tower. The originals have been conveniently lost and survive only as modern typed transcriptions. According to events that are not possible to verify, Saunière took them to Paris to consult a linguistic specialist at the church of St Sulpice, and he purchased a copy of Nicolas Poussin's *Les Bergers d'Arcadie* from the Louvre. The painting depicts shepherds gazing at an inscription on a tomb which reads

'Et in Arcadia Ego' (Even in Arcadia [am] I). The tomb and the landscape are said to resemble the scenery, including an actual tomb, around Arques, a village near Rennes-le-Château.

Saunière's behaviour became even more eccentric and suspicious when he began to renovate the cemetery. He reused the Visigothic column in a new structure, workmen reported seeing glints of metal and the priest supposedly obliterated an inscription on the tomb of an eighteenth-century countess of Hautpoul. This inscription, recorded in a book by a local author, is one of the many features of the mystery for which there is no direct evidence. Neither the documents found in the pillar nor the inscription can be dated convincingly, and the authenticity of the local book about the missing tomb inscription has been challenged. Saunière's frequent absences and his unusual prosperity brought him to the attention of the authorities. At this juncture, interpretation leads in two very different directions. One possibility is that Saunière may have been involved in fraudulent practices regarding his obligation to say daily Mass. This was a serious infringement of his duty as a priest, if true, and inconsistent with his duties as a public servant on a government salary.[10] Alternatively, he may have been involved in a conspiracy, which made the authorities nervous, although there is no direct evidence of this. However, those who favour this approach take the lack of evidence as an indication of just how deep the conspiracy went.

Saunière renovated the church, and some of his additions have been interpreted as clues to his secret espousal of the dualist beliefs of the Cathars and Templars. However, the elaborate style is in keeping with late nineteenth-century taste and has parallels elsewhere. Other projects included a villa for retired priests, the Villa Béthanie, with a tower structure to contain his library, the Tour Magdela. Here he entertained many guests, and as his expenses rose, he attracted the unfavourable attention of the new bishop, who finally suspended him. Saunière died in poverty in 1917; his housekeeper eventually sold the Villa Béthanie. She continued to live there and regaled the new owner with tales of secret treasure whose whereabouts she would one day reveal – but she had a stroke and died with the secret, if there ever was one, intact.

The modern legend of Rennes-le-Château began in earnest with a publication written by a journalist, which added significant details to the framework of the already available accounts.[11] The journalist, Gerard de Sède, introduced two manuscripts said to have been found by Saunière, a copy of a tombstone inscription supposedly obliterated by him, and the account of his acquisition of a copy of Poussin's painting. There are hints about secret societies, unexplained coincidences and secrets found by a poor village priest. The theory resurfaced with further elaborations in television documentaries that fleshed out some of the hints in de Sède's book and reformulated the earlier rumours into a more coherent legendary narrative. It is very much a 'what if' approach to history, asking readers and observers to consider that seeming coincidences in an otherwise pedestrian story reveal a world of extraordinary events and cosmic conspiracies.

It does indeed lead to an extraordinary narrative, but not an ancient or a historically convincing one. The Priory of Sion (Prieuré de Sion) was founded in 1956 and was duly registered with the French authorities. Through the activities of one of its members, Pierre Plantard, what was originally a local organization has become the centrepiece of pseudo-historical books on alternative Christianity, theories about the Holy Grail, and mass-market fiction. Plantard envisaged an organization based on a quasi-Masonic concept of chivalry that would provide a platform for the revival of the French monarchy. He even presented himself as the last Merovingian, a descendant of the line of Clovis, the first Christian king, and therefore a pretender to the French throne. Thus his claim pre-dated not only the Bourbon dynasty ousted by the French Revolution, but also the Carolingian dynasty of Charlemagne and the Holy Roman Emperors. This is important in understanding the background to the creation of the priory, since there were already a number of esoteric theories about the Grail linking it with Charlemagne and the foundation of the Holy Roman Empire. Existing interpretations owed much to ideas put forward by men like Eugene Aroux, Joséphin Péladan and Walter Stein. They had, however, acquired a distinctly Germanic flavour after writers like Otto Rahn adopted them. However fanciful the interpretations were, southern France had, historically, been the stronghold of the Cathar sect. Although the documentation is undoubtedly based on 'gossamer evidence',[12] the original members of the Priory of Sion produced a striking innovation to this legend by adapting, or perhaps readapting, these ideas to a distinctly French setting.

Pierre Plantard and his associates, including Phillippe de Cherisey and a professional author, Gerard de Sède, created documents linking the priory with an historical Abbey of Sion founded during the Crusades. These were deposited under the title 'Les Dossiers Secret de Henri Lobineau' in the Bibliothèque nationale de France in Paris. These documents claimed that a secret code found by a nineteenth-century priest, Abbé Bérenger Saunière at Rennes-le-Château, led, by way of Poussin's famous seventeenth-century painting of Arcadian shepherds, to the existence of a lost Merovingian heir to the French throne. The protection of this heir had been entrusted to a secret cabal, the Priory of Sion, operating within the medieval Cathar sect and the Order of the Knights Templar. A succession of distinguished intellectuals and artists, including Leonardo Da Vinci, had been grand masters of this secret organization. Pierre Plantard's claims were focused on inserting himself into French royal history, specifically as the heir of a dynasty founded by Clovis, King of the Franks, who had converted to Christianity, something which supported Plantard's very traditional Catholicism. This fantastic history was put forward in de Sède's book *Le Trésor maudit*. At this point two things occurred. An English television writer read the *Trésor maudit* and wrote three programmes for the BBC about the lost treasure at Rennes-le-Château and a French researcher began to explain the fictional background to the priory.[13]

The BBC's popular history series, *Chronicle*, screened the programmes showing this highly speculative decoding of the Rennes-le-Château material based on equally speculative theories about Templars and Cathars.[14] The presentation was intense and compelling. One programme included an interview with Pierre Plantard, and all made reference to an 'obvious and startling truth', but came to no clear conclusion. In the Plantard/de Cherissey version, the role of the priory was to protect a lost heir to the French throne. For the authors of *Holy Blood Holy Grail*, the story was altogether more grandiose. The priory protected the actual descendants of Christ and Mary Magdalene, and the activities of the medieval Church against Cathars and Templars were transformed into a conspiracy to eradicate the hereditary succession of Christ and his wife and maintain the apostolic succession of St Peter and the Vatican popes. The goals of the Priory of Sion were extended onto a global stage to encompass a messianic mystery religion (the 'real' Christianity) that would sustain a 'Holy European Empire' of peace and world stability. By this time, however, other authors were criticizing the pseudo-historical fictions behind the documentation of the Priory of Sion. In the decade after the book first appeared, the idea of an alternative, and of course suppressed, form of Christianity became linked to another popular theme associated with conspiracy and suppression, namely the search for the divine feminine. Margaret Starbird in *The Woman with the Alabaster Jar* (1993)[15] added the idea that the medieval veneration of Mary Magdalene concealed the remnants of an ancient cult devoted to a pre-Christian goddess, traces of which still existed in southern France. The Priory of Sion documents listed Leonardo as one of its grand masters, and other writers offered further refinements to this convoluted secret world by suggesting that his paintings contained clues to unorthodox Christian beliefs, which, among other things, caused him to fabricate the Shroud of Turin.[16]

The exact nature of this alternative Christianity is somewhat vague, since it focuses on conspiracies and cracking codes rather than the practicalities of doctrine. The motivation for the conspiracy, however, is worked out in some detail, beginning with a struggle between a patriarchal faction of St Peter and a supposedly more gender-tolerant group led by Mary Magdalene. The notion of a sacred bloodline has given rise to one of the most productive versions of the modern Grail legend, namely that Gnostics, Cathars, Templars and finally an organization known as the Priory of Sion protected a secret heritage. The only obvious historical thread linking these groups is that they were all targets for criticism or suppression by the power structures of Church and State. However, in terms of conspiracy thinking, this antagonism was not a sporadic response to differing historical circumstances, but a sustained campaign to counter an alternative religion practised in secret and passed from one set of guardians to another. These secret practices apparently stretched back before the actual founding of Christianity to form an unbroken link with the pagan world or with some even more ancient universal cosmological doctrine. Hints and pointers to the secret were sought in various works of art, church monuments and landscape features.[17]

Although the book was hugely popular, it did not garner much critical acclaim. Antony Burgess immediately saw its potential as the plot for a novel, while cultural critics like Marina Warner summed it up succinctly as 'a load of hooey'. Both comments are among the quotations prefaced to the paperback reissue of the book.[18] The controversy did not hurt sales, but neither did the 'shocking revelations' seem to have an especially negative effect on Christianity. The claims of *Holy Blood Holy Grail* surfaced again in the wake of Dan Brown's immensely successful *The Da Vinci Code*, the second in a trilogy of conspiracy thrillers published in 2003.[19] Brown's preface seemed to claim a degree of authority for details of the rituals and institutions mentioned in the book. Writers of Grail romances, such as Chrétien de Troyes and Wolfram von Eschenbach, used such authors' conceits to add authority, but many of Brown's readers took his statements literally. By this time, several tangential mysteries mentioned in the original *Holy Blood Holy Grail* book had become attached to other sites, such as Rosslyn Chapel and Shugborough Hall, while other publications had appeared pointing out some of the more notable historical fallacies in the argument.[20] At first glance, the *Holy Blood* book presents a complex theory built on an enormous array of facts supported by a vast bibliography – it is partly that which makes it so attractive. Another significant factor in its continuing success has been the Internet, which provides the widest possible access to both supportive and critical opinion.

The exact motivations of the French amateur antiquarians who created the Priory of Sion fiction are rather murky. Critics have suggested everything from surrealistic role-playing to right-wing politics, or just that authors of modern popular Grail books have interpreted local rumours too literally. The founding members of the Priory of Sion were not concerned with theology or even with the Grail as such. The secret cabal they created echoed earlier theories that historicized the Grail romances in the courts of Charlemagne and his successors, the German Holy Roman Emperors. By shifting the secret organization back to the Merovingian rulers, who were ousted by the Carolingian dynasty, the ironic, and rather clever, fiction created by the priory put a distinctly French spin on this version of alternative history, adding for good measure the politics of nineteenth-century French Catholicism, Poussin and various prominent figures of the European Enlightenment.

The Franks were among the so-called barbarian tribes who gained power and influence as the Roman Empire declined. A Frankish clan, which became known as the Merovingians, established a base in what is today France, eventually giving their name to what had been Roman Gaul. The Merovingian king Clovis I converted to Christianity and is regarded, at least in retrospect, as the first true king of France. The first in the Carolingian line of kings, Pippin the Short, deposed the last Merovingian. His son, Charlemagne, was crowned Holy Roman Emperor in 800. Although Charlemagne's world was very different from the Roman one, his title harked back to their glory days. In 987 Hugh Capet became the first king of another dynasty, the Capetians. In 1589, Henry IV initiated the Catholic Bourbon dynasty of France, and the Bourbon kings, Louis XIII and Louis XIV, together with their respective ministers, Cardinal Richelieu and Cardinal Mazarin, represent the height of French cultural and political power. Absorbing the earliest French kings into their origin legend placed the Priory of Sion at the very fountainhead of French national identity. In *Holy Blood Holy Grail* the bloodline is associated with the legendary birth of Merovech, eponymous founder of the Merovingian royal line, son of a human mother and a sea-beast called a Quinotaur. This creature was half fish and half bull. The story sets up the Merovingians as legitimate European kings by association with the well-known classical myth of Europa carried off by Zeus.[21] However, in order to turn the Merovingians into divine kings, *Holy Blood Holy Grail* adopts the popular, if somewhat naive, notion that there is always some historical reality behind such legends, suggesting that the Quiniotaur represents Christ. The link between the French dynasty and the descendants of Christ is one of the points where even an argument as speculative as this one rather strains credibility.

NICOLAS POUSSIN AND
THE ARCADIAN LANDSCAPE

The painting *Shepherds Gazing at a Tomb in Arcadia* by the French artist Nicolas Poussin (1594–1665) provides another path into the secret world of the modern Holy Grail legend. According to the Priory of Sion documents, Poussin was a member of that organization. Clues found in his painting of Arcadian shepherds, such as the hidden geometry of the picture and the tomb itself, supposedly point to the landscape features close to Rennes-le-Château and are connected with the secret guarded by this organization. The artist spent most of his life in Italy, not France, and there is controversy about whether Poussin consciously put coded messages into his painting, or whether the secret meaning exists only in retrospect as part of the pseudo-history of the Priory of Sion.[22]

The painting is certainly striking. In the context of the classical world, which Poussin revered, the very existence of a tomb in Arcadia is unsettling and the mysterious phrase 'Et in Arcadia Ego' only adds to the ambiguity. Poussin's classical art was especially concerned with the didactic and philosophical possibilities of painting, and it aimed to engage the viewer on a rational and intellectual level. 'All your actions being guided by reason you can do nothing which will not lead to a really virtuous end' is just one of the quotes from his numerous letters with which the art historian Anthony Blunt supports the idea that a philosophy of stoicism, as understood by the intellectual elite of the seventeenth century, informed Poussin's life, personal morality and artistic aesthetic.[23] The artist executed commissions for important patrons such as Louis XIII and Cardinal Richelieu, and several of his paintings eventually came into the royal collection. The *dossiers secrets*, however, present a different interpretation, namely that this painting contains a secret code available not to rational intellect but only to the initiated or the code-breaker. While classical and mythological themes abound in Poussin's work, there are no hints in his letters or in the comments of his early biographers that he had any leaning towards symbolic codes and secret messages. Rather, his paintings illustrate orthodox, albeit rather intellectualized, moral or religious precepts. The one oblique reference to a possible secret cited by the authors of *Holy Blood Holy Grail* comes not from Poussin's numerous letters but from a letter written by the soon to be disgraced royal financial minister, Lois Fouquet, to his brother, Nicolas.[24]

According to works advocating a secret history such as *Le Trésor maudit* and *Holy Blood Holy Grail*, Poussin's 'Et in Arcadia Ego' illustrates a code from a document concealed in an ancient pillar and on a tomb in the Rennes-le-Château cemetery. It has also been suggested that lines drawn from the inscribed tomb in the painting link features in the landscape around Rennes-le-Château and form a pentagram. The authors of *Holy Blood Holy Grail* describe a structure that once stood by the road between Serres and Arques as a tomb 'identical to the one in the painting' where 'if one stands before the sepulchre the vista is virtually indistinguishable from that in the painting'. The tomb is the pivot for the Rennes mystery and subsequent theories, but it presents something of a conundrum. The landscape does not match Poussin's painting with the exactness implied here. An even more pertinent fact, mentioned in the book then passed over, is that there is no record of such a structure when Poussin painted his Arcadian shepherds. A roadside monument is mentioned no earlier than the beginning of the twentieth century, and photographs of a squat rectangular structure date from the mid-twentieth century, the very period when the Priory of Sion was being created. This raises the possibility that the 'tomb' was adapted to fit in with the modern Priory mythology. The authors rely on vague 'according to the peasants' traditions and a reference, in a work by someone called Jean Delaude, to a passage conveniently 'missing' from the memoirs of someone roughly contemporary with Poussin. Delaude is one of the pseudonyms used by the writers of the *dossiers secret*.[25] Even the authors of *Holy Blood Holy Grail* admit 'there is no indication of the age of the tomb', but they rephrase their speculation as a question: 'how did its builders ever locate a setting which matches so precisely that of the painting?' The question invites the reader to think that despite clear indications that this is a modern structure, it really is not. Jessie Weston and Arthur Waite used much the same technique in creating the link between tarot cards and the Grail.[26] An equally plausible answer to the question posed by the authors at this point is not that there is a centuries-old secret, but that Pierre Plantard and his friends created a series of documents to link the environs around Rennes-le-Château with Poussin's painting retrospectively.

Poussin painted two versions of *Les Bergers d'Arcadie*. The first is a dramatic work depicting shepherds around a tomb half hidden by a twisted tree. A skull rests on a tomb inscribed with the words 'Et in Arcadia' (Yet even in Arcadia). In one corner a river god is pouring water from a jug. This work, now in the Chatsworth collection, belonged to the Duke of Devonshire. Lady Elizabeth Anson, whose marital home of Shugborough is the setting for another Holy Grail mystery, made a copy of it in the eighteenth century.[27] The appearance of death in the deathless world of Arcadia reflects a popular literary theme. It recalled the classical tradition of pastoral poetry as embodied in the work of the Roman poet Virgil. Poussin's painting owes something to earlier studies of the subject, and his first depiction of the Arcadia image had a pendant piece with the same river god pouring out the water of time and Midas washing himself, free of his accursed golden touch. This adds the futility of riches to the idea of mortality, and here at least Anthony Blunt's suggestion that Poussin was influenced by the philosophy of stoicism makes sense. The same tomb, floating in the air above dancing figures, appears in another Poussin evocation of time slipping away to death, *Dance to the Music of Time*, now in the Wallace Collection in London.

The second Arcadian shepherd picture is also set in a carefully painted landscape. The shepherds still gaze on the inscription, but without the skull as a *memento mori* or the river god pouring out water to mark the passing time. The 'code' implies that lines connect the tomb to the sacred geometry of the landscape that leads eventually to the 'secret' of the book. This secret varies in different alternative accounts. The most popular version opted for a divine Merovingian dynasty, but others suggest it points to the tomb of a mortal Christ who did not die on the cross in Jerusalem, but much later in France.[28] Of course a further possibility is that the 'sacred geography' of these paintings has been created in retrospect, and it is difficult to find anything in Poussin's life or work to support a mystery of this type. Poussin drew inspiration for his paintings from the sixteenth-century epic poem *Gerusalemme Liberata*, written by the Italian poet Torquato Tasso. Without doubt Tasso presented an idealized and glorified view of the Crusades, but there is no mention of secrets or the Knights Templar. Nor is there much evidence for unorthodox theology in any of Poussin's work. He depicted the institution of the Eucharist as part of two series of paintings of the Seven Sacraments. The imagery conforms to descriptions in the Gospels. Christ holds both a chalice and bread; St John appears among the Apostles, beardless, but hardly feminine. In both series, St Peter holds a key, the papal symbol, further suggesting an orthodox interpretation.[29]

DIVINE FANTASIES: THE BLOODLINE AND THE IDEAL FRENCH STATE

One of the pivotal themes of modern Grail legends is that there is an elaborate conspiracy whose purpose is to ensure the continued dominance of the patriarchal Rome-centred Church. Gnostic texts excluded from the

Bible supposedly contain hints about a marriage between Mary Magdalene and Jesus Christ, the secret protected by the Priory. The New Testament recounts the story of the life, death and resurrection of the Messiah, Jesus Christ, as well as the history of the early Christian Church during the ministry of the Apostles. Its content evolved over time and was not fixed until the second century at the earliest, but the life of Christ is told from four points of view in the four Gospels of the Evangelists, Matthew, Mark, Luke and John. The first three are relatively straightforward accounts presenting Christ's life as a series of episodes epitomizing the religious message he offered to his followers. Details differ, but they tell the same essential story. The tone of the Gospel of St John, however, is more impressionistic and philosophical.

The Passion of Christ, the events surrounding his death, includes the Last Supper, which took place on the Thursday and coincided with the Jewish festival of Passover. On this occasion Christ blessed bread and wine, an action commemorated as the Christian sacrament of the Eucharist. The cup used at this meal became identified with the Grail. The events of the following day, Friday, the day of the Crucifixion, also found their way into the Grail romances and into the modern Grail legends as well. Christ's mother, the Virgin Mary, St John the Evangelist and Mary Magdalene witnessed the Crucifixion. This ended when a soldier, later identified as a Roman centurion named Longinus, pierced Christ's side with a lance. The body was removed from the cross, an event referred to as the Deposition. At this point a man named Joseph of Arimathea enters the story. He offered his own tomb for the burial. Traditions not recounted by the four Evangelists claim that Joseph collected the blood from Christ's wounds in the same cup used at the Last Supper, given to him by the Roman governor Pontius Pilate. Three days later, Mary Magdalene and two other women visited the tomb only to find it empty. The fact of the Resurrection was revealed to Christ's disciples in a series of events, most notably through the words of the angel at the empty tomb, Christ's words to Mary Magdalene and later by the risen Christ to the Apostles at a supper at Emmaus. The New Testament also records the beginning of the spread of Christianity as St Paul and other Apostles preached the Christian message to the Roman world. The so-called 'canonical' books were established as the authentic record of the Christian faith. However, a number of alternative texts, referred to collectively as 'Apocrypha' since the fifth century, existed but were excluded. Indeed, the summary of the Passion given above is based on both canonical and non-canonical accounts. These non-canonical texts give different accounts of events and record variant forms of belief and ritual practised by this new Christian religion. Some of these ideas came to be viewed as heretical, but the Apocrypha as a whole were never condemned as heresy. Some apocryphal texts fell out of use or were known only through fragments, but others remained part of Christian devotion. Some even found their way into medieval Grail romances and modern Grail legends. Of these, the most pertinent for the Grail legend were texts associated with the Gnostics.[30]

Gnosticism is a collective name for a wide variety of sects that flourished in the early centuries of the Christian era. It drew elements from Greek neo-platonic philosophy as well as from the new, and still developing, Christian religion. In contrast to the hierarchical structure of Latin Christianity in which God represented the forces of good, and evil was the absence of good, and therefore of God, the dualist position embodied in Gnosticism perceived the cosmos as motivated by two opposing but equal forces. In the Gnostic (and neo-platonist) system, categories like spirit and matter, male and female complement one another in a 'balanced tension'. This differs from the clearer hierarchical categories adopted by Latin Christianity. In Gnostic systems, for example, the principle of *Sophia* (wisdom) can be actively female, rather than the ungendered dove, which usually represents the Holy Spirit in western art. For Gnostics the ultimate goal of all beings is to overcome the restrictions of the material world and be reunited with a creator spirit. This was an intensely personal, rather than public process, although for some Gnostic sects the return would be inaugurated or facilitated by the appearance of a God-sent saviour. The discovery of the Nag Hammadi library in 1945 enabled scholars to provide a fuller context for many of the lost or fragmentary Gnostic writings. The find consisted of a number of texts copied into papyrus manuscripts, known as codices. Comments, both popular and academic, about the newly discovered Gnostic Gospels have made a major contribution to the modern Grail legends.[31]

By its very nature, Gnosticism is an elastic concept, but the notion of dualism and the tension between opposed but balanced forces underpins its view of the world. This elasticity no doubt makes it easier to create links between dualist groups at different periods of history. The medieval Cathars undoubtedly held dualistic beliefs. Whether there was an unbroken line between them and the Gnostic sects of early Christianity is less easy to establish, and the assumption that some specific secret doctrine was preserved is difficult to demonstrate. The suggestion that the Templars were dualists is even more tenuous. It stems from the accusation that they worshipped an idol. Some writers suggest that the 'idol' was somehow connected to dualistic belief in two cosmic forces. Unfortunately, there is no real proof that the idol was real, much less that dualistic beliefs lay behind it.

The idea of a Gnostic religion, real or imagined, was an important aspect of the occult revival of the nineteenth century, and one which had political as well as esoteric overtones. It reflected the growth of individual spirituality, and the possibility of union with a higher being. It expressed a new sense of freedom as well, in particular the growing power of women in society and the liberation from social norms. The fact that Gnosticism was attached to groups such as Cathars and Templars, which had been suppressed by both religious and political authorities, gave this project an anti-establishment overtone as well. It could be associated with a new and growing nationalism, one that used the past, in particular a hidden or suppressed past, as a metaphor for a new identity. This identity was expressed through the revival of an ancient culture and the use of some symbol that could link that culture to the present.[32] The 'ancient world' favoured by the creators of the Priory of Sion myth was the world of the Albigensians and the troubadours in the Languedoc region of France. The esoteric Celticism so important in the development of Glastonbury, and the idea of an initiation ritual behind the Grail romances employed many of these same concepts, and often looked to the same texts for inspiration.

One of the most influential occultists to develop the Cathar myth in a French context was Joséphin Péladan, founder of the Order of the Rosy Cross and the Temple of the Grail (1890). His enormous output drew on existing legend motifs and on his own vision of the glorious heritage of France. As part of this project, he wrote a treatise on a secret neo-platonic religion practised by the troubadour poets of Provence.[33] Early editors of Wolfram von Eschenbach's medieval romance, *Parzifal,* had identified one of Wolfram's fictional sources, Kyot, with the Provençal troubadour poet Guyot de Provins. There is no evidence that Guiot wrote romances, but the identification provided an imaginative link between the German romance and the culture of the Languedoc where both Templars and Cathars were active. It remains popular with alternative writers seeking a unifying principle to the Grail material. Péladan incorporated Cathars and troubadours into the Grail legend by identifying the Cathar stronghold of Montségur with Wolfram's Grail castle, Montsalvat (Munsalvaeche). The Grail as a link between history and some inner esoteric meaning appealed to the anthroposophist Rudolf Steiner. He suggested that the Grail quest was actually a personal initiation experience coded into a narrative.[34] The idea of quest as a personal experience also figures in Jungian interpretations[35] and in the Celticism of the late twentieth century.[36] Walter Johannes Stein (1891–1957), a disciple of Rudolf Steiner, extended these intuitions about the Grail as an initiation symbol by inserting 'Grail experiences' into European history. His thoughts on the Grail romances, published in 1928, were subsequently translated into English as *The Ninth Century and the Holy Grail*.[37] The suggestion that the Grail is a person rather than a thing, a lost royal heir, owes much to Stein's ideas. He interpreted the Grail legend as it appeared in Wolfram's romance as a hidden history of the Carolingian court and identified the Grail guardians with Charlemagne's heirs. As the first Holy Roman Emperor, Charlemagne provided a link to later Germanic Holy Roman Emperors and of course to the Roman Empire. Stein also layered his approach with esoteric interpretations derived from Steiner's theories of personal development. Although it was not the first study to claim that the Grail romances referred to real historical events and contained messages for humanity, it has been an influential one. The Merovingian dynasty favoured by the Priory of Sion simply transferred the powerful secret to a French royal line.

The *dossiers secrets* presented Pierre Plantard as a lost heir to the French throne, but there is no indication that he claimed divine ancestors. The traditionalist Roman Catholic Plantard seemingly denied this emphatically. One has to look to other esoteric theories for the source of the divine bloodline. The Grail's role in this alternative history is linked to the rise of a new world order, and this is its ultimate function in the work of Julius Evola (1898–1974), another esoteric writer who looked at the Grail romances in terms of European history. For Evola the line stretched back to a primordial sacred Aryan kingship through Charlemagne and the later Hohenstaufen kings, and outwards to a new moral order purged of decadence and restored to its traditional purity.[38] The Grail studies of Walter Johnannes Stein and Julius Evola had already linked the Grail kings of the romances to historical dynasties, specifically Charlemagne and the Holy Roman Emperors. Evola had even made them ancient priest kings. In a curious foreshadowing of the divine bloodline elaboration, the writer Saki (Hector Hugh Munro) used the name Clovis Sangreal for his fictional alter ego.[39] There are no grounds for suggesting that the Merovingian kings were regarded as 'priest kings', certainly not on the basis of their long hair or from objects found in their tombs. Nor is it convincing to suggest that the Quinotaur sea beast represents the Christian symbol of the fish and is therefore a coded indication that one of the children of the Jesus/Mary divine bloodline married into this royal dynasty.[40] However, the idea of kings with divine links echoes Evola's primordial priest-kings whose return would usher in a European superstate and fits in with the messianic tone so prominent in books like these.

MARY MAGDALENE AND
THE DIVINE FEMININE

The figure of the repentant sinner, an important saint in the medieval Church, is a composite of three biblical women. The first, Mary of Magdala, was present at the Crucifixion: she was the beloved 'disciple' and the supposed author of the Gospel of Mary. In the company of Mary Salome and Mary the mother of the Apostle James, she also visited Christ's tomb. It was she who told Peter and John that the tomb was empty and was the first to see the risen Christ. The second figure, Mary of Bethany, the sister of Lazarus and Martha, anointed Jesus' feet with ointment from an alabaster jar. A third, unnamed figure, is a repentant woman mentioned in the Gospel of Luke (Luke 7:36–50) who approached Jesus while he was visiting the house of a disciple. Gradually Mary of Magdala took over Mary of Bethany's role as sister to Lazarus. Putting these biblical references together, Pope St Gregory the Great concluded, 'She whom Luke calls the sinful woman, whom John calls Mary [of Bethany], we believe to be the Mary from whom seven devils were ejected according to Mark.'[41] Gregory's writings stabilized the figure of St Mary Magdalene as the embodiment of Christian repentance. In fairness this seems to be a genuine attempt at exegesis, trying to get the accounts in the Gospels to balance. On the other hand, Eastern Christianity retained two saints, Mary Magdalene and Mary of Bethany with separate feasts, and important medieval theologians, including St Thomas Aquinas and St Augustine of Hippo, also doubted that the two were the same figure. Neither of these two theological heavyweights was pro-female, and if they were prepared to accept two figures, it is difficult to see a conspiracy.

The incomplete text of the Gospel of Mary is one of the apocryphal, that is, non-canonical gospels. There are references to it in the writings of the Christian theologians in the third century, and a few early Greek fragments and a fifth-century translation into Coptic. In this text, Mary's right to bear witness to the teachings of Christ is challenged by the Apostles. Other apocryphal texts are among the sources for the character of Joseph of Arimathea in Robert de Boron's medieval romances. Like the New Testament Gospels themselves, these apocryphal texts were composed in the early centuries of Christianity and are not contemporary with the events they describe. They present the character of Mary Magdalene in a somewhat different light, and texts like the Gospel of Philip from the Nag Hammadi codex suggest that women had more authority and influence in religious matters than is the case at present. Two passages are cited as support for a marriage between Christ and Mary Magdalene. The arguments for and against are complicated by the fact that the text is incomplete, and there is some dispute over the correct translation of terms. One passage describes Mary Magdalene by a term which some translate as 'lover' and others as 'companion'. The text for the second passage can only be partially recovered because the papyrus itself is damaged at exactly the critical point. The Gospel says that Christ loved Mary Magdalene more than the others and would often kiss her, but there is no reliable way to resolve whether the passage indicated the intimate kiss of a married couple or an affectionate salutation among friends.[42]

Legend, however, supplied a wealth of missing details about the life of this extremely popular saint. Legendary sources presented the feast at Cana as the marriage of Mary Magdalene and St John and used it to explain her fall from grace. The groom, St John, decided to leave his wife to follow Christ, and Mary Magdalene abandoned herself to promiscuity, but eventually repented. Another influential legend concerned her arrival in France. She and her companions were set adrift in a boat without sails, oars or supplies. They drifted across the Mediterranean until they came ashore at Marseilles in southern France. The earlier versions of her legend stressed Mary's apostolic mission. She preached the message of the new religion and converted many pagans. Eventually she retired to a cave at Baume where she lived for many years, her long hair covering her as her clothing rotted. Her legend included a mystic element as well. Angels brought her divine food, and, when she died on a mountaintop above her hermitage, these angels escorted her soul to heaven. Several French sites claimed her relics, notably the basilica at Vézelay in Burgundy and the cave sanctuary at Baume. The identities of the refugees in the boat vary with different accounts, but they were always important French saints. They included Mary Jacoby, the mother of the Apostle James Minor, and Mary Salome, the Blessed Virgin's sister and mother of the Apostles James Major and John, together with Lazarus and his two sisters, Mary Magdalene and Martha. Two other saints who became important in medieval France, St Maximinan, one of the original disciples, and St Sidonius, the man born blind who was cured by Christ, were also in the boat. A servant girl called Sarah or Marella accompanied them.[43] Among the prominent French saints associated with Mary Magdalene, Santa Sara, is especially popular. She is a comparatively late addition to the Magdalene legend and does not appear before the sixteenth century. Santa Sara is a traditional rather than an official saint, but the Roma people make an annual pilgrimage to her shrine at Saintes-Maries-de-la-Mer in the Camargue in southern France. At this time, Camargue horsemen escort an effigy of Sara and the two Marys (Salome and Jacoby) from the church to the seashore.

The *Legenda Sanctae*, a thirteenth-century book of saints' legends, includes accounts of St Joseph of Arimathea and the Grail, and a very full account of the apocryphal legends of Mary Magdalene in France.[44] This book was so popular that it became known as *Legenda Aurea* or *The Golden Legend*. The author, a Genoese bishop called Jacopo de Voragine, also wrote a chronicle of the history of Genoa in which, for the first time, he linked the Genoese relic the *sacro catino* with the Grail.[45] The author was an ordinary Christian bishop, not a Templar, heretic or Cathar. *The Golden Legend* was a medieval bestseller and dozens of manuscripts still exist. Laymen and clergy alike read the book. It was printed by William Caxton, illustrated, and is still in print. Nobody has tried to suppress it or lock it away in the Vatican.

The life of St Mary Magdalene was at the centre of a widespread cult, and her legend contains a number of traditional motifs. Among them are the rudderless boat which miraculously brings saints to their appointed home, the hermit covered with hair instead of clothing who receives miraculous food, numerous miracles resulting from the intercession of a powerful saint, an unusual death, and the even more unusual means by which a saint's relics are dispersed, saved, stolen and found. In the earliest versions of the Mary Magdalene legend, she was buried in Ephesus and her body later taken to Constantinople. She is often depicted in art covered with long hair instead of clothing, a motif transferred from the cult of another saint, Mary the Egyptian. Gradually her role as reformed sinner became that of reformed prostitute.[46] Although the apostolic mission of Mary Magdalene was well known in medieval accounts of the saint's life, it was eventually subsumed in the image of her as a reformed prostitute. The process by which the legend was re-localized in France is not unlike that by which St Joseph became established at Glastonbury. Local traditions became attached to a core narrative and different traditions developed to explain how her relics came into the possession of various churches and abbeys. Both Robert Graves in *King Jesus* and the Cretan-born writer Nikos Kazantzakis in *The Last Temptation of Christ* wrote novels in which Christ is involved in ordinary human relationships.[47] However, none of the early or medieval sources suggests that the idea of a divine marriage was part of her legend.

The discovery of texts like the Gospel of Philip coupled with new techniques for analysing the cultural milieu of the eastern Mediterranean created a more complete picture of this early period, making it easier to understand the way saints' legends developed in response to changing social contexts. In addition, the weakening of trust in the authority of Christianity encouraged new speculations suggesting that not only did the Christian religion develop over time, but also at the expense of other alternatives.[48] The vast bibliography appended to *Holy Blood Holy Grail* cites the work of theologians like William E. Phipps, who suggested that only married men would have been allowed to teach as rabbis. Phipps cites the much-quoted line from the Gospel of Philip, which reads that Jesus kissed Mary Magdalene, as evidence that she was his wife.[49] Critics have pointed out that although unmarried rabbis were rare, they did teach, at least at this early period, and the incomplete line from the Gospel of Philip need not refer to a connubial gesture.[50] Even if this ambiguous and incomplete text did read 'kissed her on the mouth', one can only speculate that it referred to an act between married people or that they had children.[51] Within the context of a conspiracy legend, however, lack of evidence is often taken as proof that a conspiracy exists. Although the proposition is tenuous, the idea of a conspiracy of repression had already taken hold; the lack of tangible evidence seemed only to strengthen this.[52]

The supposed significance of Mary Magdalene was extended even further once she became associated with a lost feminine aspect of religion. This notion of the sacred feminine is very broad. It can encompass the female aspect of the divine principle, or the idea that a male and female deity pair maintained the cycle of fertility.[53] Margaret Starbird interpreted the story of Sara, the servant girl of the French saints, as a survival of an ancient sacred feminine cult. Her argument, which includes as much intuition as textual study, claimed that as the name 'Sara' means princess, she must have been the daughter of Mary and Jesus and therefore the 'holy Grail', which they brought to France. The author relied on the inspiration of prayer for some of her conclusions, but her technique of historical reconstruction is a perfect mirror for that used by folklorists and mythographers during the nineteenth century. The voice of simple folk and the intangibles of art and literature become the remnants of an untainted tradition. 'The other version of the life of Jesus . . . appeared in places where the Inquisition and the establishment could not root it out – in the folktales of Europe, its art and its literature – always hidden, often coded in symbols, but ubiquitous.'[54] The elements considered most authentic are not in actual fact the most ancient. The legends bringing Mary Magdalene to France are medieval, the interpretation of the Sangreal as 'sang real' is fifteenth-century, and Santa Sara is a sixteenth-century addition to the Magdalene legend. Despite the fact that Sara's story and the procession at Saintes-Maries-de-la-Mer are comparatively recent, they have been put forward here and elsewhere, as survivals of an ancient goddess cult.[55]

Although Christianity moved away from the 'secret' knowledge and 'continuing revelation' that characterized Gnosticism, the idea that a mystery cult was somehow displaced by the patriarchal aspect of Christianity encapsulated the romantic belief that human imagination cannot be shackled.[56] The question of whether 'proof' of Mary Magdalene's marriage to Christ would somehow shake the foundations of the Church distracts from the serious issues about the nature of female participation in Christian ritual or the question of married clergy, and adds little to our understanding of the Grail texts. Robert Graves's work *The White Goddess*, a fusion of his personal poetic vision with his prodigious classical scholarship, is one of the most influential statements that religion and myth record the gradual victory of male-dominated religion over the original worship of the Goddess. The idea did not originate with Graves, but he applied it in his novel *King Jesus* (1946). Here Jesus is a sacred king, heir to the Israelite throne through the matriarchal line of his mother, princess of a royal line, and Mary Magdalene appears as his consort. In part the novel developed from Graves's interest in the controversies which surrounded the life of the historical Jesus, and it was followed two years later by *The Nazarene Gospel Restored*. The idea of a sacred matriarchal kinship is more *White Goddess* than New Testament history,[57] but it fits into the inherent conflict necessary for a conspiracy and clarifies why the explanation of Santa Sara as 'princess' was so attractive.

Less than half a century after it was founded, the Priory of Sion had changed from an attempt to renationalize a romantic fantasy to a myth about alternative religion that fused the Templars, as custodians of Gnostic wisdom, with a benign eastern goddess cult. Cathars and the Templars provide a mythic dimension to French history much like that of the Celts in Britain. As such they embody the liberal secular values of a modern state, provide theosophical and occult links back to Gnosticism or, as here for Plantard and his associates, revive the traditionalism of the *ancien régime* as a pure unadulterated cultural strain in a mixed society. Different aspects of this legend have been embraced by tourism, new age spirituality and fiction. The religion of the medieval Grail romances was Christian, but, by reviving the dying god myth first set out by James Frazer in *The Golden Bough*, the authors of alternative histories created a new twentieth-century Grail legend, the sacred bloodline. Frazer's myth was transformed into a mystery-religion based on sexual initiation that combined elements from the theosophical view of mythology with an emphasis on conspiracy, a secret theocracy and the noble destiny of mankind. Criticism, especially from an academic source, could be dismissed as confirmation that vague, conspiratorial forces were trying to suppress a secret that transcended mere historical and cultural circumstances. Claims about occult geometrical patterns in certain classical paintings have been applied to the French landscape to 'locate' the tomb of Christ or to link the Rosslyn Chapel 'Grail' in Scotland with buildings constructed by 'Templars' in Nova Scotia and Scandinavia.

SHUGBOROUGH: EIGHTEENTH-CENTURY GARDEN AND TWENTIETH-CENTURY GRAIL

The garden of the Shugborough estate in Staffordshire contains a monument with a carved relief based on Nicolas Poussin's painting of Arcadian shepherds gazing at a tomb inscribed with the words 'Et in Arcadia Ego'. The architect, Thomas Wright of Durham, designed the earliest phase of this eighteenth-century monument. The relief, based on a reversed print of Poussin's painting, was executed by the Antwerp-born sculptor Peter Scheemakers, while another architect and designer, James Stuart, added the Doric-style arch. These three designers worked under the patronage of Thomas Anson, the owner of Shugborough and an important figure in the revival of classical art and culture in eighteenth-century Britain. The dates of the individual elements of this complex and interesting monument are not completely clear, but it was standing in some form by 1759.[58] Carved into the space under the relief is a series of letters D.O.U.O.S.V.A.V.V.M. with the first and last ones lower than the rest. This inscription, and the fact that the carved relief is a mirror image of the original Poussin painting, has attracted the attention of cryptologists and Grail hunters. The members of the Priory of Sion used details in the painting to create an imaginative, albeit completely synthetic, history for their society, and the authors of *Holy Blood Holy Grail* extended the original speculations to include the Shugborough monument with its seemingly mysterious inscription.[59] Since then a location with no prior links to Templars or the Grail has been absorbed into a dynamic modern legend and has attracted new motifs of its own. The mystery at Shugborough is not in any way related to medieval romance, nor does it concern any physical Grail relic; its primary focus is the meaning of the mysterious cipher and its possible link to esoteric ideas.

The earliest of the various elements of the monument were designed by Thomas Wright (1711–86), a mathematician, architect, antiquarian and astronomer, born in Durham in the early eighteenth century. His interests, which mirrored those of his patrons, were erudite, elitist, intellectually playful and, on the whole, confident about the harmony of knowledge and creation, and stoical about the vicissitudes of fate. When Lord Admiral

George Anson and his new wife, Elizabeth Yorke, came to live at Shugborough in 1748, Wright designed additions to the house and the garden, including a structure that has become known as 'the Shepherd's Monument'. His interests in astronomy and the past fit in well with the classical revival style of the architectural scheme at Shugborough. Wright's scientific fame rests on his explanation of the earth's position in the Milky Way, but he also wrote utopian fiction, *Voyage to the Fortunate Isles* (1733), and a treatise that attempted to integrate all divine, moral and scientific views into one cosmology.[60] Secret codes are all too easy to manufacture if details are strung together independently of their historical and cultural context, and at first glance the imaginative Thomas Wright seems an ideal purveyor of codes and secrets. He was a Freemason, and the decorations of his home near Durham contained a ciphered version of his motto. A tradition about him as a youth claimed that his father, thinking his son mad, burned all the young man's books. The original design of a rustic arch on which the Shugborough monument is based appeared as a garden design in 1750 and later in one of Wright's architectural pattern-books. His antiquarian interests favoured druidic interpretations: in his drawings, for example, he linked ancient monuments to druid practices, and his belief in reincarnation no doubt owed something to the idea that this was a druidic doctrine.[61] He used the fashionable images for past wisdom to describe his rustic follies as 'suitable for a Brahmin or a druid'. Eighteenth-century notions about druidism, not the Templars, provided the source for his fantasies about the past and the inspiration for many of his designs.

Wright was not involved in the creation of the mirror-image bas-relief adaptation of Poussin's painting whose imagery and inscription have suggested so many secret meanings. The reason for the mirror image is not at all mysterious. The sculptor Peter Scheemakers worked from a print based on an etching by Bernard Picart (1693–4), which was printed in reverse. In addition, the rectangular landscape shape of the original picture had to be fitted into a vertical 'portrait' space. Thus pragmatic considerations, rather than esoteric concerns, account both for the reversal and the distortions in the arrangement of the figures.[62] The sudden death of Anson's intimate friend and political patron Henry Pelham in 1754 may also shed some light on the meaning of the monument without recourse to esoteric speculation. Pelham's monument, a funerary urn on a pediment, bears a Latin memorial inscription that addressed his widow as *placens uxor* ('pleasing wife') and the words 'Et in Arcadia Ego', an unambiguous reference to death in the midst of life. Another architect, James Stuart, completed the final phase of the Shugborough monument with a Doric portico and designed other structures for the garden. Some esoteric interpretations go so far as to suggest that these monuments constitute a map of the location of the Holy Grail, but most of the speculations centre on the Shepherd's Monument.

Several solutions have been suggested for the meaning of the letters. These include a Grail code, a lover's message, a memorial verse or a stoic philosophical cipher. The ten letters are separated by full stops. This implies that they are abbreviations for words and suggests a cipher rather than a code. Margaret, Countess of Lichfield, a member of the family presently occupying Shugborough, proposed a solution that recalled to her mind a story she had heard as a child. 'Out of your own sweet vale Alicia vanish vanity twixt Deity and Man, thou Shepherdess the way.' A direct source for this story has never been identified. However, it shares an atmosphere of vanity and Arcadia not unlike the background reading to Lady Anson's letter to her brother-in-law in 1750, namely Honoré d'Urfé's Arcadian fantasy *L'Astrée*, with its contemplative shepherds and shepherdesses.[63] The Anson family were members of an erudite circle with a particular interest in the classical philosophy of stoicism, which stressed that life and its blessing were transitory, and Arcadia was a favourite symbol. An alternative solution also echoes the notion of life's transience: '*Orator Omnia Sunt Vanitas Ait Vanitas Vanitatum*', based on a paraphrase of a biblical verse in Ecclesiastes, 'Vanity of vanities, saith the preacher, all is vanity.'[64] Through the efforts of two code-breakers, who worked at Bletchley Park during the war, the meaning of the inscription and several new solutions were suggested and aired to the media, and for a time at least the estate was keen to engage visitors in the endeavour.[65]

The solution linking the letters to the Grail is attributed to an unnamed code-breaker occupying a senior position in some unspecified intelligence network. It explains the letters as a reference to the Holy Grail and to the belief that Templars preserved secret truths. The letters were submitted to a series of code-grids and produced a phrase, 'Jesus H Defy'. This is not a very satisfactory solution, as it makes little sense as it stands and needs further clarification. The code-breaker identified H with the Greek letter X (chi), equated it with 'messiah' or 'Christ' and translated it as 'deity'. The reasoning behind this is unclear, since the Greek letter 'H' usually refers to the letter 'e' in the name Jesus, as in the abbreviation IHS, the first three letters of his name in Greek. Also, the words 'messiah' and 'Christ' mean 'the anointed one' not 'deity'. In any case, this alteration to 'Jesus (the Deity) Defy' does not clarify the original phrase. So, the code-breaker adds more speculative history about the Templars and the Priory of Sion and the supposed secret doctrine that Jesus was human, not divine. Unfortunately, the result has no more inherent sense than the original series of letters. It owes more to the popularity of romanticized Templars than any convincing attempt to solve a code and might very well have been suggested by the discussion of the Shugborough Hall monument in popular literature. No code-breaker need look farther than a reference to the 'denial of Jesus' divinity' in *Holy Blood* itself, which occurs immediately after the reference to Shugborough Hall's so-called code.[66] However, code-breaking grids, an unknown code-breaker 'high up' in some intelligence network, the Templars, and the Priory of Sion are just the elements that make the contemporary Grail legend so compelling. It is also these very elements that take this explanation so unequivocally into the world of modern legend.[67]

The first and last letters, an abbreviation of the phrase 'Diis Manibus' ('To the Souls of the Departed'), appear frequently on Roman tombs. Olive Marchand Bishop, who catalogued the Shugborough Hall papers in the 1950s, suggested that the remaining letters might stand for the Latin phrase, '*Optimae Uxoris, Optimae Sororis, Viduus Amantissimus Vovit Virtutibus.*' A possible translation would be, 'Best wife, best sister, the most loving widower dedicates [this] to [your] virtue.' The sentiments fit the poetic ambiguities of Arcadian symbolism popular with the Anson family and their circle. The phrase '*optimae uxoris*' appears in Roman grave inscriptions and provides another link between the Pelham and Shugborough memorials. Depending on the date of the inscription, the cipher could be a memorial to the parents of the Anson brothers who died before the alterations to the garden took place, or to Elizabeth, Lady Anson, who had died by 1760. It is even possible that the memorial commemorates an early and brief marriage of Thomas Anson.[68] Any of these would make sense of the Latin inscription and would mean that the solution to the code is clear once it is 'cracked'.

It is the Ansons, the owners of the estate, and how they fit into eighteenth-century intellectual interests that can tell us most about the monument. Admiral George Anson, famous for his circumnavigation of the globe, came to live at his brother's estate, Shugborough, with his wife, Lady Elizabeth Yorke. His brother, Thomas, was a founder member of the Society of Dilettanti, a club devoted to the revival of classical art, and also a member of the Royal Society. Neither organization was a secret society, and neither brother was a Freemason. The final element, the Doric surround, was added to the Shepherd's Monument by Thomas's friend, the architect and designer, James 'Athenian' Stuart (1713–88). Stuart is widely recognized for his role in making neo-classical design popular in the late eighteenth century. His publication of the *Antiquities of Athens* contained detailed architectural drawings and sketches of the actual antiquities in romantically idealized landscapes. These imaginative scenes were translated by men like Stuart, and Wright before him, into the landscaping of eighteenth-century gardens like that at Shugborough. The opening page of Stuart's book also has a drawing enclosing a dedication in the classical style incorporating the phrase '*Diis Manibus*'.[69] This raises the possibility that the Shugborough inscription was based on, or at least influenced by Stuart, although it would date the inscription to the 1760s, a little later than the original rustic frame and Arcadian carving.

References to the monument and the Latin inscription occur in poems and family documents, and while none of these sources offers an explanation of the cipher, there is nothing about the Grail, mystery religions, or the Templars. For example, a poem on 'An Emblematical Basso Relievo after a famous picture of Nicolas Poussin' mentions Arcadia and contains the phrase 'life's fleeting moments gently steal away'.[70] The poet clearly understood the meaning of the scene emblematically with overtones of ambiguity about the meaning of life, but there is no esotericism. George Anson's wife, Elizabeth, described Shugborough as 'Arcady' in a letter to her brother-in law whom she addressed as Shepherd (*Gentil Berger*). This letter may throw light on Lady Margaret Lichfield's solution, as it has oblique references to the Arcadian heroine in a work by the French writer Honoré d'Urfé. Elizabeth Anson had copied Nicolas Poussin's earlier, and less well-known, version of the Arcadia picture owned by the Duke of Devonshire, and there is a portrait of her with the drawing. Both the letter and the portrait date to the middle of the eighteenth century, exactly the time when the monument was under construction.

The contrast in Poussin's *Les Bergers d'Arcadie* between the pastoral scene and the inscribed tomb suggests the clever ambiguity so beloved of sophisticated baroque painters and their classically educated patrons. The image of a tomb in Arcadia recalls descriptions of pastoral bliss in Virgil's *Eclogues*, while the phrase 'Et in Arcadia Ego' appears in paintings by several artists, and on a funeral urn commemorating the untimely death of Henry Pelham, a friend and political ally of the Ansons. The phrase implies both the transience of life 'even in Arcadia am I [i.e., Death]' and the beauty of eternity 'I [the occupant] am in Arcadia'. A poem of 1758 mentions the Poussin bas-relief on the monument at Shugborough, but there is nothing about a cipher until 1767. During that period both Lady Elizabeth and her husband had died and Thomas Anson had engaged his friend, the architect James Stuart, to make further additions to the park and garden. The first volume of Stuart's *Antiquities of Athens* appeared in 1762, the year before he started working at Shugborough, and one of his drawings shows a tomb with the letters D.M.[71] The cipher on the monument commissioned by the Anson family may commemorate the affection between Lady Elizabeth (the wife and sister) and the husband (widower) who survived her by only a few years, or perhaps the parents of George and Thomas Anson, or even someone close to Thomas Anson himself. The monument is often said to have had a personal meaning for the owner of Shugborough, and it is possible that Thomas had married as a young man. This would fit with comments by Thomas Pennant, a famous eighteenth-century traveller and friend of Thomas Anson who visited Shugborough in 1782. 'The scene is laid in Arcadia. Two lovers expressed in elegant pastoral figures appear attentive to an ancient shepherd who reads to them an inscription on a tomb "Et in Arcadia" the moral resulting from this seems to be that there are no situations of this life so delicious but which death must at length snatch us from. It was placed here by the owner as a momento of the certainty of that event perhaps as a secret memorial of some loss of a tender nature in his early years for he was wont often to gaze on it in affection and fine meditation.'[72]

Details relating to the Anson family and their interests place the monument firmly within the theme of an elegiac Arcadia; nothing links it to the Grail or the Templars. It has been clear for some time that Poussin painted an imaginary tomb. Only much later was a structure built on this site in the French countryside, and even later still was it linked to the tomb in the painting.[73] Since the inscribed tomb did not exist when Poussin painted his vision of shepherds in Arcadia, a connection with a family who commissioned the Shugborough monument in the eighteenth century is unlikely in the extreme. The reversed composition and the changed angles have practical explanations relating to the construction, not the secret meaning, of the monument. In this context, suggestions that 'Staffordshire was a hotbed of Masonic activity',[74] or that the symbols point to 'the location of the treasure- the tomb of god the holy blood and the holy Grail',[75] or that Admiral Anson captured the Poussin bas-relief at sea from the Templars appear far-fetched. However, an aristocratic family with a mysterious possession attracts just this type of legend. The announcement that the code had been cracked produced a flurry of interest, and, although this died down somewhat, the Shugborough website still contains a 'Holy Grail' section.[76]

Arguments about Templar secrets may be more smoke and mirrors than history. One prominent historian, speaking on a television documentary produced in the wake of *The Da Vinci Code* novel, stated quite bluntly that such works 'dismiss reputable evidence . . . Accept disreputable evidence and fill in the gaps where there was no evidence at all.'[77] Certainly one cannot simply appropriate the mechanics of scholarly research without applying some criteria of judgement, but no matter how well founded the criticism presented by professional historians, it is not going to convince those who search for mysteries that there are none. As a counter to such critics, it is all too easy to retreat farther into the secret world in which manufactured documents function as an elaborate double-bluff, hiding the real secret code. There is no need for proof, just an assertion that a conspiracy exists to hide the truth. The fictional origins of the Priory of Sion have been made clear in television documentary and, as it happens, through the testimony of at least one founding member, but the legend lives on.

The aim of the esoteric and occult approach in any case is not really history, but a search for a principle that will unify diverse aspects of mythology, literature and culture, and with this universal principle, enable one to reach the deep metaphysical doctrine assumed to lie beneath all ritual. As a consequence, mythic themes and symbols are interchangeable, and this accounts for the discursive nature of so much of the writing, which moves dizzyingly across time periods and cultures.[78] The underlying assumptions illustrate two essential features of much of this writing. This is detective story analysis in which similarities are taken as proof of influence and connection, and they are increasingly self-referential, using other popular works on the subject rather than original source material. The world of secret sects and the quest for the Holy Grail mirrors the dynamics of contemporary legend in so far as these legends are able to 'challenge definitions of the real world and leaves itself suspended relying for closure on each individual's response'.[79] This allows us to draw in the reactions to alternative theories with all their attendant paraphernalia of cultural information and direct involvement of readers. Even the commentaries adopt the language of revelation. The cover of one of the code commentaries claims that it is 'revised and expanded with important new revelations and discoveries'.[80]

The argument about the alternative Grail has shifted somewhat. Many writers now claim that theirs is a plausible interpretation of the material or that their ideas are the result of psychic intuition or spiritual enlightenment. This is certainly a way of bridging the hiatus between the end of organizations such as the Templars and the appearance of modern revivals claiming esoteric links with them. Media attention, especially television specials and websites, have also contributed to the changing character of this popular research. Sites range from personal blogs to advertisements for products, and there is a positive explosion of new books. It has also produced a more vigorous questioning from sceptics who gleefully point out the errors, major and minor, in this kind of argument. Conspiracy theory itself has been transformed from an elite view of sinister cabals operating in the shadows to an everyday explanation of how the world works. It provides a framework in which to organize blame and assign responsibility, but there is also a nostalgic sense that what is suppressed by the conspiracy is somehow better.[81]

CONCLUSION

The Grail Legend Today: Conspiracy and Beyond

IN *A GLASTONBURY ROMANCE* (1932), the Grail is called 'a fragment of the absolute known in those parts for five thousand years as a cauldron, a horn, a krater, a mwys, a well, a kernos, a platter, a cup and even a nameless stone'.[1] The description provides a complete checklist of all the theories about the Grail up to the time the novel was written. John Cowper Powys (1872–1963) called the Grail a 'magnet gatherer of all that came to Glastonbury'.[2] His novel is not a *roman à clef*, but it includes the full range of personalities that made Glastonbury into the new age spiritual centre it is today. It needs only an author of alternative history, a woman writer seeking the divine feminine and perhaps a television producer for a complete up-to-date cast.

Powys helped popularize the idea of Glastonbury as the legendary isle of Avalon, home of the Holy Grail. He described the region as 'shifty wavering undulating fluctuating country full of Phantoms . . . by far the most enchanted ground in England'.[3] His novel belongs to the world of 'Avalon of the heart' in which mystic visionaries oppose the forces of modern reactionary industrialism. Powys's personal interests were esoteric, and the idea of the Grail as a psychic force uniting both paganism and Christianity was very much in tune with what was happening at the time. As the plethora of references in this long and detailed novel show, he had an exceptionally wide-ranging knowledge of the subject. Even in the throes of a personal Grail vision, Owen Jones, the mystic-cum-antiquarian hero of *A Glastonbury Romance*, lists the poetry of Taliesin, the Triads, Charlotte Guest and John Rhŷs among the sources for his knowledge of the Grail.

It is worth noting that in medieval romance, the Grail quest is always accomplished. The object may be withdrawn when its keepers prove unworthy or if the knights are not yet ready, but eventually the destined knight finds it. This contrasts sharply with modern uses of the term 'holy

Grail'. These imply something desired and sought but never found, or a secret just out of reach. R. S. Loomis suggested that romances reflect an oral tradition of Celtic mythology and folklore adapted to the needs of medieval culture. The motifs do resonate with Celtic material such as food producing vessels, but it is difficult to reduce the romances to a single source and attempts to reconstruct a coherent earlier narrative are invariably speculative. The antiquarian nature of such textual studies made them the direct heirs of the Romantic Movement with its quest for the original, pure and authentic voice of a people unadulterated by civilization.[4] Equally perilous is any attempt to interpret the formal logical structure shared by folk narratives and romances as a code that points the way to a more hopeful future. The contemporary fashion for secret codes is also heir to the romantic imagination, and many of the scholarly perspectives on the meaning of romance established in the nineteenth and early twentieth centuries still drive modern Grail legends. Was the Grail an authentic relic of the Passion of Christ brought back from the Holy Land during the Crusades? Did it originate as a Celtic myth? Was it a religious relic associated with early British Christianity? Or does it have a link to some mystery tradition from the distant past? However revolutionary modern Grail theories claim to be, they fall into one of these categories and conform to a pattern established not by antiquity, but by attempts to understand these texts only a century ago. Nevertheless, modern interpretations of the Grail do link the narrators with the past, perhaps a romantic past, but one that, by sharing in these legendary narratives, forges a shared sense of identity.

The structure of a Grail romance is broadly similar to the structure of a folktale of magic and wonder in that both focus on the actions of a character undergoing a series of life-changing adventures leading to an ultimate achievement. Narratives involving contact with the supernatural are often worked out in terms of conflict and resolution. Likewise, the core of the Grail legend involves the possession of some powerful object not associated with the real world. As a literary form, the medieval Grail romance reached something of a peak with Malory's *Morte Darthur*, but as a legend it has continued to develop in response to new intellectual paradigms. The core remains, but it is no longer just a medieval theme linked to the cultural aspirations of a courtly elite. As a symbol of personal transformation and cultural renewal, it continues to fascinate a particular corner of the publishing industry. Print is an important stabilizing factor for modern legends, and the Internet plays a special role in the appeal of Grail legends. Besides the growing number of sites that offer comment on the Grail, code-breaking and quest plots are used frequently as computer game formats. Modern literary fiction also uses the Grail legend in interesting ways, sometimes as a direct reworking of Arthurian themes, sometimes as a symbolic quest. Through character and situation, writers critique and comment on changing worldviews, and in this way literary fiction also contributes to the development of legend.[5] Scholarship has undoubtedly worked its way into fiction as the academic debate spilled over into the important market for popular books.[6] Alfred Nutt published a volume on the meaning and origin of the Grail romances in a series on mythology intended for the general public, but it was Jessie Weston's readable and attractive speculations about the ritual origins of the Grail that reached the widest audience. The Grail as a way to expose the negative aspects of secular modernity, to express positive aspects of cultural pluralism, or as a defence against conspiracy now crosses the boundaries of literary, artistic, popular and even academic imagination.

In his notes to 'The Waste Land', T. S. Eliot attributed 'not only the title, but the plan and a good deal of the incidental symbolism of the poem' to Jessie Weston's *Ritual to Romance* and to Frazer's *Golden Bough*, especially the volumes on Adonis, Attis and Osiris. The Hanged Man of the tarot pack, he associated with 'the Hanged god of Frazer' as well as the biblical journey to Emmaus. The Man with Three Staves was identified 'quite arbitrarily with the Fisher King himself'. The wasteland image provided a rich poetic metaphor to express the alienation of modern humanity. When the poem first appeared, critical reaction focused on the idea of fertility rite,[7] and in 1928 Mary Butts specifically compared the subject of her own novel about the Grail, *Armed with Madness,* with seasonal myths and with the main image of Eliot's poem.[8] Later, Eliot repudiated 'certain references to vegetation ceremonies'.[9] The cards in Madame Sosostris's tarot reading (lines 43-56) resemble A. E. Waite's revised tarot pack,[10] but they evoke literary references rather than the esoteric meanings ascribed by their creator. The Phoenician sailor in the card reading and the fisherman on the canal undoubtedly suggest Perceval's host, the Fisher King, but they also evoke the supposed drowning of Ferdinand's father in Shakespeare's *Tempest*. The tarot references are perhaps best understood in the context of other allusions to Grail literature, the empty chapel (lines 296–393), the dry wasted land, like the 'brown land' and its departed nymphs (line 175), the man fishing in the dirty canal thinking of kings (lines 185–192).

Like the Glastonbury setting in Powys's romance, the cast list of Charles Williams's novel *War in Heaven* (1930) runs the gamut of personality types involved in the occult and esoteric revivals that shaped the modern Grail legend. Using the appropriate anthropological and archaeological techniques, the folklorist Sir Giles Tumulty has written a book assembling the

'Historical Vestiges of Sacred Vessels in Folklore' that reveals the location of the Grail in an idyllic English country village. The occultist and publisher Gregory Persimmons covets its power, while the Archdeacon of Fardles, the Duke of North Ridings, and the publisher's clerk, Kenneth Mornington, seek to protect it. The archdeacon's position is closest to that of Williams himself. Both reject the sterile historicism of the folklorist and the selfish occultism of Persimmons. Mornington is the mediating figure, repelled by the occult and wary of the supernatural. For Williams the power of ritual was very real. He had been a member of A. E. Waite's esoteric order, and the evocation of Persimmons's occult rituals is very convincing. For him, the Grail is a Christian symbol, a means of communal experience as well as a defence against evil. The climax, a Grail Eucharist with echoes of medieval romance, embodies his mystical Christian ideal that the eucharistic sacrament unites the individual with God and with the rest of humanity.[11] In both his esoteric novels, the intersection between everyday situations and fantastic events reveals the deeper meaning beneath what is seemingly ordinary. *War in Heaven* presents a relatively straightforward account of the discovery of the Holy Grail. In his other esoteric novel, *The Greater Trumps* (1932), a magic talisman evokes supernatural forces in the form of archetypal figures represented by the greater trumps of the tarot. Once again there is a struggle between the forces of order and chaos, and only the efforts of those who refuse to harness these energies for selfish ends can restore order.[12] Although the novels explore the nature of supernatural experience, Williams was dubious of pagan interpretations and stressed the Grail's symbolic associations with Christianity. As in T. S. Eliot and C. S. Lewis, events are played out amid the social and spiritual wasteland of modernity, rather than the enchantments of romance.[13]

The characters in *War in Heaven* fall into clearly defined and opposing camps, both wanting the Grail. This tension of oppositions is essential to the thriller genre, but it is also characteristic of conspiracy writing, which demands an oppressor and an oppressed. It is not found in medieval romances, however, where the Grail is not an object of contention, but rather one to be sought. Williams has a lighter touch than many writers of Grail thrillers, especially when he satirizes the researches of such figures as Sir Giles. He also incorporates creatively nonsensical philology, which is a salient feature of alternative writing, in his explanation that the village, Fardles, was originally 'Castra Parvulorum' (the camp of the children). Two legends, one about Merlin and the other about the attempt by the medieval Oxford scientist, Roger Bacon, to bring a brazen head to life clash in C. S. Lewis's novel *That Hideous Strength* (1945).[14] A lame Oxford don, Ransom, now using the name Mr Fisher King, presides over the struggle between the forces of false progress and real humanity. The forces of sterile alien science that seeks to sanitize humanity in the name of progress have taken over an Oxford college. Opposed to them are Ransom and his friends who represent Arthurian Logres, Lewis's vision of a spiritual Britain. The Grail is missing from this particular romance and the quest is centred on a young married couple. The couple are reunited at the end of the novel, and Mr Fisher King (Ransom) departs for Avalon. The novel appeared at the end of the Second World War, and the group gathered around Ransom have something of Spence's secret Arthurian cult, struggling against the forces of totalitarianism. The novel even introduced a female principle to teach the young wife about the sensual spirituality of marriage. Lewis was not looking for an object of mystic contemplation, but the Wasteland and the Fisher King had a particular meaning for C. S. Lewis. Ransom's wound is that of fallen humanity struggling against a Wasteland of sterile materialism.[15]

For Weston, the Grail legend was an external record of an esoteric initiation that would lead to theosophical experience of higher consciousness. Her ideas about Celtic origins and seasonal rituals continue to influence fiction and popular writing where the need to find an origin for the Grail coincides with the need to find that meaning in a mythical context. Although writers responded in different ways, the idea of a pre-Christian fertility ritual was a useful metaphor for those concerned with the alienation brought about by secular modernity. A secret tradition was a reality for writers like Charles Williams and Arthur Machen, although they saw the Grail as essentially Christian rather than pagan. C. S. Lewis's position was similar to that of Williams on the dangers of secular modernity, but his fantasy did not advocate any mysticism. Powys found resolution in a life principle that transcended both paganism and Christianity. Like Powys, Dorothy James Roberts constructed a Grail that was both pagan and Christian in *Kinsmen of the Grail* (1963). The cycle of seasons, fertility and replacement of rulers are interwoven with Weston's myth in the book's climatic image in which Gawin (the old knight) sees only a ruined castle and no Grail, while the young Perceval enters into a magnificent castle and experiences a vision of the Holy Grail.[16] The Morgan figure in John Boorman's film *Excalibur* (1981) frustrates the attempts of the knight to reach the Grail. She plays a relatively minor role in the medieval romances, but here she suggests the powerful female of ritual theory. Perceval's return to bring the sick and feeble Arthur the curing power of the Grail, however, dramatically evokes the images of wounded king and quest knight.[17] Weston's ritual origins show no signs of becoming unfashionable either in fiction or alternative writing. A. A. Attanasio's *The Serpent and the Grail* (1999), part of his

Arthor series, similarly recasts the Arthurian tale in terms of a wounded king connected to his land. Here, too, a powerful female opposes the king and attempts to obtain the *graal*, an object of power, for her son.[18]

Scholarly perspectives on the origin of the Grail romances have provided a useful paradigm for modern Grail interpretations. The influence of origin scholarship remains strong in fictional and alternative approaches concerned with the conflict between absolutism and pluralism in twentieth-century society.[19] This perspective is more spiritual than religious, and it can accommodate concepts of pluralism and tolerance, secret wisdom and individual enlightenment. It also coincided with interest in non-Christian spirituality and the engagement of self so characteristic of modern forms of neo-paganism.[20] Increasingly, novelists like Rosemary Sutcliff depicted the Arthurian world as a time of spiritual pluralism where native pagan cults and Christianity coexisted or competed.[21] Marion Zimmer Bradley also rewrote the Grail search as a conflict between a native goddess cult and Roman Christianity.[22] These writers inherited the notion of a lost belief system capable of resolving the contradictions of competing cults from the evolutionary mythographers and scholars of comparative religion who had been their forebears. This view of cultural history was supported by works like Robert Graves's *The White Goddess*, which equated the Grail with the cauldron of a pagan Celtic goddess. This seamless hybrid of poetic imagination and scholarship incorporated exactly the kind of mythic historicizing so familiar from Frazer and Weston, and it reflected the attitudes of the occult revivals that pitted Christian absolutism against a more humanistic and relativist message of paganism.[23]

The debate about the origin and meaning of the Grail parallels the way in which history too was reshaped to accommodate the possibility of a historical Arthur. Archaeology played an important role in this debate as a way to investigate the physical traces of the past on the landscape and provide a means for accessing and displaying that past.[24] This has great potential in the context of modern Grail legends, where meaning is often linked to the authenticity that science can bestow. Placing the objects uncovered by archaeology on display, in, for example, a museum, fixes their place in temporal history. In the film *Excalibur*, the Grail appears as a shimmering object enclosed in sheets of light, protected by sombre walls and dramatically illuminated, rather like a museum exhibit. In Susan Cooper's *The Dark is Rising*, a group of children finds a sixth-century Celtic chalice in a sea cave in Cornwall. Here the Grail is both a relic of Celtic paganism and a physical archaeological antiquity.[25] But a museum can also rob objects of their sacredness. A striking use of the museum as an ambiguous repository for such objects occurs in the cyberpunk science fiction of James

P. Blalock where a mysterious museum is the setting for the search for a rare Japanese print folded origami-style into a paper Grail.[26] Archaeology also provides a framework for understanding magical events in fantasy novels. The author Susan Cooper was influenced by the work of writers like Leslie Alcock, John Morris, E. K. Chambers and R. S. Loomis, all of whom examined possible connections between Arthurian tradition and archaeology.[27] The character Merriman is both an archaeologist and a wizard, and the Grail discovered by the children in *The Dark is Rising* is eventually put on display in a museum as 'a gold chalice, probably of Celtic workmanship, probably 6th century'. However, the children, and we the readers, know its true worth. The same contrast between cultural categorization and secret inner value characterizes the Grail in Penelope Lively's *Astercote*.[28] Indiana Jones has to choose the least prepossessing object, and therefore the most convincing from an archaeological point of view, in order to identify the true Grail and save his father.

In the medieval period relics were authenticated by miracles, although this did not prevent the custodians of relics from creating a history. Some modern writers still feel that sincere veneration is sufficient, but in general authority is sought elsewhere. As a result, the Grail carries the dual identity of artefact and sacred object in many modern reinterpretations. The pivotal event in many modern Grail treatments hangs on a character's ability to recognize the true nature of an object seemingly found by chance, like the one found in a well in Mary Butts's novel, or in a churchyard in Williams's *War in Heaven*. The hero of Bernard Cornwell's Grail books, Thomas of Hookton, and the Tudor sleuth Roger Shallot in *The Grail Murders*[29] present their masters with elaborate gold goblets, while the real Grail remains hidden and safe. Jonathan Gash's bad-boy antiques dealer, Lovejoy, has a brush with the Grail, a pewter cup kept in an ornate box. Thieves try to steal the valuable box and are uninterested in the authentic relic.[30] Archaeology has been used more controversially as a way of accessing a secret history through narrative. A tension between miraculous relic and authentic history surrounded the discovery of the Nanteos cup, the Hawkstone cup, and the glass bowl in St Bride's Well, Glastonbury. This creates an interesting irony, since novelists and Grail enthusiasts who use the medieval legend to confront modernity usually see it as a reaction against rational materialism. Attempts to use scientific methods to validate relics such as the *sacro catino* or the *santo caliz* often create further controversy about their authenticity. Where once miracles and personal revelations were sufficient, now these are suspect and need the validation of science.

Some fictional retellings of the Grail story retain its Christian source. Thomas Costain's biblical novel *The Silver Chalice* (1952) is a typical tale of pagan boy meets Christian girl. The Grail was based on an object found during archaeological investigations near Antioch, and suggestions that this might be the real Holy Grail had been set out on serious archaeological grounds.[31] Monty Python's 'Holy Hand Grenade of Antioch' may be a distant comic cousin of this controversy. *The Crimson Chalice* (1976), part of Victor Canning's historical trilogy set in Roman Britain, also presented the Grail as a Christian relic. The format is (Roman) girl meets (British) boy, but the fifth-century British setting resonates with an increased interest in the historical context for Arthur and with the origin legend attached to the Hawkstone cup.[32]

At the beginning of the twenty-first century, new themes linked to conspiracies entered Grail fiction. Alternative theories, like the Priory of Sion myth, were a major influence in this changing emphasis. Bernard Cornwell's use of the Grail motif in *The Warlord Chronicles* (1995–7) illustrates this.[33] The Grail originates in the sacred cauldron of Celtic folklore and still has echoes of Celtic paganism in a changing Arthurian world. A very different Grail, however, is at the centre of a later trilogy, *The Grail Quest* (2000–03).[34] Set during the Hundred Years' War, it tells the story of Thomas, illegitimate offspring of a noble family who were lords in the Languedoc at the time of the Cathar heresy. A raid to steal a sacred lance kept in the church in Thomas's village initiates the adventure to find the Holy Grail. His companion is a heretic girl with psychic powers. The dominant themes are obsession and intolerance among those who wish to possess or destroy the Grail. Thomas's opponents desire the Grail for its inherent power, or, like the ambitious archbishop, wish to create a false relic of gold to deceive the world. The Grail seekers find a mysterious empty box in the Languedoc and realize that the Grail has been in Thomas's home village all the time. The true Grail, an ordinary clay vessel, contrasts with the false gold chalice created by the ambitious archbishop. Cornwell's is a very modern treatment of the legend. Like the hero, Indiana Jones, the Grail seeker's defining characteristic is not to ask a question, but to be able to distinguish between real and false Grails. The novels are played out against a backdrop of historic battles, which are a hallmark of Cornwell's writing, while the Cathar background and the prominence of a young woman in the Grail search reflect contemporary Grail themes.

The last of Cornwell's *Grail Quest* books appeared in the same year as Dan Brown's *The Da Vinci Code* (2003). This novel drew directly on contemporary legend motifs found in popular writing. Brown was already a successful novelist specializing in conspiracy thrillers, and this one might have remained just that except for a prologue headed 'FACT'. This asserted that the Priory of Sion 'is a real organization' and 'all descriptions of artwork, architecture, documents and secret rituals' were accurate. This authorial conceit is about as reliable as Wolfram von Eschenbach's Kyot and his mysterious parchment. However, as with Wolfram, those who try to read such statements as true are taken into the world of conspiracy, rumour and secrets, in short into the world of modern contemporary legend. Certain religious groups reacted against the book's message, and a raft of handbooks, web blogs and television documentaries followed.[35] Nor was Dan Brown's preface the only arena in which fact and fiction collided. Two of the authors of *Holy Blood Holy Grail* brought an unsuccessful court action claiming theft of intellectual property.

The plot combined several alternative themes about a covert Christian sect protected by a mysterious secret organization hunted by an equally mysterious enemy. Leonardo Da Vinci's *Last Supper* painting provided the key. If interpreted correctly, it revealed that St John was actually Mary Magdalene, the real Grail. The immediate sources were undoubtedly popular books about the female aspect of divinity, a divine bloodline, and supposed connections between Leonardo Da Vinci and the Turin Shroud.[36] However, as the previous chapters have shown, these in turn drew on a number of speculative ideas about the New Testament, popular myths about Templars and Cathars, hidden treasure legends, conspiracy rumours and vague esoteric ideas which had become popular with the rise of new age spirituality. Like so many thrillers, the emphasis in Brown's novel is on action and the characters are stereotyped. The material is, however, repackaged in an inventive way. Character names reflect earlier work. Sophie is the embodiment of *Sophia*, the divine feminine; Bezu Fache and Jacques Sauniere echo the Rennes-le-Château story, and the anagrammatic name 'Teabing' is a nod in the direction of conspiracy genre authors. The plot involves familiar Grail thriller motifs such as the museum and the academic hero opposed by obsessed police detectives and sinister villains, and, of course, the Templars are involved in absolutely everything.

Umberto Eco's satirical mystery novel *Foucault's Pendulum* also combines a group of occult book enthusiasts, a translation of Wolfram's *Parzival*, the Grail, Templar secrets, an object sought by Hitler and his Nazis, and a conspiracy that starts out as a fiction, but eventually engulfs its creators.[37] Eco was by no means the first to use satire in dealing with the Grail. Mark Twain's *Connecticut Yankee* dismissed the activity of going 'Grailing' as a summer pursuit among Arthur's knights.[38] Naomi Michison's anachronistic medieval reporters get up to all sorts of ridiculous antics in *To the Chapel Perilous*,[39] and Charles Williams provides an amusing folklorist, Sir Giles Tumulty. Eco however, specifically satirized the conspiracy methodology of alternative writers, although at least one alternative writer has drawn Eco himself into the secret world.[40] Although written over a decade before Dan Brown's book, Eco's novel has achieved the accolade of being described as 'the thinking man's *Da Vinci Code*'. Undoubtedly, the alternative books of the 1980s and Brown's twenty-first-century thriller created a new audience for ideas which had been circulating for some time. In Kate Mosse's time-shift thriller *Labyrinth* (2005),[41] Alice, a young woman working on an archaeological dig in southern France, finds a cave containing two skeletons with a labyrinth inscribed on the walls. Subsequent events reveal her connection to Alais, a young woman who guarded the secret of the Holy Grail during the Cathar crusade. The novel follows a familiar pattern in Grail literature. The forces of good fight the forces of evil for possession of a secret talisman. One character acts as mediator, and his, or in this case her, journey of self-discovery drives the plot. Maurice Magre and Joseph Péladan had explored links between the Grail and the Cathar crusade in earlier novels, but the importance of a feminine principle brings this one up to date.

Video and role-play gaming present such an obvious fusion of traditional plot structure, technology and popular culture that it is surprising it is not more widely used. The main character of the Gabriel Knight adventure games series is a bookstore owner with special abilities to hunt down evil beings. The context for *Gabriel Knight 3: Blood of the Sacred, Blood of the Damned*[42] is a guided tour and treasure hunt in Rennes-le-Château. Legends about the Templars and the Holy Grail are important elements in playing the game successfully, with vampires thrown in for good measure. The games workshop scenario *Queen Victoria and the Holy Grail* combines fantasy, history, comic book heroes and many of the themes of Grail conspiracy thrillers. A mysterious theft from Buckingham Palace reveals the British monarchy as 'the guardians of a gold chalice reputedly the true Holy Grail'.[43] The complex *Pendragon* fantasy role-play game also uses the Grail as a storyline.[44]

The thread that connects scholarship, alternative writing and fiction is a particular attitude to how meaning can be created out of tradition. The way tradition was used by folklorists at the end of the nineteenth century had much in common with the comparative approach used by early anthropologists. There was broad consensus that the romances contained mythic elements that could be recovered and could illuminate a genuine mythic source. Both isolated elements in their respective body of texts and then reconstructed backwards, often without concern for their function in the original source. For those seeking access to a secret tradition, the methodology was much the same. The secret tradition was reflected in myth and legend and attempts were made to recover the authentic history of the Grail as spiritual or esoteric alternative through the examination of texts.[45] It is therefore not surprising that the link between those writing in the occult tradition and writers of fiction, especially gothic, fantastic and supernatural fiction, has always been strong.[46] Jessie Weston's ancient ritual provided a way to critique the failures of contemporary society, as well as a metaphor for aesthetic and imaginative continuity. The idea of a mystery cult as a precursor of Christianity fitted into a view of the past and of human nature prevalent in the occult revival and in theosophy. Likewise, paganism provided a way to envisage a pluralistic society, and alternative Christianity helped resolve the dislocations of patriarchy. Whether any of these assumptions were ever true of ancient civilization is a moot point. However, the theory of evolution provided the nineteenth-century occult revival with a useful paradigm. Social evolution, according to Frazer, was dominated by progress. In the context of the revival of esotericism, it became a programme for the development of humanity rather than just a description of how societies developed. If the primordial world was good, and the present situation is bad, then esoteric evolution could ensure a better future once the secret key was found.[47]

The pattern of code, revelation and secret message repeats itself endlessly in modern Grail traditions; but how do such theories sit in the context of ideas about knowledge? Current debates about interpretation centre on a credible view of the past. Presenting history as a secret code leads to a clear solution, unlike the constant revisions of academic research, but these theories can be true only if there actually is a conspiracy to suppress an alternative reality. The numerous historians who take issue with the assumptions behind these theories have a point. The plethora of sources so characteristic of this alternative genre do not in fact suggest that tortuous plots of conspiracy and suppression ever existed. Modern Grail legends reach a global audience through mass media and publishing, newspaper and television. Beliefs, images, and the array of localized legends surrounding the Grail place it at the centre of a complex web of conflicting religious visions, millennial anxieties and nostalgic reimaginings supported by a mix of science, pseudo-science, and popular culture. This book has tried to trace the process by which these narratives became charged with multiple layers of cultural meaning. They belong to a general impulse often called new age, but they depend on ideas that pre-date this movement. They reflect an interest in sources outside the Judeo-Christian tradition, and a strong vein of individualism in which personal feeling based on an eclectic array of sources is more important for determining what is true than mainstream sources of authority.[48] The famous bricolage image used by

Lévi-Strauss of a workman who builds with the materials to hand encapsulates the process very well. The past is reassembled in a way that makes the present understandable and the future more assured. Thus the sense of disorder and discontinuity in the events and experiences of everyday life is balanced by a countermovement that embodies a desire to re-establish a universal principle for cultural action. In this way, the past can be reclaimed and the present overcome in order to usher in a new era of harmony and spiritual fulfilment on personal, ecological and cosmic levels.

The earliest Grail narratives appeared as romance fictions in the twelfth century. While Grail fictions written in the past century have realigned some of the polarities found in medieval story, both medieval and modern versions narrate the actions of a character on a life-changing journey. Another constant is the enduring struggle for control of a talisman. Initially, folk elements such as these were viewed as part of a peasant realm, where tradition was passed on orally from one generation to the next and where the way of life was rural and stable. Traditions changed over time, but this was a gradual process that could be tracked and controlled. Now folklore moves rapidly through conduits such as the Internet and other forms of mass media, and the elements of this myth are constantly re-localized and reinvented. As a result, the treatments of the Grail and the relationship between Grail and seeker have changed. Modern Grail narratives may favour conspiracies and secret codes, but what links them to the medieval Grail romances is the idea of quest. In treatments that emphasize the personal and internal, the seeker must be able to distinguish between real and false Grails, rather than ask the question which opens the way to a vision of the Holy Grail; but it is a quest all the same.

A publicity blurb for a book on the holy bloodline reads 'What links the Vatican, the CIA, the KGB, the Mafia, Freemasonry, P2, Opus Dei and the Knights Templar? What mysterious modern crusade implicates British industry, Churchill and de Gaulle, the EEC and Solidarity?'[49] The idea of a secret society that controls, or attempts to control, world events and maintains a malevolent conspiracy to cover the fact is not new. Conspiracy in early modern Europe flourished in court situations where power was based on access to a ruler. On this level, it was a seemingly rational way of understanding a court-centred political culture in which a relatively small number of people actively participated. Court situations with disproportionately powerful ministers were often targeted by extreme measures such as assassination attempts and plots. It still has a modern reflection in popular attitudes to institutions that retain some of the pageantry of the past, such as the papacy and religious orders.[50] However, this situation, rooted in the reality of court life, has been extended and elaborated with the passage of time into a more glamorous world of billowing tapestries which conceal decadent churchmen and dashing musketeers, and it is this more romantic and glamorous view that finds its way into alternative writing and thriller novels.

Conspiracy, or at least the perception of it, flourishes at times of ideological conflict. The impact of the Reformation, for example, reinforced the conspiratorial mindset. Religious rivals interpreted each other's actions in terms of plots whose consequences could be very real, especially when the politics of conspiracy combined with popular fears. Accusations created scapegoats who embodied those fears and who could therefore be persecuted. Although the idea of conspiracy as a political and social model was challenged by the new paradigms that arose at the time of the Enlightenment, it never completely lost its hold. 'Physical and social sciences offered alternative methods of analysing human actions as did a conception of history that was increasingly connected to the movement of impersonal forces.'[51] Perhaps it is the impersonal nature of these forces that contributes to the problem. We are confronted, on the one hand, with an explosion of information and opinion, and on the other, given the widespread distrust of traditional channels of authority with no obvious way to sort through these data. In these circumstances conspiracy, whether real or not, gives a face to the complexity of experience and offers a way of explaining the seemingly random chaos of daily life.[52] Conspiracy theory endows the opponent with personality and restores a gothic frisson in which conspirators lurk in the shadows of a past world. Furthermore, the reader of modern conspiratorial literature is cast in the role of code-breaker, the hero or heroine of an excellent adventure.

In Steven Spielberg's film *Indiana Jones and the Last Crusade*, the hero Indiana asserts that 'we cannot take mythology at face value', while his friend, the museum curator Marcus Brody, says that the search for the Grail is the search for the divine in all of us. The film is one of the most lighthearted treatments of the Grail legend, but it illustrates the ways in which the legend today inherits not just the content of the medieval romances, but also all the interpretations that have been suggested over the years. The characters express two of the dominant trends in the way in which Grail legends have developed. Indiana, a hero more like the savvy Gawain than the naive Perceval, seeks meaning in archaeology and history, while Brody, despite his comic turns, hankers after an inner experience. The film mixes old and new themes. The historian father pursues the quest through texts, while the archaeologist son battles his way through exotic landscapes. The villains of the thriller genre beset them and a conspiracy of stereotyped satanic militarism seeks to acquire the Grail for its own ends. Indiana's father acts as advisor and guide, much like Perceval's uncles did in the earliest Grail romances, and at the end he is cured by water from the Grail, just like the Fisher King. The Grail choice is very modern. Indiana must choose the right Grail, not the glittering false ones, but the simple cup that served a simple man. In many ways the Grail legend has become independent of its origins. Sometimes the object is physical, sometimes it is knowledge expressed in words or actions, sometimes it is a mystic experience. The Fisher King's Grail is now a psychic or spiritual mediator between the land and the people who populate it. However it changes, the eternal chalice retains its power to draw us into its magic orbit.

Notes

Introduction

1 Clare Birchall, *Knowledge Goes Pop: From Conspiracy Theory to Gossip* (Oxford: Berg, 2006), 65–90; Peter Knight, *Conspiracy Culture: From the Kennedy Assassination to The X-files* (London and New York: Routledge, 2000).

2 Alfred Nutt, *Studies in the Legend of the Holy Grail: With Especial Reference to the Hypothesis of its Celtic Origin*, Folklore Society Publication 23 (London: David Nutt, 1888).

3 Bill Ellis, *Aliens Ghosts and Cults: Legends We Live* (Jackson: University of Mississippi, 2001), xiii–ix, 46–57, 60.

4 Linda Degh, *American Folklore and the Mass Media* (Bloomington: Indiana University Press, 1994).

5 Philip Cousinauu, *Once and Future Myths: The Power of Ancient Stories in Modern Times* (Berkeley: Conari, 2001), 11.

6 John Girling, *Myths and Politics in Western Societies: Evaluating the Crisis of Modernity in the United States, Germany and Great Britain* (New Brunswick: Transaction, 1993), 3–4, 170–2.

Chapter 1 – Romances and Relics

1 Tony Hunt, 'The Prologue to Chrétien's Le Conte del Graal,' *Romania* 92 (1971), 359–79; Sarah Kay 'Who Was Chrétien de Troyes?' *Arthurian Literature* 15 (1997), 1–36; Richard Barber, *The Holy Grail: Imagination and Belief* (London: Allen Lane, 2004), 10–14; Constance Bullock Davies, 'Chrétien de Troyes and England', *Arthurian Literature* I (1981), 1–61.

2 Chrétien de Troyes, *Perceval the Story of the Grail*, tr. Nigel Bryant (Cambridge and Totowa: Brewer, 1982).

3 William Roach, *The Continuations of the Old French Perceval of Chrétien de Troyes* (Philadelphia: University of Pennsylvania Press, 1949–83).

4 Lenora Wolfgang, *Bliocadran: A Prologue to the Perceval of Chrétien de Troyes* (Tubingen: Niemeyer, 1976).

5 Albert Wilder Thompson, *The Elucidation: A Prologue to the Conte del Graal* (1931) (Geneve: Slatkine, 1982).

6 Barber, *The Holy Grail: Imagination and Belief*, 38.

7 Robert de Boron, *L'estoire del Saint Graal*, ed. Jean-Paul Ponceau, Classiques Francais du Moyen Age (Paris, 1997); *Merlin and the Grail: Joseph of Arimathea, Merlin and Perceval: The Trilogy of Prose Romances Attributed to Robert de Boron*, tr. Nigel Bryant (Cambridge and Rochester: Brewer 2001).

8 Robert de Boron, *Le roman du graal: Manuscrit de modène* ed. and tr. Bernard Cerquigliani (Paris: Champion 1981).

9 The term Apocrypha has been used since the fifth century for the non-canonical books of the Bible which are not considered to be divinely inspired.

10 Robert de Boron, *Le roman de L'Estoire dou Graal*, ed. William A. Nitze (Paris: Champion 1927; repr. 1983).

11 *The Didot Perceval*, ed. William Roach (Philadelphia: University of Pennsylvania Press, 1971); tr. D. Skeeles (Seattle: University of Washington Press, 1966).

12 *The High Book of the Grail* or *Perlesvaus*, tr. Nigel Bryant (Cambridge: Cambridge University Press, 1978).

13 Robert Williams, *Y Seint Greal* (London: T. Richards, 1876); Thomas Jones, J. E. Caerwyn Williams, Ceridwen Lloyd-Morgan and Daniel Huws, eds, *Ystoryaeu seint greal*. Text from Peniarth 11, NLW 3063E, Peniarth 15 (Cardiff: University of Wales Press, 1992).

14 Wolfram von Eschenbach, *Parzival*, tr. Cyril Edwards (Oxford: University Press, 2006); Barber, *The Holy Grail: Imagination and Belief*, 78–9.

15 Will Hasty, ed., *A Companion to Wolfram's Parzival: Studies in German Literature, Linguistics, and Culture* (Columbia, SC; Camden House, 1999), 92–3.

16 Hasty, 'Doing His Own Thing: Wolfram's Grail', 77–97; Carl Lofmark 'Wolfram's source references in Parzifal', *Modern Language Review* 67 (1972), 820–44; 'Zur Interpretation der Kyotstellen im Parzifal', *Wolfram-Studien* 4 (1977), 33–70; A. D. Horgan, 'The Grail in Wolfram's Parzifal', *Medieval Studies* 36 (1964), 354–81.

17 *Lancelot-Grail: The Old French Arthurian Vulgate and Post-Vulgate in Translation*, ed. Norris J. Lacy (New York and London: Garland 1993–6).

18 *The Vulgate Version of the Arthurian Romance*, ed. H. O. Sommer, 8 vols (repr. New York: The Carnegie Institution, 1979); *The Grail Quest*, ed. and tr. P. M. Matarasso (Harmondsworth: Penguin, 1969).

19 'Peredur vab Efrog', 65–102 in *The Mabinogion*, tr. Sioned Davies (Oxford: Oxford University Press, 2007).

20 Barber, *The Holy Grail: Imagination and Belief*, 20–5; Norris J. Lacey, *The New Arthurian Encyclopaedia* (Chicago and London, 1991), 'Post vulgate Cycle', 430–2.

21 *The Works of Sir Thomas Malory*, ed. Eugene Vinaver, rev. P. J. C. Field (Oxford: Oxford University Press, 1990), Books 1, 5 and 6 lines, Malory incorporates Grail material into the story of Balin and the Dolorons Blow as well as the actual quest section.

22 Barber, *The Holy Grail: Imagination and Belief*, 215–21; Sandra Ness Ihle, *Malory's Grail Quest: Invention and Adaptation in Medieval Prose Romance* (Madison: University of Wisconsin Press, 1983), 117, 127ff.

23 Barber, *The Holy Grail: Imagination and Belief*, 187.

24 Heinrich von der Türlin, *The Crown* (Diu Crône), tr. J. W. Thomas (Lincoln and London: University of Nebraska Press, 1989).

25 *Fouke le Fitz Waryn*, ed. E. J. Hathaway *et al.*, Anglo-Norman Text Society (Oxford: Blackwell, 1975).

26 *Le Roman de Tristan en prose,* ed. Gilles Roussineau (Geneva: Librairie Droz, 1991).

27 Henry Lovelich, *History of the Holy Grail*, ed. F. J. Furnivall, Early English Text Society Extra Series (London: K. Paul, Trench, Trübner & Co., 1874–1905).

28 *The Chronicle of Iohn Hardyng . . .*, together with the continuation of Richard Grafton, to the thirty-fourth year of King Henry the Eighth ed. Henry Ellis (London: F. C. and J. Rivington, 1812).

29 H. M. Gillett, *The Story of the Relics of the Passion* (Oxford: Basil Blackwell, 1935), 95–110.

30 Rose Jeffries Peebles, *The Legend of Longinus in Ecclesiastical Tradition and English Literature and Its Connections with the Holy Grail* (Baltimore: J. H. Furst 1911).

31 Adamnan, *De Locis sanctis*, ed. Denis Meehan (Dublin: Institute for Advanced Studies, 1958), 51; Liam S. Gogan, *Ireland's Holy Grail* (Dublin: Browne & Nolan, 1932), 10.

32 Barber, *The Holy Grail: Imagination and Belief*, 167.

33 Gogan, *Ireland's Holy Grail*, 80–2; Gillett, *The Story of the Relics of the Passion*, 106–12.

34 C. E. Clifton, tr, *Historical, Literacy and Artistic Travels in Italy by M. Valery* (Paris: Baudry's European Library 1859), 684 n.1.

35 Domenico Calcagno, *Il mistero del sacro catino* (ECIG Colla Nuov Atlantide, 2000).

36 Johann Zahlten, 'Der "sacro catino" in Genua. Auflärung über eine mittelalterliche Gralsrelique', 121–31 in Reinhold Baumstark, *Der Gral artusromantik in der Kunst des 19 Jahrhunderts* (Köln, 1995); Sir Martin Conway, 'The Sacro Catino at Genoa', *Antiquaries Journal* 4 (1924), 11–18.

37 Barber, *The Holy Grail: Imagination and Belief*, 168–9.

38 Iacopo de Voragine, *Chronica civitatis Ianuensis*, ed. Giovalli Monleone (Rome, 1941), ii, 311–12; Barber, *The Holy Grail: Imagination and Belief*, 168.

39 Barber, *The Holy Grail: Imagination and Belief*, 167.

40 See Chapter 2.

41 Alex Owen, *The Place of Enchantment* (Chicago: University of Chicago Press, 2004), 10–13.

42 Antonio Beltran Martinez, *Estudio sobre el Santo Caliz de la catedral de Valencia*, 4th edn (Zaragoza octavio y Feles, 1984), 37–8; Juan Dominguez Lasierra, 'Argon legendario: el Santo Grial', *Turia* 18 (1991), 140–59. http://www.aragonesasi.com/libros/santocaliz.php http://www.geocities.com/Athens/Rhodes/3946/santocaliz/ (accessed 5 July 2007); http://www.catholicculture.org/library /view.cfm?recnum=6985 (accessed 17 July 2007); http://thenewliturgicalmovement.blogspot.com/2006/07/ cns-story-at-mass-in-valencia-pope.html (accessed 17 August 2007).

43 Asunción Alejor Morán, *Presencia del Santo Cáliz en al arte* (Valencia: Ajuntament de Valencia, 2000).

44 Barber, *The Holy Grail: Imagination and Belief*, 168–70.

45 Janice Bennett, *St Laurence and the Holy Grail* (Denver: Ignatius Press 2004); 'New Book Says the Holy Grail Exists', Roxanne King *Denver Catholic Register*, 11 September 2002, www.arch.den.org/dcr/archive/20020911/20029112n.htm (accessed 7 January 2007).

46 See Chapter 3.

47 See Chapter 2.

48 S. W. Gentle-Cackett, *The Antioch Cup* (London, 1935), 7, 23–7; Barber, *The Holy Grail: Imagination and Belief*, 300.

49 Gustavus Eisen, *The Great Chalice of Antioch*, 2 vols (New York: Konchakji Freres, 1923), http://century.lib.uchicago.edu/. In the introduction to a booklet prepared for the Chicago World's Fair, Eisen wrote, 'My monograph, the great chalice of Antioch, ... is both technical and expensive ... In response to ... demand ... this brief untechnical account has been prepared', 'The Great Chalice of Antioch' (New York, 1933), 6–7.

50 Barber, *The Holy Grail: Imagination and Belief*, 301; 'Antioch Chalice', *Timeline of Art History* (New York: The Metropolitan Museum of Art, 2000), http://www.metmuseum.org/toah/ho/06/waa/hod_50.4.htm (October 2006) (accessed 17 July 2007).

51 Thomas Costain, *The Silver Chalice* (New York: Doubleday, 1952).

52 Ordine del Tempio S.M.T.H.O. http://web/cheapnet.it/smtho/stampa.htm (accessed 7 January 2007).

53 Peebles, *The Legend of Longinus*, 173–7, 181–8; see also A. C. L. Brown, 'The Bleeding Lance', *Publications of the Modern Language*

Association of America 25/1 (1910), 59. For a survey of this motif see
Konrad Burdach, *Der Gral: Forschungen über seinen Ursprung und
seinen Zusammenhang mit der Longinuslegende Forschungen zur
Kirchen-und Geistesgeschichte*, vol. 14 (Darmstadt: Wissenschaftliche
Buchgesellschaft, 1974).

54 Steven Runciman, 'The Holy Lance Found at Antioch', reprinted from
Analecta Bollandiana, vol. 68, 197–209 (Bruxelles: Société des
Bollandistes, 1950); Barber, *The Holy Grail: Imagination and Belief*,
126–7; Laura Hibbard Loomis, 'The Holy Relics of Charlemagne and
King Athelston: The Lances of Longinus and St Mauricius', *Speculum* 25
(1950), 437–56; H. L. Adelson, 'The Holy Lance and the Hereditary
German Monarchy', *The Art Bulletin* 48 (1966), 177–91.

55 Joe Nickell, *Relics of the Christ* (Lexington: University Press of Kentucky,
2007), 111–79.

56 Noel Currer-Briggs, *The Shroud and the Grail: A Modern Quest for the
True Grail* (London: Weidenfeld and Nicolson, 1987); *The Shroud: Mafia
Creation of a Relic?* (Lewes: Book Guild 1995).

57 Lynn Picknett and Clive Prince, *Turin Shroud: In Whose Image? The
Shocking Truth Unveiled* (London: BCA by arrangement with
Bloomsbury, 1994); and their *The Templar Revelation: Secret Guardians
of the True Identity of Christ* (Reading: Corgi, 1998).

58 Joséphin Péladan, *La philosophie de Léonard de Vinci d'après ses
manuscrits* (Paris: F. Alcan, 1910).

59 Richard A. Turner, *Inventing Leonardo: The Anatomy of a Legend* (New
York: Knopf, 1993).

60 www.sacred-destinations.com/belgium/bruges-basilica-of-holy-blood.html
(accessed 2 June 2007).

61 Barber, *The Holy Grail: Imagination and Belief*, 212–17; Felicity Riddy,
Sir Thomas Malory (Leiden: Brill, 1987), 123–5, 130–1.

Chapter 2 – *The Grail at Glastonbury*

1 Dion Fortune, *Glastonbury: Avalon of the Heart* (Boston, MA: Weiser
Books, 2000), 1.

2 Antonia Gransden, 'The Growth of the Glastonbury Traditions and
Legends in the Twelfth Century', in James P. Carley (ed.), *Glastonbury
Abbey and Arthurian Tradition* (Cambridge: D.S. Brewer, 2001), 30–1.
[Hereafter *Glastonbury Abbey*.]

3 John Scott, ed., *The Early History of Glastonbury*, an edition, translation
and study of William of Malmesbury's *De antiquitate Glastonie Ecclesie*
(Woodbridge: Boydell & Brewer, 1981).

4 Gransden, 'The Growth of the Glastonbury Traditions', 34, 37.

5 Ibid., 39.

6 Valerie M. Lagorio, 'The Evolving Legend of St Joseph of Glastonbury', in *Glastonbury Abbey*, 56–63.

7 Ibid., 60–2; R. S. Loomis, *The Grail from Celtic Myth to Christian Symbol* (Cardiff, University of Wales Press, 1963), 223–48,

8 Lagorio, 'The Evolving Legend of St Joseph of Glastonbury', 62–4; J. Armitage Robinson, *Two Glastonbury Legends: King Arthur and St. Joseph of Arimathea* (Cambridge, 1926), 28–50; R. F. Treharne, *The Glastonbury Legends: Joseph of Arimathea, the Holy Grail and King Arthur* (London, 1967), 28–9.

9 Robinson, *Two Glastonbury Legends*, 48, 64; James P. Carley, 'A Grave Event: Henry V, Glastonbury Abbey, and Joseph of Arimathea's Bones', in *Glastonbury Abbey*, 285–302.

10 James P. Carley, 'Melkin the Bard and Esoteric Tradition at Glastonbury Abbey', *The Downside Review* 99 (1981), 8; Lagorio, 'The Evolving Legend of St Joseph of Glastonbury', 66; Robinson, *Two Glastonbury Legends*, claims it was a fourteenth-century forgery, 26.

11 Carley, 'Introduction', in *Glastonbury Abbey*, 4–5.

12 Ibid., 8; Rachel Bromwich, ed., *Trioedd Ynys Prydein: The Triads of the Island of Britain*, 3rd edn (Cardiff: University of Wales Press, 2006), 428–32; Juliette Wood, 'Maelgwn Gwynedd: A Forgotten Welsh Hero', *Trivium* 19 (1984), 103–17.

13 There is a response from Professor Rhŷs to a 'Mr Murray'. See Caroline Oates and Juliette Wood, *A Coven of Scholars: Margaret Murray and Her Theories of Witchcraft* (London: Folklore Society, 1998), 79–80.

14 Robinson, *Two Glastonbury Legends*, 42; Lagorio, 'The Evolving Legend of St Joseph of Glastonbury', 64–8; see *The Chronicle of Glastonbury Abbey: An Edition, Translation and Study of John of Glastonbury's 'Chronica sive antiquitates Glastoniensis ecclesie'*, ed. James P. Carley, tr. David Townsend (Woodbridge: Boydell and Brewer, 1985).

15 Lagorio, 'The Evolving Legend of St Joseph of Glastonbury', 68.

16 William Good, a Jesuit priest, was an acolyte at Glastonbury. He gives useful details of the function of the St Joseph cult during the last years of the abbey. See Robinson, *Two Glastonbury Legends*, 46–9, 66–7; James P. Carley, 'The Discovery of the Holy Cross of Waltham at Montacute, the Excavation of Arthur's Grave at Glastonbury Abbey and Joseph of Arimathea's Burial', in *Glastonbury Abbey*, 303–08; Carley, 'A Grave Event', 296–302.

17 Jeanne Krochalis, 'Magna Tabula: The Glastonbury Tablets', in *Glastonbury Abbey*, 477–525.

18 Lagorio, 'The Evolving Legend of St Joseph', 65–6, 68–72.

19 Edward Donald Kennedy, 'John Hardyng and the Holy Grail', in *Glastonbury Abbey*, 249–67, 250–1 nn. 7, 9.

20 John Hardyng, *The Chronicle of Iohn Hardyng: . . .* from the earliest

period of English history to the beginning of the reign of King Edward the Fourth; together with the continuation of Richard Grafton, to the thirty fourth year of King Henry the Eighth. An index, ed. Henry Ellis (London, 1812), 83ff.

21 Kennedy, 'John Hardyng and the Holy Grail', 251–5; Felicity Riddy, 'Glastonbury, Joseph of Arimathea and the Grail in John Hardyng's Chronicle', in *Glastonbury Abbey*, 269–84.

22 Kennedy, 'John Hardyng and the Holy Grail', 120, 131, 148–9; Riddy, 'Glastonbury, Joseph of Arimathea and the Grail in John Hardyng's Chronicle', 282–4.

23 Lagorio, 'The Evolving Legend of St Joseph of Glastonbury', 74–6.

24 Carley, 287.

25 My thanks to C. and N. Hollinrake for photographs and information on Beckery Island and its history.

26 Geoffrey Ashe: Collins, *King Arthur's Avalon: The Story of Glastonbury* (London: Collins, 1957; repr. 1982), 117, 348–9.

27 Adrian J. Ivakhiv, *Claiming Sacred Ground: Pilgrims and Politics at Glastonbury and Sedona* (Bloomington: Indiana University Press, 2001), 69–70.

28 Patrick Benham, *The Avalonians* (Glastonbury: Gothic Image Press, 1993), 6.

29 John Arthur Goodchild, *The Light of the West: An Account of the Dannite Settlement in Ireland* (London: Kegan Paul & Co., 1898).

30 Benham, *The Avalonians*, 88–100.

31 Rosamund Lehmann, *My Dear Alexias, Letters from Wellesley Tudor Pole to Rosamund Lehmann* (Sudbury: Neville Spearman, 1979), 32–52, 67–8, 71, 83, 183, 195, 199.

32 Letter to the *Daily Express* is quoted by Benham, *The Avalonians*, 78–81.

33 Benham, *The Avalonians*, 60–1.

34 Quoted by Benham, *The Avalonians*, 59; see also Rosamund Lehmann's letter to Tudor Pole, 183; Oliver G. Villiers, *Wellesley Tudor Pole, Appreciation and Valuation* (Canterbury, 1977), 26–9.

35 Benham (*The Avalonians*) has the most sympathetic view of this discovery. It is less sympathetically handled in the correspondence between A. E. Waite and Arthur Machen: see Chapter 3. See also Stephen Scammell, *Mary of Nazareth, Joseph of Arimathea and the Early Celtic Church* (Cumbria: David Grayling, 1995), 36–46.

36 Benham, *The Avalonians*, 74; Juliette Wood, 'The Creation of the Celtic Tarot', *Folklore* 109 (1998), 15–24.

37 Benham, *The Avalonians*, 118–19; *The Enigma of Good Versus Evil; Notes on Healing; God is Love*, booklets by W. Tudor Pole (Glastonbury: The Chalice Well Trust, 1983).

38 Tracy Cutting, *Beneath the Silent Tor, the Life and Work of Alice Buckton* (Appleseed Press, 2004).

39 The Rev. Lionel Smithett Lewis, *St. Joseph of Arimathea at Glastonbury* (London: James Clark, 1955; repr. 1964), 101–04.

40 Benham, *The Avalonians*, 189–250, 197–9, 202.

41 Catherine Crowe, *The Night Side of Nature*, 1848 (London: Wordsworth, 2000), 9–14.

42 Benham, *The Avalonians*, 215; William Kenawell, *The Quest at Glastonbury: A Biographical Study of Frederick Bligh Bond* (New York: Helix Press, 1965).

43 Frederick Bligh Bond, *An Architectural Handbook of Glastonbury Abbey, with a Historical Chronicle of the Building* ... (Glastonbury: Central Somerset Gazette, 1920); *The Gate of Remembrance* (the story of the psychological experiment which resulted in the discovery of the Edgar Chapel at Glastonbury), (Oxford: B. H. Blackwell, 1918); *The Company of Avalon: A Study of the Script* [i.e. automatic writing], *on the Subject of Glastonbury Abbey* (Oxford: Basil Blackwell, 1924); Henry John Wilkins, *A Further Criticism of the Psychical Claims concerning Glastonbury Abbey* [made in *The Gate of Remembrance* by F. B. Bond] (Bristol: J. W. Arrowsmith, 1923).

44 For Arthur Machen and the legend of the Holy Grail see Chapter 3. For a similar discussion of the work of Lewis Spence, see Chapter 4.

45 Frederick Bligh Bond, *The Hill of Vision* forecast of the First World War and of social revolution with the coming of the new race gathered from automatic writings through the hand of John Alleyne (London: Constable & Co., 1919), *The Glastonbury Scripts: Tales of Glastonbury Abbey Purporting to be Automatic Writings* (Glastonbury, 1921), 'The Story of King Arthur and How He Saw the Sangreal, of His Institution of the Quest of the Holy Grail, and of the Promise of the Fulfilment of that Quest in the Latter Days/ Founded on Scripts Partly Metrical Received in 1924' (Glastonbury: Central Somerset Gazette, 1925).

46 Charles Fielding and T. Carr, *The Story of Dion Fortune* (Loughborough: Thoth Publication, 1998); Benham, *The Avalonians*, 251–63.

47 John Clark, *The Avalonian Guide to the Town of Glastonbury and its Environs*, 2nd edn (Bridgwater, 1814; first publ. 1810). This continued to be republished during the nineteenth century.

48 Dion Fortune, *Glastonbury: Avalon of the Heart*; Benham, *The Avalonians*, 256–7.

49 Ivakhiv, *Claiming Sacred Ground*, 81.

50 Lehmann, *Dear Alexias*, 135; Roger Dobson, Godfrey Brogham and Robert Andrew Gilbert (eds), *Arthur Machen: Selected Letters* (Wellingborough: Aquarian Press, 1988), 38. See Chapter 3.

51 James Ussher, *Britannicarum ecclesiarum antiquitates: quibus inserta est ecclesiam inductae haereseos historia, Collectore Jacobo Usserio* (Dublin: Societatis Bibliopolarum, 1639).

52 Robert Buick Knox, *James Ussher, Archbishop of Armagh* (Cardiff: University of Wales Press 1967), 98–118.

53 Quote about 'Sangreal vocem hic usurpat sanguinis realis . . . Pretiosissimum enim illium sanguinem, quem in Cruce essidet Servator moster', cap II, p. 18

54 *Britannicarum ecclesiarum antiquitates*, cap II, 17: 'exodem nugacisssimo libro, qui sanctum Graal appellatur; 'de catino illo . . . in quo Dominus caenavit cum discipulis suis, ac quo ab eodem eremita descripta et historia que dicitur Gradal.' 'Gradalis autem vel Gradale Gallice dicitur scutella lata . . . dicitur vulgari nomine Graal'.

55 'The Spirit of Prophecy Has not Wholly Left the World: The Stylization of Archbishop James Ussher as a Prophet', in Helen Parish and William G. Naphy (eds), *Religion and Superstition in Reformation Europe* (Manchester: Manchester University Press 2002) 119–132.

56 'Bishop Ushers second prophesie which he delivered to his daughter on his sick-bed' (London: John Hunt, 1681); 'The Prophecies and Predictions of the Late Learned Rev James Usher' (London: Benjamin Tooke, 1687); James Ussher, *Strange and Remarkable Prophecies and Predictions: To Which is Prefaced a Short Sketch of his Life* (Dublin, 1840).

57 He gives the name of this correspondent as H. Kendra Baker, see *Glastonbury Traditions Concerning Joseph of Arimathea: Being a Translation from the Latin by H. Kendra Baker of the Second Chapter of Britannicarum ecclesiarum antiquitates of James Ussher* (London: Covenant Publishing Co., 1928).

58 *St Joseph of Arimathea at Glastonbury* (1955, repr. 1964).

59 See Chapter 3 for a discussion of the Grail at Nanteos.

60 Sebastian Evans, *The High History of the Holy Graal* (London: J. M. Dent & Co., 1898).

61 Sebastian Evans, *Brother Fabian's Manuscript and Other Poems* (London, 1865), trans. *Histories of the Kings of Britain* by Geoffrey, of Monmouth, Bishop of St. Asaph (London: J. M. Dent, 1904).

62 Sebastian Evans, ed., *Leicestershire Words, Phrases, and Proverbs, Collected by the Late Arthur Benoni Evans* (London: Trubner, 1881).

63 Sebastian Evans, *In Quest of the Holy Grail: An Introduction to the Study of the Legend* (London: Dent, 1898).

64 *High History* (London: Dent, 1904), 378–9.

65 This expectation of a mysterious redeemer also influenced their joint work W. Tudor Pole and Rosamond Lehmann, *A Man Seen Afar* (1965; C. W. Daniel, 1988).

66 Katherine Maltwood, *The Enchantments of Britain*, with illustrations (Victoria, BC: Victoria Printing & Publishing Co., 1944); *King Arthur's Round Table of the Zodiac*; with map (Victoria, BC, 1946); *A Guide to Glastonbury's Temple of the Stars*: their giant effigies described from air

views, maps, and from 'The High History of the Holy Grail' (London:
John Clarke, 1964); Rosemary Alicia Brown, *Katherine Emma
Maltwood, Artist, 1878–1961*, exhibition held at the Maltwood Art
Museum and Gallery, University of Victoria, June–July 1981 (Victoria
BC, 1981). Maltwood and her husband founded a museum at the
University of Victoria in British Columbia where many of her works are
among the collections.

67 John Michell, *New Light on the Ancient Mystery of Glastonbury*
(Glastonbury: Gothic Image, 1990), 62

68 Benham, *The Avalonians*, 266–8; Ivakhiv, *Claiming Sacred Ground*, 108.

69 Mary Williams, ed., *Glastonbury: A Study in Patterns* (London: Research
into Lost Knowledge, 1969).

70 *The High Book of the Grail* or *Perlesvaus*, tr. Nigel Bryant (Cambridge:
Cambridge University Press, 1978); W. A. Nitze and T. Atkinson Jenkins,
eds, *Le haut livre du Graal: Perlesvaus*, Oxford University Bodleian
library. MS. Hatton 82 (Chicago: The University of Chicago Press,
1932–7); Thomas E. Kelly, *Le haut livre du Graal: Perlesvaus; A
Structural Study* (Geneva, 1974).

71 Nitze and Jenkins, *Le haut livre du Graal: Perlesvaus*, I, 409, lines
10188–10192.

72 James P. Carley, 'A Glastonbury Translator at Work: Quedan Narracio
de nobili rege Arthuro and De Origine Gigantum in their Earliest
Manuscript Contexts', in *Glastonbury Abbey*, 340–4.

73 James P. Carley, 'A Fragment of Perlesvaus at Wells Cathedral Library',
309–35; Carley, 'A Glastonbury Translator at Work', 340.

74 Carley, 'A Fragment of Perlesvaus', 312.

75 Ceridwen Lloyd-Morgan, 'From Ynys Wydrin to Glasynberi: Glastonbury
in Welsh Vernacular Tradition', in Carley, *Glastonbury Abbey*, 161–77.
The name appears in various spellings and mutated forms (Lasynbri)
(G)lastynbri or (G)lassymbri.

76 Bromwich, *Trioedd Ynys Prydein*, 254–75; Lloyd-Morgan, 'From Ynys
Wydrin to Glasynberi', 163.

77 Lloyd-Morgan, 'From Ynys Wydrin to Glasynberi', 67–72.

78 Ibid., 175–6.

79 Dom Aelred Watkin, 'The Glastonbury Legend', in *Glastonbury Abbey*,
24; Kennedy, 'John Hardyng and the Holy Grail', 260.

Chapter 3 – *The Grail in Welsh Tradition*

1 'Peredur vab Efrog', in *The Mabinogion*, tr. Sioned Davies (Oxford:
Oxford University Press, 2007), 73.

2 Brynley F. Roberts, 'A Text in Transition', *Arthuriana* 10/3 (2000), 59–61;

the four texts of *Peredur* are found in *The White Book of Rhydderch* (MS. Peniarth 4), *The Red Book of Hergest* (MS. Oxford, Jesus College 111), Peniarth 7, Peniarth 14. See *Corff Electrinic o Ryddiaith Cymraeg Canol* / The Electronic Corpus of Medieval Welsh Prose, available online at. http://www.cardiff.ac.uk/cymraeg/welsh/research/CorffElectronig.shtml.

3 Charlotte Guest, *The Mabinogion from the Llyfr Coch o Hergest and other Ancient Welsh Mss*, 3 vols (London and Llandovery: Longmans, Rees, 1838–49); Revel Guest and Angela John, *Lady Charlotte: A Biography of the Nineteenth Century* (London: Weidenfeld & Nicolson 1989), 98.

4 Guest and John, *Lady Charlotte*, xv–xxiii, 92–119, 264–9; Juliette Wood, 'A Welsh Triad: Charlotte Guest, Marie Trevelyan, Mary Williams', in *Women and Tradition: A Neglected Group of Folklorists*, ed. Carmen Blacker and Hilda Davidson (Durham, NC: Carolina Academic Press, 2000), 259–76.

5 Guest, *The Mabinogion*, I, 375–6; III, 136; Roberts, 'A Text in Transition', 57–8.

6 Alfred Nutt, *The Mabinogion*, tr. Charlotte Guest, notes by Alfred Nutt (London: David Nutt, 1902).

7 Anne Ross, *Pagan Celtic Britain: Studies in Iconography and Tradition* (London: Cardinal, 1974), 94–171.

8 Richard Barber, *The Holy Grail: Imagination and Belief* (London: Allen Lane, 2004), 239.

9 Juliette Wood, 'Folk Narrative Research in Wales at the Beginning of the Twentieth Century: The Influence of John Rhŷs (1840–1916)', *Folklore* 116 (2005), 324–43.

10 John Rhŷs, *Studies in the Arthurian Legend* (Oxford: Clarendon Press, 1891), 303–11; John B. Marino, 'The Grail Legend in Modern Literature', *Arthurian Studies* 59 (Cambridge: Boydell & Brewer, 2004), 37, 50.

11 Rhŷs, *Arthurian Legend*, Preface.

12 Vincent Evans, 'The Late Right Honourable Sir John Rhŷs, Appreciation by Some of His Friends and Fellow-workers', *Transactions of the Honourable Society of Cymmrodorion* (1916), 223–5.

13 Charles Squire, *Mythology of the British Isles* (1920), intro. J. Wood (Kent: Wordsworth Editions, 2000). For Spence see Chapter 4.

14 Wood, 'A Welsh Triad', 259–76 ; M. Williams, *Essai sur la Composition du Roman Gallois de Peredur* (Diss., Paris 1909); *eadem*, 'The Story of Peredur: Its Sources', *Journal of the Welsh Bibliographical Society* 3 (1927), 73–81; *eadem*, 'Arthuriana: Chrétien's Perceval', in *Mélanges Bretons et Celtiques Offerts a M.J. Loth* (Rennes: Plihon et Hommay and Paris: Champion, 1927), 418–21.

15 Mary Williams, 'Some Aspects of the Grail Problem', *Folklore* 71 (1960), 85–103.

16 Mary Williams, 'The Dying God in Welsh Literature', *Revue Celtique* 46
    (1929), 167–214; *eadem*, 'The Keepers of the Threshold in the Romance
    of Perlesvaus', in *A Miscellany of Studies in Romance Languages &
    Literatures Presented to Leon E. Kastner*, ed. Mary Williams and James
    A. de Rothschild (Cambridge: W. Haffer, 1932), 560–67; *eadem*,
    'Apropos of an Episode in *Perlesvaus*', *Folklore* 43 (1937), 263–6;
    eadem, 'The Episode of the Copper Tower in the *Pelesvaus*', in *Mélanges
    à Rita Lejeaune* (Paris: Editions J. Duculot, 1969), 159–62.

17 A pamphlet among Williams's papers suggests that St David's Cathedral
    was built on the ruins of a Mithraic temple. *A Schedule of Papers Given
    and Bequeathed by Dr Mary Williams 1968–78* compiled by Ceridwen
    Lloyd Morgan (Aberystwyth: The National Library of Wales 1983).

18 Davies, *The Mabinogion*, 65–102; Guest, *The Mabinogion*, 183–227;
    Historia Peredur vab Efrawc, ed. Glenys Geotinck (Cardiff: University of
    Wales Press, 1976); Meirion Pennar, tr. *Historia Peredur vab Evrawc*,
    English and Welsh, a facsimile of the Welsh text, ed. J. Gwenogvryn
    Evans (Felinfach: Llanerch, 1991).

19 James Douglas Bruce, *The Evolution of Arthurian Romance from the
    Beginnings Down to the Year* 1300, 2nd edn, 2 vols (Baltimore: The
    Johns Hopkins University Press, 1928), vol. 1, 342–7; vol. 2, 59–74; Ian
    Lovécy, 'Historia Peredur ab Efrawg', in Rachel Bromwich, A. O. H.
    Jarman and Brynley F. Roberts, eds, *The Arthur of the Welsh: The
    Arthurian Legend in Medieval Welsh Literature* (Cardiff: University of
    Wales Press, 1991), 171–82; John K. Bollard, 'Theme and Meaning in
    Peredur', *Arthuriana* 10 (2000), 73–5; Ceridwen Lloyd Morgan,
    'Y Cyd–Destun Ewropeaidd', in Sioned Davies and Peter Wynn Thomas,
    eds, *Canhwyll marchogyon: cyd-destunoli Peredur* (Cardiff: University of
    Wales Press, 2000), 113–27.

20 Lovécy, 'Historia Peredur ab Efrawg', 173; W. A. Nitze, *Perceval and the
    Holy Grail* (Berkeley: University of California Press 1949); Roger
    Sherman Loomis, *The Grail: From Celtic Myth to Christian Symbol*
    (Cardiff: University of Wales Press, 1963); Glenys Goetinck, *Peredur: A
    Study of Welsh Tradition in the Grail Legends* (Cardiff: University of
    Wales Press, 1975); Jean Marx, 'Le cortège du château des merveilles
    dans le roman gallois de Peredur', *Etudes celtiques* 9 (1961), 92–108;
    idem, 'Observations sur la structure du roman gallois de Peredur', *Etudes
    Celtiques* 10 (1963), 88–108.

21 Stephen Knight, 'Resemblance and Menace: A Post-Colonial Reading of
    Peredur', in Davies and Thomas, *Canhwyll marchogyon*, 133–41.

22 John K. Bollard, 'Theme and Meaning in *Peredur*', 78.

23 Rachel Bromwich, *Trioedd Ynys Prydein, the Triads of the Island of Britain*,
    3rd edn (Cardiff: University of Wales Press, 2006), see 'Peredur', 478–9.

24 The romances of Owein and Gereint also have analogues in Chrétien.
    See Davies, *Mabinogion*, 116–78.

Notes

25 Barber, *The Holy Grail: Imagination and Belief*, 240; Roberts, 'A Text in Transition'; Ian Lovécy, 'The Celtic Sovereignty Theme and the Structure of Peredur', *Studia Celtica* 12/13 (1978), 133–46.

26 J. K. Bollard, 'Peredur: The Four Early Manuscripts', *Bulletin of the Board of Celtic Studies* 28 (1979), 365–72; Daniel Huws, 'Y Pedair Llawsgrif Ganoloesol', 1–9; and Peter Wyn Thomas, 'Cydberthynas Y Pedeir Fersiwn Ganoloesol', in Davies and Thomas, *Canhwyll marchogyon*, 10–49.

27 Roberts, 'A Text in Transition', 60–2; Brynley Roberts, 'Y Cydcyniad O Destun', in Davies and Thomas, *Canhwyll marchogyon*, 50–64.

28 Glenys Goetinck, *Peredur: A Study of Welsh Tradition in the Grail Legends* (Cardiff: University of Wales Press, 1975).

29 Goetinck, *Peredur*, 127, 130, 313–16; Marino, *The Grail Legend in Modern Literature*, 16–17; Lovécy, 'Historia Peredur ab Efrawg', 175–6, 179; Lovécy, 'The Celtic Sovereignty Theme', 139–45.

30 Bollard, 'Theme and Meaning in *Peredur*', 84–5; Knight, 'Resemblance and Menace', 137–8.

31 M. Williams, *Essai*, 18; Lovécy, 'Historia Peredur ab Efrawg', 172–3.

32 Ceridwen Lloyd-Morgan, '*Breuddwyd Rhonabwy* and Later Arthurian Literature', in Bromwich, Jarman and Roberts, *The Arthur of the Welsh*, 193–8, 203. According to a contemporary poem, Hopcyn ap Thomas owned a copy of 'Y Greal'.

33 *Y Seint Greal*, ed. Robert Williams (London, 1876; repr. Pwyllheli, 1987); Ceridwen Lloyd-Morgan, 'A Study of "Y Seint Greal" and "Percevel" in Wales: Late Medieval Welsh Grail Tradition', in Alison Adams, Armel H. Diverres, Karen Stern and Kenneth Varty, eds, *The Changing Face of Arthurian Romance* (Cambridge: Cambridge University Press 1986), 78–91; Ceridwen Uryd Morgan '*Breuddwyd Rhonabwy* and later Arthurian Literature', in Bromwich, Jarman and Roberts, *The Arthur of the Welsh*, 193–8.

34 Leslie Richards, ed. *Gwaith Dafydd Llwyd o Fathafarn* (Cardiff: University of Wales Press, 1964), 120. My thanks to Professor Helen Fulton for pointing this out to me.

35 Lloyd-Morgan, 'Breuddwyd', 200–02; Bromwich, *Trioedd*, Triads 81 and 86, 211–13, 225–7, 405–06.

36 Samuel Rush Meyrick, *The History and Antiquities of the County of Cardiganshire* (London: Longman 1809), xli, 254–65. In 1992, the Department of Further Education at Aberystwyth under the aegis of Gerald Morgan organized a conference on the history of the Nanteos estate. At that time the owners very kindly allowed me to examine the cup.

37 John Stow, *The Chronicles of England 1580, the Annals of England ...* till 1592. (London 1605), f. 572a; NLW 3297B, 'Archaeological Notes and Queries: The Cup at Nanteos, Cardiganshire', *Archaeologia Cambrensis* 5 (1888), 5th ser., 170–1.

38 Bruce Rosenberg, *Custer and the Epic of Defeat* (Harrisburg:

Pennsylvania State University Press, 1964), 217–50.

39 Sidney Wright, *Up the Claerwen* (Birmingham: Cornish Bros 1948), 61; S. M. Powell, 'Pilgrim Routes to Strata Florida', *Cardiganshire Antiquarian Society Transactions* 8 (1931), 9–24.

40 Thomas Nicholas, *Annals and Antiquities*, vols 1 and 2 (London, 1872), 168; Meyrick, *Antiquities of Cardiganshire*, 265.

41 Powell family correspondence, The National Library of Wales Handlist vol. 3 no. 4624–4996. See letter no 4624; S. W. Gentle-Cackett, *The Antioch Cup* (London: Bible Lands Mission Aids Society, 1935), 7, 23–7.

42 'Catalogue of the Local Museum Exhibited in the Hall of St David's College 1878', *Archaeologia Cambrensis* 10 (1879), 4th ser., 66; 'Report of the Lampeter Meeting', *Archaeologia Cambrensis* 9 (1878), 4th ser., 337–9; Stephen J. Williams, 'The Cup at Nanteos', *Archaeologia Cambrensis* 5 (1888), 170–1.

43 *Archaeologia Cambrensis* 5 (1888) 170–2; Stephen J. Williams, *The Cistercian Abbey of Strata Florida: Its History, and an Account of the Recent Excavations Made on Its Site* (London: Whiting, 1889).

44 George Eyre Evans, *Cardiganshire Antiquarian Transactions* 12 (1937), 29–30; another description of the *Cwpan Nanteos* occurs in the folklore section of the same number, 58.

45 Juliette Wood, 'Nibbling Pilgrims and the Nanteos Cup: A Cardiganshire Legend', in Gerald Morgan, ed., *Nanteos: A Welsh House and its Families* (Llandysul: Gomer, 2001), 137–50: Ethelwyn M. Amery, *Sought and Found* (n.p. 1905; repr. 1910).

46 See Chapter 2 for a discussion of Archbishop's Ussher's ideas and the role of Lionel Smithett Lewis at Glastonbury. *The National Library of Wales Handlist*: Powell family correspondence no. 4778–4793.

47 Samuel Williams, *The Aberystwyth Guide* (Aberystwyth, 1816), 126–8; John E. Lloyd, *A Guide to Walks and Places of Interest Around Aberystwyth* (Aberystwyth, 1885).

48 *Aberystwyth, Official Guide and Souvenir*, issued by Aberystwyth Corporation (Gloucester, 1923), 89; *Official Guide* (1924), 80; *Official Guide* (1934), 47–8.

49 *Nanteos Historic Monument* (Aberystwyth, 1966), 7–8.

50 S. M. Powell (1931) 'Pilgrim Routes to Strata Florida', 9–24.

51 'A Welsh Relic' by JJB, *The Church Times*, vol. 55, no. 2247, 16 February 1906, 195.

52 Personal communications from Aberystwyth University students; Emily Pritchard Cary, 'In Search of Noah's Ark, Mary's Grave and the Holy Grail', *Y Drych*, September 1995, 14; 'More of the Nanteos Cup', *Y Drych*, March 1996.

53 Bob Danvers-Walker, 'Is the Holy Grail in Wales? The Chalice of Nanteos', photocopy n.d.; John Cottrell, 'My Search for the Holy Grail', photocopy

n.d.; Peter Bloxham, 'Is this the Cup that was Used at the Last Supper?', *Sunday Express*, 1 August 1961; A. G. Prys-Jones, 'The Healing Cup of Nanteos', *Western Mail*, 17 March 1953.

54 Douglas Hague, Royal Commission on Ancient Monuments in Wales NLW ex 720, 'An Object of Romantic History', *Cambrian News*, 13 May 1988, 'Report on Nanteos Cup 16/3/85', Handlist, vol. 3, 60.

55 *Church Times*, 195; Bloxham, *Sunday Express*, 1961.

56 David Salmon, 'The Nanteos Cup', *Notes & Queries* 26 (October 1940), 174, 295.

57 E. R. Horsfall-Turner, *Walks and Wanderings in County Cardigan* (Bingley: T. Harrison & Sons, 1902 (?)), 25; *Archaeologia Cambrensis*, (1888), 170–1.

58 See Powell correspondence no. 4784–4790.

59 Frederick Blight, 'The Nanteos Cup', *Western Mail*, 21 March 1953; 'The Future of the Nanteos Cup', *Country Life*, 12 November 1967; Byron Rogers, *The Bank Manager and the Holy Grail* (London: Aurum Press, 2003).

60 Fortean TV, Channel 4; broadcast March 1997.

61 Jacqueline Simpson, 'Rationalising Motifs and Contemporary Legends', *Folklore* 92/2 (1981), 203–07.

62 Richard Dorson, *Folklore and Fakelore: Essays Toward a Discipline of Folk Studies* (Cambridge, MA: Harvard University Press, 1976).

63 Charles R. Beard, *Lucks and Talismans: A Chapter of Popular Superstition.* (London: Sampson Marston and Co., 1934).

64 *Archaeologia Cambrensis* (1879), 99, 140.

65 *Western Mail*, A. G. Prys-Jones, 17 March 1953, Blight, 'The Nanteos Cup', 21 March 1953. Continuing interest in the Nanteos cup is reflected in an ever-changing array of Internet sites. See, for example, 'My Search for the Holy Grail (the Nanteos Cup)' at http://www.bbc.co.uk/wales/mid/sites/weird/pages/nanteos.shtml (accessed 8 May 2006).

66 'The Nanteos Cup,' *Country Life*, 12 November 1967.

67 Bloxham, *Sunday Express*, 1 August 1961.

68 D. Silvan Evans and John Jones, *Ysten Sioned* (Aberystwyth, 1882), 83–5.

69 E. B. Morris, 'Ystrad Fflur', *Cymru* (1907), 85–90. This magazine published a range of articles on poetry, folklore and other matters of Welsh interest aimed at a literate Welsh-speaking readership.

70 Arthur Machen, 'The Great Return', in *Holy Terrors: Collected Short Stories* (London: Penguin, 1946), 108–40; R. A. Gilbert, 'Arthur Machen and A. E. Waite: A Forgotten Collaboration', *Antiquarian Book Monthly Review*, 11/4 (April 1976), 7–8.

71 See Chapter 4. R. A. Gilbert, *A. E. Waite: A Magician of Many Parts* (Wellingborough: Crucible, 1987), 159.

72 Gilbert, 'Arthur Machen and A. E. Waite'. A similar theory about the

Grail as a powerful religious talisman belonging to a Welsh saint was put
forward by Professor Mary Williams.

73 Tudor Pole dismissed the Nanteos cup, while Arthur Machen rejected
Tudor Pole's 'Bristol Grail'. Rosamund Lehmann, *My Dear Alexias,
Letters from Wellesley Tudor Pole to Rosamund Lehmann* (Sudbury:
Neville Spearman, 1979), 135, 183; Oliver Villiers, *Wellesley Tudor Pole:
Appreciation and Valuation* (Canterbury: Hardcastle, 1968), 26–9;
Arthur Machen: Selected Letters, ed. R. Dobson and R. A. Gilbert
(Wellingborough: The Aquarian Press, 1988), 38.

74 Graham Phillips, *The Search for the Grail* (London: Century, 1995),
idem, The Marian Conspiracy (London: Sidgewick and Jackson, 2000);
Andrew Collins, *Twenty-First Century Grail: The Quest for a Legend*
(London: Virgin Books, 2004).

75 J. F. Matthews, 'Olympiodorus of Thebes and the History of the West',
Journal of Roman Studies (1970), 79–80, 91–3.

76 R. C. Blockley, *The Fragmentary Classicising Historians of the Later
Roman Empire (1981–3)*, vol. I, part I, 40–1; vol. II, 171–3; Photius,
Biblioteca or Myriobiblion, Cod. 1–165, Tr. Freese section 80. See
http://www.ccel.org/p/pearse/morefathers/photius_03biblioteca.htm
(accessed 6 November 2005).

77 http://www.grahamphillips.net/Books/Grail.htm (accessed 23 July 2007).

78 Justin Griffin, *The Holy Grail: The Legend, the History, the Evidence*
(London: McFarland, 2001).

79 *Autobiography of Thomas Wright of Birkenshaw in the County of York
1736–1797 Edited by His Grandson Thomas Wright* (London: J. R.
Smith, 1864).

80 *The History and Antiquities of the Town of Ludlow and Its Ancient
Castle by Thomas Wright of Ludlow* (Ludlow: Proctor and Jones, 1822;
1st edn c.1822; 2nd edn 1826).

81 The source for Wright's edition was British Museum MS. Reg.12, c.xii;
Fouke le Fitz Waryn, ed. E. J. Hathaway *et al.*, Anglo-Norman Text
Society (Oxford: Blackwell, 1975); *The History of Fulk fitz-Warine* tr.
Alice Kemp-Welch, intro. Louis Brandin (Cambridge: Ontario, 2001).

82 See notes 16, 18, 77 in Wright's edition of *The History of Fulk fitz-
Warine*, 'The White Land was evidently the district around Wittington,
but I have not met with the name elsewhere applied to it'; Wittington
from the Anglo-Saxon name 'Hwitta', *English Place Name Society*,
vol.62/63, 312, part I.

83 Robert William Eyton, *Antiquities of Shropshire* (London: John Russell
Smith, 1854–60); Joseph Morris, 'The Family of Fitz-Warine', *Transactions
of the Shropshire Archaeological Society*, 1st ser. 5 (1882), 214–50.

84 Thomas Wright, 'The Local Legends of Shropshire', Collectanea
Archaeologica: communications made to the British Archaeological
Association 1 (1862), 50–66.

85 Thomas Wright, ed., *Fouke le Fitz Waryn & Early English Miscellanies in Prose and Verse*, ed. J. O. Halliwell (London: Warton Club, 1855); *idem, Early Christianity in Arabia: A Historical Essay* (London: Bernard Quaritch, 1855). No such volume appears in Wright's entry in the *Dictionary of National Biography*, nor among the list of Wright's publications in British copyright libraries, such as the British Library, the Bodleian Library, Oxford, or the National Library of Wales, the National Library of Scotland; nor among the considerable material held at the Shropshire Record Office. 'Thomas Wright' s.v., *Dictionary of National Biography*, ed. Brian Harrison and H. C. G. Matthew (Oxford: Oxford University Press, 2004); Shropshire Record Office. I would like to express my thanks to the librarians for making all the Thomas Wright material available to me.

86 William Cathrall, *History of Oswestry* (Oswestry: George Lewis, 1855). See bottom of the final page for comparison, www.grahamphillips.net/newGrail/ (accessed 5 July 2007).

87 *Early English Miscellanies in Prose and Verse,* ed. J. O. Halliwell (London: Warton Club, 1855). The Warton Club edition has both works bound together, but they do occur separately, which only adds to the confusion.

88 D. H. S. Cranage, *An Architectural Account of the Churches of Shropshire* (Wellington: Shropshire Hobson and Co., 1894–1912), part 8. In 1846 extensive restoration to the church was carried out under the auspices of Mr Algernon Heber-Percy.

89 Wright's comments are included among the occasional papers. *Narratives of Sorcery and Magic, from the Most Authentic Sources,* 2 vols (London: R. Bentley, 1851); see vol. 1, 41.

90 See *Early Christianity in Arabia,* 1855.

91 *Narratives of Sorcery and Magic,* vol. 1, n. 41.

92 Peter Partner, *The Knights Templar and Their Myth* (Rochester: Destiny Books, 1987), 166–7; Thomas Wright, ed., *A Discourse of the Worship of Priapus by Richard Payne Knight. Essay on the Generative Powers during the Middle Ages* (London: printed privately, 1865).

93 Collins, *Twenty-first Century* Grail, 186–95.

94 Ibid., 190.

95 Partner, *The Knights Templar and Their Myth,* 62–6.

96 http://www.catholic.net/RCC/Periodicals/Inside/sep95/rome1.html (accessed 20 June 2007).

97 *Y Greal* (London: S. Rousseau, 1805–07).

98 William Owen Pughe, *Dictionary of the Welsh Language* (London: E. Williams, 1803).

99 Tom Parry, *Saint Greal y chwedl wedi ei hailadrodd* (Llandysul: Gwasg Gomer, 1933).

100 Edward Tegla Davies, *Y Greal Sanctaidd* (Wrecsam: Hughes, 1922).

101 John Dyfnallt Owen, Y *Greal a cherddi eraill* (Gwasg Aberystwyth, 1946), 9–46.
102 Gereint Elfyn Jones, *Bywyd a Gwaith John Dyfnallt Owen* (Swansea: Ty John Penry, 1976), 43–6.
103 Lewis Spence, *Mysteries of Britain* (London: Rider, 1928) ch. 10, 'On the Writings of Morien', www.morien-intitute.or/morieniog.html (accessed 15 January 2006).
104 Owen Morgan (Morien), *The Light of Britannia, the Mysteries of Ancient British Druidism Unveiled* (Cardiff: Daniel Owen, 1894); *idem, The Royal Winged Son of Stonehenge and Avebury* (Pontypridd, 1911); *idem, A History of Wales from the Earliest Period, Including Hitherto Unrecorded Antiquarian Lore* (Liverpool: Edward Howell, 1911).
105 Owen Morgan, *The Light of Britannia*, ch. 5.
106 John Michael Greer, 'Phallic Religion in the Druid Revival', 12, the Order of Bards Ovates & Druids Mount Haemus Lecture for the year 2003, available online at http://www.druid.org/pdfs/third_mt_haemus_lecture/pdf.
107 Partner, *The Knights Templar and Their Myth*, 166–7; Wright, *A Discourse of the Worship of Priapus*.
108 Mark Valentine, *Arthur Machen* (Bridgend: Wales Poetry Press, 1995); Marino, *The Grail Legend in Modern Literature*, 124–30.
109 Arthur Machen, *War and the Christian Faith* (Steffington, 1918); Wesley D. Sweetser, *Arthur Machen* (New York: Twayne, 1964), 37–8.
110 'The Holy Things', 75–8, in *Holy Terrors: Short Stories by Arthur Machen* (Harmondsworth: Penguin, 1946); Arthur Machen, *Things Near and Far* (London: Richards Press, 1951).
111 Arthur Machen, *The Secret of the Sangraal: A Collection of Writings* (East Sussex: Tartarus Press, 1994); *idem,* 'The Secret of the Sangraal', 1–39; *idem,* 'Celtic Magic', 142–5; *idem,* 'The Holy Graal', 146–50; *idem,* 'The Holy Grail', 228–32.
112 'Chapter V and VI of *The Secret Glory*', (East Sussex: Tartarus Press, 1991), 86.
113 Arthur Machen, *The Secret Glory* (East Sussex: Tartarus Press, 1998), 252. Machen kept notebooks on the Grail, and these included material on the Nanteos cup. *Arthur Machen: Selected Letters*, ed. Dobson and Gilbert, 40–1; Sweetser, *Arthur Machen*, 32–4.
114 'The Great Return', in *Holy Terrors*, 108–40.
115 Machen, *Things Near and Far* (1927); Sweetser, *Arthur Machen*, 33, 63.
116 Gilbert, 'Arthur Machen and A. E. Waite', 7–8; A. E. Waite, *The Holy Grail: Its Legends and Symbolism* (London: Rider. 1933), 615. He refers to the 'enchanting essay by my familiar friend of more than forty years'; *Arthur Machen: Selected Letters*, ed. Dobson and Gilbert, 31–81.
117 Arthur Machen, *The Secret of the Sangraal*, 20–30, 391, 48–9; *Arthur Machen: Selected Letters*, ed. Dobson and Gilbert, 42–3.

118 David Jones, *The Anathemata* (London: Faber, 1952; repr, with corrections 1955); *idem, In Parenthesis* (London: Faber, 1937); *idem, The Sleeping Lord and Other Fragments* (London: Faber, 1974).

119 Joe Moffett, 'Anglo-Saxon and Welsh Origins in David Jones's *The Anathemata*', *North American Journal of Welsh Studies* 6/1 (Winter 2006), 1–6.

120 *The Anathemata*, 17, 20.

121 There is a substantial body of criticism on Jones's use of myth in his poetry. See for example Jeremy Hooker, 'David Jones and the Matter of Wales', in David Blamires, *David Jones: Artist and Writer*, 2nd edn (Manchester: Manchester University Press, 1978), 11–25.

122 Muriel Whitaker, 'The Arthurian Art of David Jones', *Arthuriana* 7/3 (Autumn 1997), 137–56. A drawing of the journey to the Chapel Perilous exists in private hands.

123 David Jones, 'The Arthurian Legend', in *Epoch and Artist* (London: Faber, 1959), 216. The essay originally appeared as a review of *The Arthurian Torso* for *The Tablet* in 1946.

124 Harman Griseweed, ed., *Epoch and Artist: Selected Writings by David Jones*, 203, 205, 221.

Chapter 4 – Celtic Origins and the Grail Romances

1 *The Golden Bough*, 3rd edn, 13 vols (London: Macmillan, 1906–15; 1st edn 1890; abridged edn, Robert Fraser, Oxford: Oxford University Press, 1994); Robert Fraser, *The Making of the Golden Bough: The Origins and Growth of an Argument* (Basingstoke: Palgrave, 2001).

2 As late as 1922, the abridged edition of *The Golden Bough* suppressed this material.

3 Alfred Nutt, *Studies in the Legend of the Holy Grail: With Especial Reference to the Hypothesis of Its Celtic Origin* (London: David Nutt, 1888); Richard M. Dorson, *The British Folklorists* (Chicago: University of Chicago Press, 1968); Richard Barber, *The Holy Grail: Imagination and Belief* (London: Allen Lane, 2004), 233–40. Dr John Carey's new study, *Ireland and the Grail* (Aberystwyth: Celtic Studies Publication, 2007), appeared too late to be included in the research for this book, but it offers a comprehensive reassessment of the Irish texts suggested as sources for the Grail story.

4 Jessie Weston, 'Obituary for Alfred Nutt (1856–1910)', *Folklore* 21 (1910), 512–14.

5 Juliette Wood, 'Alfred Nutt: Publisher and Folklorist', *Folklore* 110 (1999), 3–12.

6 Alfred Nutt, 'The Aryan Expulsion and Return Formula in the Folk and

Hero Tales of the Celts', *Folklore* 4 (1881), 1–44; *Folklore* 5 (1881), 147–9; *idem*, 'Monsieur Sébillot's Scheme for the Collection and Classification of Folklore', *Folklore Review* 3, section ii (1881), 195–200; *idem*, 'Folklore Terminology', *Folklore Journal* (1884), 2, 311–15.

7 Alfred Nutt, 'Recent Archaeological Research-no II-Folk-lore', *Archaeological Review* 3 (1889), 79, 88.

8 Nutt, 'Monsieur Sébillot's scheme', 'Folklore Terminology,' *Folklore Journal* (1884), 311–15; 'Jottings from the South-west of Ireland', *Folklore Journal* 1 (1883), 330; Douglas Hyde, *Beside the Fire: A Collection of Irish Gaelic Folk Stories* (London: David Nutt, 1890). Nutt's introduction to Hyde's collection of Irish folktales emphasized the importance of collecting.

9 Dorson, *The British Folklorists*, 393–401, 419–26, 432–6.

10 Jessie Laidley Weston, tr.: *Wolfram von Eschenbach's Parzival*, 2 vols (London: David Nutt, 1894), *Four lais: Guningamor, Lanval, Tyolet, Bisclaveret*, Arthurian Romances 3 (London: David Nutt, 1900), *Morien, A Metrical Romance Translated from the Mediaeval Dutch*, Arthurian Romances 4 (London: David Nutt, 1901); *Sir Gawain at the Grail Castle*, Arthurian Romances 6 (London: David Nutt, 1904); *The Legend of Sir Gawain*, Grimm Library 7 (London: David Nutt, 1897); *The Legend of Sir Lancelot du lac*, Grimm Library 12 (London: David Nutt,1901); *The Three Days Tournament: A Study in Romance and Folk-lore*, Grimm Library 15 (London: David Nutt, 1902); *The Legend of Sir Perceval: Studies upon its Origin, Development, and Position in the Arthurian Cycle*, Grimm Library 17, 19, 2 vols (London: David Nutt, 1906–09); *King Arthur and His Knights*, Popular Studies 4 (London: David Nutt, 1905).

11 Eleanor Hull, *Pagan Ireland* (London: David Nutt, 1904); *eadem*, *Early Christian Ireland* (London: David Nutt, 1905).

12 Sean O'Luing, *Kuno Meyer 1858–1919, A Biography* (Dublin: Geography Publications, 1991), 17; Nutt, *Legends of the Holy Grail*, Romance Popular Studies 14 (London: David Nutt, 1902).

13 A significant portion of Nutt's output deals with matters relating to Celtic culture and to the Grail. See for example, 'Mabinogion Studies: Branwen Daughter of Lyr', *Folklore Review* 5 (1882–3), 1–32, 149–50; 'Les derniers travaux allemands sur la legends du Saint Graal', *Folklore* (1891), 2, i–xlviii; 'The Legend of the Buddha's Alms Dish and the Legend of the Holy Grail', *Archaeological Review* 3 (1889), 267–71; *Studies in the Legend of the Holy Grail; The Influence of Celtic upon Medieval Romance*, Popular Studies in Mythology Romance and Folklore 1 (London: David Nutt, 1899); *The Legends of the Holy Grail*, Popular Studies in Mythology Romance and Folklore 14 (1902); Notes and Appendix to Matthew Arnold, *On the Study of Celtic Literature* (London: David Nutt, 1900); Lady Charlotte Guest, *The Mabinogion:*

Mediaeval Welsh Romances with notes by Alfred Nutt (London: David Nutt, 1902).

14 John B. Vickery, *The Literary Impact of the Golden Bough* (Princeton: Princeton University Press, 1973), 5–7, 5–13.

15 Nutt, 'The Fairy Mythology of English Literature: Its Origin and Nature', Presidential Address, *Folklore* 8 (1897), 29–53.

16 Nutt, 'Recent Archaeological Research- no II-Folk-lore', 88.

17 Dorson, *British Folklorists*, 229–39; Nutt, Notes and Appendix to Matthew Arnold, *On the Study of Celtic Literature*; John B. Marino, *The Grail Legend in Modern Literature* (Cambridge: D. S. Brewer, 2004), 33.

18 'The Influence of Celtic upon Medieval Romance', *Popular Studies in Mythology, Romance and Folklore* 1 (1899).

19 See 'Prieddeu Annwn', Theodore de la Villemarqué, *Contes populaires bretons* (Paris: W. Coquebert, 1842), 192–4.

20 Ernest Renan, *Essais de morale et de critique* (Paris, 1859); Barber, *The Holy Grail: Imagination and Belief*, 241–2.

21 See Chapter 3.

22 Sabine Baring-Gould, *Curious Myths of the Middle Ages* (Dover edn, 1976; 1st edn 1866 and 1868; new enlarged edn 1901), 16–22.

23 Baring-Gould, *Curious Myths*, 17–19.

24 Ibid., 20, 37, 45, 67, 617–27.

25 Arthur C. L. Brown, *The Origin of the Grail Legend* (Cambridge, MA: Harvard University Press, 1943), 25–9, 35, 449–50.

26 Barber, *The Holy Grail: Imagination and Belief*, 245–6.

27 Roger Sherman Loomis, *Arthurian Tradition and Chrétien de Troyes* (New York: Columbia University Press, 1949), 373.

28 Barber, *The Holy Grail: Imagination and Belief*, 245–6; Roger Sherman Loomis, *Celtic Myth and Arthurian Romance* (New York: Columbia Press, 1927; rev. 1935), 24–38, 139–310.

29 Roger Sherman Loomis, *Wales and the Arthurian Legend* (Cardiff: University of Wales Press, 1956); *idem*, ed., *Arthurian Literature in the Middle Ages* (Oxford: Clarendon Press, 1959); *idem*, *The Grail: From Celtic Myth to Christian Symbol* (Cardiff: University of Wales Press, 1963).

30 Loomis, *Celtic Myth and Arthurian Romance*, 263–70; *idem*, *From Celtic Myth to Christian Symbol*, 51–4; *idem*, 'The Irish Origin and Welsh Development of the Grail', *Speculum* (1933), 19–41.

31 Raymond J. Cormier, 'Tradition and Sources: The Jackson/Loomis Controversy Re-examined', *Folklore* 83 (1972), 101–21: the number of popular books for which this is still a basic assumption is too great to list. See Juliette Wood, 'Secret Traditions in the Modern Tarot: Folklore and the Occult Revival', *3rd Stone Archaeology, Folklore and Myth* 39 (2000/2001), 26–31.

32 Michael J. Bell, 'The Relation of Mentality to Race: William Wells Newell and the Celtic Hypothesis', *Journal of American Folklore* 92/363 (1979), 25–43; William Wells Newell, *King Arthur and the Table Round* (Boston: Houghton Mifflin, 1897).

33 A. Birch-Hirshfeld, *Die saga von Gral* (Liepsig: Vogel 1877).

34 Lisette Andrews Fisher, *The Mystic Vision in the Grail legend and in the Divine Comedy* (1917; repr. New York: AMS, 1966).

35 Marino, *The Grail Legend in Modern Literature*, 42.

36 Urban T. Holmes and M. Amelia Klenke, *Chrétien Troyes and the Grail* (Chapel Hill: University of North Carolina Press, 1959).

37 James Douglas Bruce, *Arthurian Romance from the Beginnings down to the Year 1300* (Baltimore: The Johns Hopkins University Press, 1922), 257–60.

38 Barber, *The Holy Grail: Imagination and Belief*, 243, 248–9; Marino, *The Grail Legend in Modern Literature*, 44–7.

39 Raymond J. Cormier, 'The Jackson-Loomis Controversy', *Folklore*, 101–21; Joseph Keller, 'Paradigm Shifts in the Grail Scholarship of Jessie Weston and R. S. Loomis: A View from Linguistics', *Arthurian Interpretations* 1 (1987), 10–22.

40 See Alan Bruford, *Gaelic Folktale and Medieval Romance* (Dublin: Folklore of Ireland Society, 1969).

41 Nutt, *The Legends of the Holy Grail*, iv.

42 See Chapter 2.

43 Robert Fraser, *The Making of The Golden Bough*.

44 Juliette Wood, 'The Creation of the Celtic Tarot', *Folklore* 109 (1998), 15–24; and 'Folklore Studies at the Celtic Dawn: Alfred Nutt: Publisher and Folklorist', *Folklore* 110 (1999), 3–12.

45 William A Nitze, 'The Fisher King in the Grail Romance', *Publications of the Modern Language Association* (1909), 411–13; Jessie Weston, 'The Grail and the Rites of Adonis', *Folklore* 18 (1907), 283–305.

46 Weston, 'The Nant Eos Healing Cup', *The Church Times*, no. 2, 248, vol. 55, 23 February 1906.

47 Jessie Weston, *From Ritual to Romance* (1925; repr. Princeton: Princeton University Press, 1993); Janet Grayson, 'In Quest of Jessie Weston', *Arthurian Literature* 11, ed. Richard Barber (Cambridge: Boydell and Brewer, 1992), 1–80; Marino, *The Grail Legend in Modern Literature*, 45–7.

48 Weston, *From Ritual to Romance*, 186–7.

49 Weston, *The Legend of Sir Perceval*, chs 10 and 11, 249 n. 1, 253 n. 1.

50 Annie Besant, *Esoteric Christianity* (London: Theosophical Publishing Society 1905); Weston, *The Legend of Sir Perceval*, 253 n. 1, 296 n. 1.

51 G. R. S. Mead, *Fragments of a Faith Forgotten* (London: Theosophical Publishing Society 1906); Weston, *The Legend of Sir Perceval*, 256 nn.1, 2, 3; 257 n. 2; 312 n. 1.

52 Edward Cowan, *Alba: Celtic Scotland in the Middle Ages* (East Linton: Tuckwell Press, 2000), 4; Richard J. Finlay. *Independent and Free: Scottish Politics and the Origins of the Scottish National Party 1918–45* (Edinburgh: John Donald, 1994), 38–40.

53 Lewis Spence, *Myth and Ritual in Dance, Game and Rhyme* (London: Watts, 1947); *idem*, 'The Secret Tradition in Britain: Its Sources and Affinities', *The Occult Review* (April 1940), 99–103; *idem*, 'The Arcane Cult of Arthur', *The Occult Review* (July 1940), 145–49; *idem*, 'Occult Centres of Scotland', *The Occult Review* (October 1940), 196–8.

54 Lewis Spence, *The Magic Arts in Celtic Britain* (London: Rider, 1945), 7–13.

55 Ibid., 115–20.

56 Spence, *Will Europe Follow Atlantis?* (London: Rider, 1942); *idem*, *The Occult Causes of the Present War* (London: Rider, 1940); *idem*, *The Occult Sciences in Atlantis* (London: Rider, 1943).

57 Spence, *Will Europe Follow Atlantis?*, 17–18; *idem*, *The Occult Sciences in Atlantis*, 167–85.

58 Spence, *Occult Sciences*, 230.

59 Spence, *Will Europe Follow Atlantis*, 18–19, 160, 166–85.

60 Spence, 'The Secret Tradition in Britain', 99–102.

61 Spence, 'Arcane Cult of Arthur', 146–7.

62 A. E. Waite, *The Hidden Church of the Holy Grail* (London: Rider, 1909); R. A. Gilbert, *A. E. Waite: A Magician of Many Parts* (Wellingborough: Crucible, 1987), 159.

63 Michael Dummett, *The Game of Tarot* (London: Duckworth, 1980), 10–19.

64 R. A. Gilbert, 'Arthur Machen and A. E. Waite: A Forgotten Collaboration', *Antiquarian Book Monthly Review* 11/4 (April 1976), 7–8; idem, *Magician of Many Parts*, 6–10; Roger Dobson, Godfrey Brangham and R. A. Gilbert, eds, *Arthur Machen: Selected Letters* (Wellingborough: Aquarian Press, 1988), 34–47.

65 A. E. Waite, *The Pictorial Key to the Tarot: Being Fragments of a Secret Tradition under the Veil of Divination* (New Hyde Park, NY: University Books, 1951), 59–71; *idem*, *The Secret Tradition of Freemasonry*, 2 vols (London: Rebman, 1911), II, 379;
R. A. Gilbert, ed., *The Hermetic Papers of A. E. Waite* (Wellingborough: Aquarian Press, 1987), 59–71.

66 'The Hidden Sacrament of the Holy Grail: A Mystery Play', in *Strange Houses of Sleep* (London: Welby, 1906), 140ff; Dobson *et al.*, *Arthur Machen: Selected Letters*, 34–47.

67 Alex Owen, *The Place of Enchantment: British Occultism and the Culture of the Modern* (Chicago and London; University of Chicago Press, 2004), 82–4.

68 Waite's revised tarot is referred to as 'The Rider Pack' or the Waite/Colman pack.

69 Dummett, *Game of Tarot*, 114–20; Alphonse Louis Constant (Eliphas Levi), *The Mysteries of Magic: A Digest of the Writings of Eliphas Levi*, tr. A. E. Waite (London: Temple Chambers, 1894); idem, *Transcendental Magic: Its Doctrine and Ritual*, tr. A.E. Waite (London: Redway, 1896); idem, *The History of Magic:* tr. with notes by A. E. Waite (London: Rider, 1913).

70 Waite, *The Pictorial Key to the Tarot*, 128–31; Juliette Wood, 'The Creation of the Celtic Tarot', *Folklore* 109 (1998), 15–24; eadem, 'Secret Traditions in the Modern Tarot: Folklore and the Occult Revival', 26–31.

71 Richard Cavendish, *The Tarot* (London: Chancellor Press, 1975), 26, 29–30; Christopher McIntosh, *Eliphas Levi and the French Occult Revival* (London: Rider, 1972), 104–06, 111–15; *Eliphas Levi: Letters to a Disciple*, tr. Bertram Keightley, intro. Christopher McIntosh (Wellingborough: Aquarian Press, 1980), 102; Kathleen Raine, *Yeats: The Tarot and the Golden Dawn* (Dublin: Dolmen Press, 1972), 59, illustration; Dummett, *Game of Tarot*, 76.

72 Waite, *The Hidden Church of the Holy Grail* (London: Redway, 1909), 600–14; idem, *The Pictorial Key to the Tarot*, 81–3; S. Y. Edgerton, *Pictures and Punishment: Art and Criminal Prosecution during the Florentine Renaissance* (Ithaca: Cornell University Press, 1985), 86–7; Dummett, *Game of Tarot*, 124.

73 Paul Huson, *The Devil's Picturebook* (New York: Putman and Sons, 1971), 200–02; *Eliphas Levi: Letters to a Disciple*, 102; Anne-Marie Ferguson, *A Keeper of Words,* Handbook for *Legend: The Arthurian Tarot* (St Paul, MN: Llewelyn, 1995), 77–8; Raine, *Yeats: The Tarot and the Golden Dawn*, 40–4; Cavendish, *The Tarot*, 106, Weston, *The Legend of Sir Perceval*, xxi–xxviii.

74 Howard Bayley, *A New Light on the Renaissance Displayed in Contemporary Emblems* (London: Dent and Co., 1909), 232; idem, *The Lost Language of Symbolism*, 2 vols (London: Williams and Norgate, 1851), 247–50.

75 Bayley, *A New Light*, 262–3.

76 Ibid., 65–78, and *The Lost Language of Symbolism*, 245–58; Waite, *Pictorial Key*, 10–11.

77 Steven Runciman, *The Medieval Manichee* (Cambridge: Cambridge University Press, 1947), Appendix.

78 Waite, *The Holy Grail: Its Legends and Symbolism* (London: Rider, 1933), 607.

79 Nutt, *Studies in the Legend of the Holy Grail*, 124, 209; Waite, *The Holy Grail: Its Legends and Symbolism*, 607.

80 Waite, *The Hidden Church of the Holy Grail*, 600–14; idem, *The Pictorial Key to the Tarot*, 299–305; idem, *The Holy Grail: Its Legends and Symbolism* (1933), 572–4.

81 Waite, *Key* booklet, 158. The booklet has the same dimensions as the

original Rider pack and may have accompanied the cards.

82 John and Caitlin Matthews, *The Arthurian Tarot: A Hallowquest Handbook* (Wellingborough: Aquarian Press, 1990) 128; Weston, *The Legend of Sir Perceval*, 79 n. 20; Waite, *The Holy Grail: Its Legends and Symbolism*, 574.

83 Huson, *Devil's Picturebook*, 251; John and Caitlin Matthews, *Hallowquest: Tarot Magic and the Arthurian Mysteries* (Wellingborough: Aquarian Press, 1990), 106; Ferguson, *A Keeper of Words*, 16–19.

84 Waite, 'Romance of the Holy Grail', *The Quest* (1909), 90–107.

85 Weston, *The Legend of Sir Perceval*, 77–9.

86 Ibid., 94.

87 Raine, *Yeats: The Tarot and the Golden Dawn*, 17–22; W. B. Yeats, *Stories of Red Hanrahan* (London: A. H. Bullen, 1913).

88 Charles Williams, *The Greater Trumps* (London: Paladin, 1989). My thanks to the late John Heath-Stubbs for pointing out that Williams's papers included one of Waite's pamphlets on the tarot.

89 Tom Gibbons, 'The Wasteland Tarot Identified', *Journal of Modern Literature* 2 (1972), 560–4.

90 Wood, 'The Creation of the Celtic Tarot', *Folklore* 109 (1998), 15–24.

91 Frances Yates, *The Rosicrucian Enlightenment* (London: Routledge & Kegan Paul, 1972).

Chapter 5 – Secret Relics and Hidden Codes

1 Umberto Eco, *Foucault's Pendulum*, tr. William Weaver (New York: Harcourt Brace Jovanovich, 1989).

2 Peter Partner, *The Knights Templar and Their Myth* (Rochester: Destiny Books, 1990), 92–5, 100–01.

3 Jonathan Sumption, *The Albigensian Crusade* (London: Faber and Faber, 1999), 48–9; Malcolm Barber, *The New Knighthood: History of the Order of the Temple* (Cambridge: Cambridge University Press, 1994), ch. 3.

4 Barber, *The New Knighthood*, 211 n. 20; Michael Baigent, Richard Leigh and Henry Lincoln, *The Holy Blood and the Holy Grail* (London: Corgi, 1984), 42. Although the authors admit that the phrase may be apocryphal, nevertheless they feel it typifies 'the fanatical zeal and bloodlust' of the attackers.

5 For a survey of the Church's attitude to heresy in the medieval period see Malcolm Lambert, *Medieval Heresy: Popular Movements from the Gregorian Reform to the Reformation*, 3rd edn (Oxford: Blackwell, 2002).

6 Wolfgang Behringer, 'Detecting the Ultimate Conspiracy, or How Waldensians Became Witches', in *Conspiracies and Conspiracy Theory in*

Early Modern Europe: From the Waldensians to the French Revolution, ed. Barry Coward and Julian Swann (Aldershot: Ashgate, 2004), 13–34.

7 For a comprehensive and scholarly treatment of the Order of the Knights of the Temple see the following: Malcolm Barber, *The New Knighthood*; Helen Nicholson, *Love, War and the Grail: Templars, Hospitallers, and Teutonic Knights in Medieval Epic and Romance, 1150–1500* (Leiden: Brill, 2001); *eadem, Templars, Hospitallers and Teutonic Knights: Images of the Military Orders, 1128–1291* (Leicester: University Press, 1993); *eadem, The Knights Templar: A New History* (Stroud: Sutton, 2001); Alain Demurger, *Vie et mort de l'Ordre du Temple: 1118–1314* (Paris: Editions du Seuil, 1985).

8 See Partner, *The Knights Templar and Their Myth*. This contains a comprehensive assessment of the Templar myth.

9 Malcolm Barber and Keith Bate, tr. & annot. *The Templars: Selected Sources* (Manchester: Manchester University Press, 2002), 215–26.

10 *Walter Map De Nugis Curialiam: Courtiers Trifles*, ed. and tr. M. R. James, rev. C. N. L. Brooke and R. A. B. Mynors (Oxford: Oxford University Press, 1983); Barber and Bate, *The Templars*, 29.

11 Barber and Bate, *The Templars*, 54–8.

12 Ibid., 31–53, 59–64.

13 Paul Crawford, 'Imagination and the Templars', *Epeteris* 30 (2004), 113–21; Helen Nicholson, *The Knights Templar: A New History*, 201–03; Bill Ellis, *Aliens Ghosts and Cults: Legends We Live*, 199–235.

14 Nicholson, *The Knights Templar*, 207.

15 Ibid., 218.

16 Partner, *The Knights Templar and Their Myth*, 3–14, Nicholson, *The Knights Templar*, 22.

17 Issues surrounding the trial, especially torture and political expediency, have concerned historians since Jules Michelet's revisionist history in 1841–51. New editions of the trials outside France are providing an even clearer perspective on what happened. See Jules Michelet, *Le procès des templiers*, 2 vols (Paris, 1987); Anne Gilmour-Bryson, *The Trial of the Templars in Cyprus* (Leiden, Boston: Brill, 1998), *The Trial of the Templars in the Papal State and the Abruzzi* (Città del Vaticano: Biblioteca apostolica vaticana, 1982).

18 Nicholson, *The Knights Templar*, 192–3.

19 Partner, *The Knights Templar and Their Myth*, 77–81.

20 Barber and Bate, *The Templars* contain many of the most important documents.

21 This trend has become increasingly obvious in television documentary interviews. For example 'The Real Da Vinci Code', Wildfire Television, broadcast February 2006, Channel 4.

22 Partner, *The Knights Templar and Their Myth*, Part 2, chs 5–8.

23 *Walter Map De Nugis Curialiam*, 69.

24 Sumption, *The Albigensian Crusade*, 54; Barber, *New Knighthood*, 213–14; Jean-Paul Perrin, *Histoire des Vaudois 1618 ... Luthers fore-runners: ... The second containes the historie of the Waldenses called Albingenses. ... All which hath bene faithfully collected out of the authors named in the page following the preface, by I.P.P.L.* (London, 1624).

25 Sabine Baring-Gould, *The Holy Grail* (1887; repr. Llanfynydd: Unicorn Press, 1976); Thomas Wright, *Narratives of Sorcery and Magic*, vol. I, n. 41, *A discourse of the Worship of Priapus by Richard Payne Knight Essay on the Generative Powers during the Middle Ages* (London: printed privately, 1865); Partner, *The Knights Templar and Their Myth*, 166–7.

26 Steven Runciman, *The Medieval Manichee* (Cambridge: Cambridge University Press, 1947), Appendix.

27 Lynn Picknett and Clive Prince, *The Templar Revelation* (London: Bantam Press, 1997).

28 Baigent, Leigh and Lincoln, *The Holy Blood and the Holy Grail*, 277–81, 328–30; Margaret Starbird, *Woman with the Alabaster Jar* (Santa Fe: Bear & Co., 1993).

29 Sumption, *The Albigensian Crusade*, 236–41.

30 Barber, *New Knighthood*, 203–25; Déodat Roché, *Le catharisme: son développement dans le Midi de la France et les croisades contre les albigeois* (Carcassonne: Les Imprimeries Gabelle, 1937).

31 Eugene Aroux, *Les mystères de la chevalerie et l'amour platonique en moyen âge* (Paris: V. J. Renouard, 1858).

32 Joséphin Péladan, *Constitutions de la Rose-Croix, le Temple et le Graal: Ordre de la Rose-Croix du Temple et du Graal* (Paris: Secrétariat, 1893); Maurice Magre, *Lucifer: roman moderne* (Paris, 1929); *Le sang de Toulouse. Histoire albigeoise du XIIIe siècle* (1931; rev. Paris, 1972); *Le trésor des Albigeois: roman du XVIe siècle à Toulouse* (Paris, 1938); *La clef des choses cachées* (Paris, 1935); *Magiciens et Illuminés* (Paris, 1930); *The Return of the Magi*, tr. Reginald Merton (London, 1931); Dennis Wheatley Library of the Occult, vol. 36 (London: Sphere Books, 1975).

33 Hans-Jürgen Lange, *Otto Rahn und die Suche nach dem Gral: Biographie und Quellen Engerda* (Engerda: Arun, 1999); *Engerda Otto Rahn: Leben & Werk* (Engerda: Arun, 1995), includes *Kreuzzug gegen den Gral - Luzifers Hofgesind*; Otto Rahn, *La croisade contre le Graal*, tr. Christiane Roy (1934, new edn, Paris, 1974); Nicholas Goodrick-Clarke, *Black Sun: Aryan Cults, Esoteric Nazis and the Politics of Identity* (New York: University Press, 2002), 134–5.

34 The details of development are found in J. G. Biget, 'Mythographie du Catharisme 1870–1960', *Cahiers de Fanjeaux* 14 (1979), 271–342; F. Zambon, 'Le catharisme et les myths du Graal', in J. Berlioz and J.-C. Helas, eds, *Catharisme l'édifice imaginaire*, Actes du 7e colloque du

Centre d'Etudes Cathares 1994 (Carcassonne, 1998), 215–43; M. Roquebert, *Les Cathares et le Graal*, Collection Domaine cathare (Toulouse: Editions Privat, c.1994), 33–4, 101–02, 206; S. Nelli, *Montségur: mythe et historie* (Monaco, 1996), 99–128.

35 Christian Bernadac, *Montségur et le Graal: le mystère Otto Rahn* (Paris: 1994, = rev. edn of *Le mystère Otto Rahn*. c.1978); Trevor Ravenscroft, *The Spear of Destiny* (London: Sphere Books, 1973); Jean and Michel Augebert, *The Occult and the Third Reich: The Mystical Origins of Nazism and the Search for the Holy Grail*, tr. L. A. M. Sumberg (New York: McGraw-Hill, 1974); Nicholas Goodrick-Clarke, *The Occult Roots of Nazism: Secret Aryan Cults and Their Influence on Nazi Ideology* (London: I.B.Tauris, 1992), Appendix E, 'The Modern Mythology of Nazi Occultism', 217–27.

36 Goodrick Clarke, *Black Sun*, 125–7, 148.

37 Dennis Wheatley, *They Used Dark Forces* (London: Hutchinson, 1964); Duncan Kyle, *Black Camelot* (London: Collins, 1978).

38 Owen, *The Place of Enchantment*, 133–34.

39 W. M. S. Russell, 'Tarn Wadling and Montségur', *Pendragon: Journal of the Pendragon Society*, vol. xxv/3&4 (1996), 33–34: Jean Markale, *Montségur et L'Enigme Cathar* (Paris: Loisirs, 1986).

40 See Chapter 6.

41 Wouter J.Hannegraaff, *New Age Religion and Western Culture Esotericism in the Mirror of Secular Thought* (State University of New York Press, 1998), 411–20.

42 See Chapter 3.

43 Rudolf Steiner, *Christ and the Spiritual World and The Search for the Holy Grail* (Rudolf Steiner Press, 1963).

44 Trevor Ravenscroft, *The Spear of Destiny: The Occult Power behind the Spear Which Pierced the Side of Christ* (London: Spearman, 1973, rpr. London: Sphere 1990); Trevor Ravenscroft and Tim Wallace-Murphy, *The Mark of the Beast: The Continuing Story of the Spear of Destiny* (London: Sphere, 1990); Goodrick Clarke, *Black Sun*, 118–21; *idem*, *The Occult Roots of Nazism*, 217–26.

45 Hanegraaff, *New Age Religion and Western Culture*, 411–82.

46 Robert L. D. Cooper, *The Rosslyn Hoax? Viewing Rosslyn Chapel from a New Perspective* (Lewis, 2006), 36–39; Partner, *The Knights Templar and Their Myth*, 108–09.

47 Partner, *The Knights Templar and Their Myth*, 110.

48 Andrew Michael Ramsay, *The Travels of Cyrus. In two volumes to which is annexed a discourse upon the theology and mythology of the ancients* (Dublin, 1728).

49 Partner, *The Knights Templar and Their Myth*, 110–112.

50 Ibid., 120–3.

51 Ibid., 128–9. The Illuminati are more usually associated with a sinister

world conspiracy rather than a life-affirming symbol like the Grail, but the two do cross over.

52 Partner, *The Knights Templar and Their Myth*, 133; Abbé Augustin Barruel, *Application of Barruel's Memoirs of Jacobinism to the Secret Societies of Ireland and Great Britain*: by the translator of that work [i.e. Hon. Robert Clifford] (London: E. Booker, 1798).

53 Partner, *The Knights Templar and Their Myth*, 137–45.

54 Ibid., 136.

55 Cooper, *The Rosslyn Hoax?*, 132–3; Baigent, Lincoln and Leigh, *The Holy Blood and the Holy Grail*, 152.

56 Andrew Sinclair, *The Sword and the Grail: The Story of the Grail the Templars and the True Discovery of America* (New York: Crown Publishers, 1992); *idem, The Discovery of the Grail* (London: Century, 1998); *idem, The Secret Scroll* (London: Christopher Sinclair-Stevenson, 2001); *idem, Rosslyn – the Story of Rosslyn Chapel and the True Story behind the Da Vinci Code* (Edinburgh: Birlinn, 2005); Gavin Bell, *The Scotsman*, July 2004, reception and reaction to Sinclair's theories www.rosslyntemplars.org.uk (accessed 26 December 2006). For a more positive review of Sinclair's work see the alternative magazine, *The Edge* www.theedge.abelgratis.co.uk/index.htm. Other writers have also followed this trend; see Tim Wallace-Murphy and Marilyn Hopkins, *Rosslyn: Guardian of the Secrets of the Holy Grail* (London: Element, 1999); Karen Ralls, *The Templars And the Grail* (Wheaton, IL: Quest Books, 2003): Robert Brydon, *Rosslyn: A History of the Guilds, The Masons and the Rosy Cross* (Roslin: the author, 2003).

57 Professor Bill Nicolaisen, Aberdeen University, personal communication.

58 For a detailed discussion of Rosslyn, its construction and its symbolism see Cooper's *The Rosslyn Hoax?*, 129–71. Mark Oxbrow and Ian Robertson in *Rosslyn and the Grail* (Edinburgh and London: Mainstream, 2005) take a critical stance, but do not indicate their sources clearly, and so this book is less useful.

59 Lewis Spence, 'Mystical Roslin', *Scottish Motor Traction Magazine* (1952), 29.

60 Cooper, *The Rosslyn Hoax?*, 24–5; Sinclair, *Sword and the Grail*, plates between pages 150–1.

61 Cooper, *The Rosslyn Hoax?*, 216–21.

62 Sinclair, *Sword and the Grail*, 46–8.

63 Baigent, Lincoln and Leigh, *The Holy Blood and the Holy Grail*, 74; Baigent and Leigh, *The Temple and the Lodge* (New York: Little Brown and Co, 1989), 18.

64 *The Templar Revelation*, 167.

65 See e.g. Karen Ralls, *The Templars and the Grail*, 111–13.

66 Sinclair, *Sword and the Grail*, 168.

67 Cooper, *The Rosslyn Hoax?*, 173–212 gives an exceptionally detailed critique of alternative interpretations and demonstrates how the iconography reflects eighteenth-century Freemasonry rather than a secret Templar sect; Brian Smith 'The Not-so-Secret Scroll – Priceless Relic or Floor Cloth?' www.rossyntemplars.org.uk/not_secret_scroll.htm) (accessed 26 December 2006).

68 Cooper, *The Rosslyn Hoax?*, 145–6.

69 For other collegiate churches in Scotland see www.rosslyntemplars.org.uk. In England, the Collegiate Church of St Mary at Warwick provides a good comparison. Unlike Rosslyn, the church in Warwick was completed and contains the fifteenth-century burial chapel of Richard Beauchamp, Earl of Warwick. Much of the iconography is also found at Rosslyn: angels of different grades, many with their entire bodies covered in feathers, as well as a wide range of saints, recognizable by their attributes, and illustrations of biblical stories. The Beauchamp chapel even has an Oliver Cromwell tradition, the common belief that he stabled his horses in the church and his reluctance to order the carvings defaced and removed. Perhaps, so goes the tradition, because his own ancestors were connected to the Beauchamp family.

70 Cooper, *The Rosslyn Hoax?*, 111–28.

71 Ibid., 140–2; www.rosslynchapel.org.uk.

72 Ibid., 153–4; www.rosslyntemplars.org.uk.

73 Ibid., 155–6.

74 Sinclair, *Sword and the Grail*, 78.

75 Examples from Sinclair, 86 illustration; Michel Partoureau, *Heraldry: Its Origins and Meaning*, tr. F. Garvie (London, 1997), 125.

76 Ralls, *The Templars and the Grail*, 189–90.

77 See Cooper for a detailed discussion of the problems, *The Rosslyn Hoax?*, 223–42.

78 See Rosslyn Chapel site www.rosslynchapel.org.uk.

79 Sinclair, *Sword and the Grail*, 85–6; Cooper, *The Rosslyn Hoax?*, 162–3.

80 Jennifer Westwood and Jacqueline Simpson, *The Lore of the Land a Guide to England's Legends from Spring-Heeled Jack to the Witches of Warboys* (London, Penguin, 2005), 'Oliver Cromwell', 364–5.

81 In the words of the observer 'legend even gossips so lustily', Cooper, *The Rosslyn Hoax?*, 142–6, 169 n. 48; Ralls, *The Templars and the Grail*, 185–6.

82 Westwood and Simpson, *The Lore of the Land*, 'Architects and Master Builders', 24, 415, 416, 503–04, 648, 652. The apprentice who completes the work while the master is away appears in a Swedish example. Reimund Kvideland and Henning K. Sehmsdorf, *Scandinavian Folk Belief and Legend* (Minneapolis: University of Minnesota Press, 1988), 339; Donald Ward in his translation of *The German Legends of the Brothers*

Grimm, vol. 2 (Philadelphia: Institute for the Study of Human Issues, 1981), 124–6 also gives examples of this common theme. My thanks to Jacqueline Simpson for drawing my attention to these, and to other examples, at Kingsbury Episcopi and Staple Fitzpaine in Somerset.

83 Sinclair, *Sword and the Grail*, 191; 'Was Hess on a Mission to Find the Holy Grail? Nazi's Thought Religious Icons were Hidden in Scotland', *Glasgow Evening Times*, 26 June 1999, www.geocities.com/CapitolHill/Congress/2106/hess/h_Grail.htm (accessed 26 December 2006); www.rosslynchapel.org.uk/ :www.kt-scotland.fsnet.co.uk/ (accessed 30 June 2007).

Chapter 6 – The Religion of the Grail

1 BBC *Chronicle* Programmes, *The Lost Treasure of Jerusalem?* (1972), *The Priest, the Painter and the Devil* (1974) and *The Shadow of the Templars* (1979).

2 Michael Baigent, Richard Leigh and Henry Lincoln, *The Holy Blood and the Holy Grail* (published in America as *Holy Blood Holy Grail*) (London: Corgi, 1996). In the introduction, the authors defended their conclusions, but the argument remains problematic. Michael Baigent, Richard Leigh and Henry Lincoln, *The Messianic Legacy* (London: Corgi Books, 1987); Michael Baigent and Richard Leigh, *The Temple and the Lodge* (c.1989; repr. London: Arrow, 1998). For a comprehensive assessment of the theory see Bill Putnam and John Edwin Wood, *The Treasure of Rennes-le-Château: A Mystery Solved* (Stroud: Sutton, 2003, rev. 2005).

3 A legal action was brought by two of the authors of *Holy Blood Holy Grail*, but a judge eventually dismissed the claimants' case. Sarah Lyall, 'Idea for Da Vinci Code was not Stolen Judge Says', *New York Times*, 8 April 2006.

4 Alex Owen, *The Place of Enchantment* (Chicago: The University of Chicago Press, 2004), 17–41.

5 Wouter J. Hanegraaff, *The New Age Religion and Western Culture* (State University of New York Press, 1998), 79–89.

6 http://priory-of-sion.com/ is the most comprehensive site associated with the holy bloodline and is updated regularly.

7 Putnam and Wood, *The Treasure of Rennes-le-Château*, 9.

8 January 1956, See translations in Putman and Wood, 10–14.

9 René Desdadeilles, *Notice sur Rennes-le-Château et l'Abbé Saunière*, Putman and Wood, 20–6.

10 Putnam and Wood, *The Treasure of Rennes-le-Château*, 167–74.

11 Jean-Luc Chaumeil and Gerard de Sède, *Le Trésor de Rennes ou la vie insolite de Bérenger Saunière* (The Gold of Rennes or the Strange Life of

Bérenger Saunière), later republished as *Le Trésor maudit de Rennes-le-Château*, published in English as *The Accursed Treasure of Rennes-le-Château* (2001); Putnam and Wood, *The Treasure of Rennes-le-Château*, 37–9.

12 Putnam and Wood, *The Treasure of Rennes-le-Château*, 73.

13 Ibid., 89–90.

14 *The Lost Treasure of Jerusalem?* (1972); *The Priest, the Painter and the Devil* (1974); *The Shadow of the Templars* (1979).

15 Margaret Starbird, *The Woman with the Alabaster Jar: Mary Magdelene and the Holy Grail* (Santa Fe: Bear & Co., 1993).

16 Lynn Picknett and Clive Prince, *The Templar Revelation: Secret Guardians of the True Identity of Christ* (London: Bantam, 1997), *The Turin Shroud: In Whose Image? The Truth behind the Centuries-long Conspiracy of Silence* (New York: HarperCollins, c. 1994).

17 Several writers push the bloodline idea back to the Old Testament family of David or the Temple of Solomon, and even beyond that to extraterrestrial beings. This has become a publishing area all its own, but this study is concerned only with the Grail aspect of the legend.

18 Preface to Corgi paperback edition, 1982.

19 Dan Brown, *The Da Vinci Code* (New York: Bantam, 2003).

20 The book by Jean-Luc Chaumeil and Gerard de Sède had appeared in English by this time, and at least one TV programme, *Timewatch: The History of a Mystery*, had critiqued the theory. The television documentary also demonstrated the increasingly uneasy relationship between authors and programme makers, as the authors of one popular book threatened to sue the programme for what they called a 'demolition job'. The *Oxford Times*, 27 September 1996. Recent programmes have, on the whole, taken a sceptical view, and there is even a website rating them according to the degree of scepticism. 'Da Vinci code documentaries' on the www.Priory-of-Sion.com website.

21 Ian Wood, *The Merovingian Kingdoms* (London: Longman, 1994), 37.

22 Putnam and Wood, *The Treasure of Rennes-le-Château*, 98–9.

23 Anthony Blunt, *The Paintings of Nicolas Poussin* (London: Phaidon Press, 1967), 160–7.

24 For quotes and a fuller explanation, see www.Priory-of-Sion.com.

25 *Holy Blood Holy Grail*, 39, 96–7, 481; Putnam and Wood, *The Treasure of Rennes-le-Château*, 98–9, 191.

26 See Weston *From Ritual to Romance* and Waite *The Hidden Church of the Holy Grail*, ch. 4.

27 http://www.shugborough.org.uk/AcademyShepherdsMon-169.

28 Richard Andrews and Paul Shellenberger, *The Tomb of God, the Body of Jesus and the Solution to a 2000 Year Old Mystery* (London: Little, Brown, 1996).

29 Blunt, *The Paintings of Nicolas Poussin*, 159.

30 Elaine Pagels, *The Gnostic Gospels* (London: Wiedenfeld & Nicolson, 1980).

31 Occasionally, as in *The Da Vinci Code*, the Dead Sea scrolls are confused with the Nag Hammadi texts. The former contain the writings associated with a Jewish Essene community active somewhat earlier. See Sharan Newman, *The Real History Behind the Da Vinci Code* (New York: Berkeley Books, 2005), 62–4, 178–80.

32 Hanegraaff, *The New Age Religion and Western Culture*, 302–17.

33 Eugene Aroux, *Les mystères de la chevalerie et l'amour platonique en moyen âge* (Paris: V. J. Renouard, 1858); Joséphin Péladan, *Constitutions de la Rose-Croix, le Temple et le Graal Ordre de la Rose-Croix du Temple et du Graal* (Paris: Secrétariat, 1893); *idem, Le Secret des Troubadours de Parsifal à Don Quichott* (Paris, 1906).

34 Rudolf Steiner, *Christ and the Spiritual World and the Search for the Holy Grail* (Sussex: Rudolf Steiner Press, 1963).

35 Emma Jung and Marie-Louise von Franz, *The Grail Legend* (1960; 2nd edn tr. Andrea Dykes, Princeton: Princeton University Press, 1998); Helen Adolf, *Visio Pacis, Holy City and Grail* (Harrisburg: Pennsylvania State University Press, 1960).

36 John Matthews, *The Mystic Grail: The Challenge of the Arthurian Quest* (London: Thorsens, 1997).

37 Walter Johannes Stein, *Weltgeschichte im Lichte des heiligen Gral. Das neunte Jahrhundert; The Ninth Century and the Holy Grail* (Sussex: Temple Lodge Publishing, 2001).

38 Nicholas Goodrick Clarke, *Black Sun: Aryan Cults, Esoteric Nazism, and the Politics of Identity* (New York: New York University Press, 2002).

39 Hector Hugh Munro (Saki), *The Chronicles of Clovis* (London: John Lane 1912).

40 Baigent, Leigh and Lincoln, *The Holy Blood and the Holy Grail*, 245–57.

41 Susan Haskins, *Mary Magdelen Myth and Metaphor* (London: HarperCollins, 1993), 93–7.

42 *The Nag Hammadi Library in English*, Coptic Gnostic Library Project (Leiden: Brill, 1977).

43 Haskins, *Mary Magdelen Myth and Metaphor*, 220–8.

44 *The Golden Legend of Jacobus de Voragine,* tr. Granger Ryan and Helmut T. Ripperger (New York: Arno Press, 1969), 355–64.

45 See Chapter 1.

46 Haskins, *Mary Magdelen Myth and Metaphor*, 135–45.

47 Robert Graves, *King Jesus* (London: Cassell, 1946); Nikos Kazantzakis, *The Last Temptation of Christ*, tr. Peter Bien (New York: Simon & Schuster, 1960).

48 Hugh Joseph Schonfield, *The Passover Plot: New Light on the History of Jesus* (London: Hutchinson, 1965).

49 William E. Phipps, *Was Jesus Married? The Distortion of Sexuality in the*

Christian Tradition (New York: Harper and Row 1970)

50 Haskins, *Mary Magdelen Myth and Metaphor*, 374–5.

51 Ibid., 39–41.

52 Peter Knight, *Conspiracy Culture: From the Kennedy Assassination to the X-files* (New York: Routledge, 2000).

53 Dan Burstein, *Secret of the Code: The Unauthorized Guide to the Mysteries behind the Da Vinci Code* (rev. and expanded, CDS books, 2006); 'The Sacred Feminine', see ch. 2, 86–128.

54 Starbird, *The Woman with the Alabaster Jar*, xx–xxi.

55 Ibid.; Lynn Picknett, *Mary Magdalene: Christianity's Hidden Goddess* (London: Robinson, 2003). Graves, *King Jesus.*

56 Starbird, *The Woman with the Alabaster Jar*, xxii–xxiii.

57 Graves, *King Jesus*; Robert Graves and Joshua Podro, *The Nazarene Gospel Restored* (London: Cassell & Co., 1953) – an attempt to prove the existence of an original Aramaic narrative, orally preserved, of which the four canonical gospels are distorted adaptations; *Time Magazine* review, 'Old Heresy New Version', 30 September 1946, http://www.time.com/time/magazine/printout/0,8816,887225,00.html.

58 Letter to Elizabeth Anson and poem. See the Shugborough estate website, www.shugborough.org.uk/AcademyHome-156 (accessed 30 April 2007). The section on 'Shugborough Academy' gives a comprehensive history of the monument and incorporates information from Andrew Baker's 'The Shepherdess's Secret', unpublished MS deposited in the Staffordshire Record Office. I would like to express my thanks for their helpful suggestions.

59 Baigent, Leigh and Lincoln, *The Holy Blood and the Holy Grail*, 190–1. See *The Priest, the Painter and the Devil*, BBC *Chonicle* programme, 1974.

60 Eileen Harris, 'Cracking the Poussin Code: The Key to the Shepherd's Monument at Shugborough', *Apollo*, May 2006, 1–6, available online at http://findarticles.com/p/articles/mi_moPAL/is_531_163/ai_n16462475/print

61 *Arbours and Grottos: A Facsimile ... / Thomas Wright; with a catalogue of Wright's Works in Architecture and Garden Design*, ed. Eileen Harris (London: Scolar Press, 1979), plate A; T. Wright, *Louthiana: Or, An Introduction to the Antiquities of Ireland ... the principal ruins, curiosities and ancient dwellings in the county of Louth* (London, 1758).

62 Baker, Shugborough Academy website; Harris, 'Cracking the Poussin Code'.

63 For text of letter, see Baker. At the time she was reading Honoré d'Urfé's *L'Astrée*, which incorporates shepherdesses and Arcadian imagery with philosophical sentiment.

64 *Billings Gazette*, 'City Lights: Parmly Plus Pluck Solve Old Puzzle', www.billinggazette.com/newdex.php?display=rednews/2004/06/06/build/local (accessed 18 January 2007).

65 'Has the Mystery of the Holy Grail been Solved?', *Guardian*, 26

November 2004, 3; 'War Codebreaker Cracks an Enigma of Love', *The Times*, 26 November 2004, 'Letters Remain the Holy Grail to Code-breakers', *Daily Telegraph*, 26 November 2004, Shugborough site.

66 Baigent, Leigh and Lincoln, *The Holy Blood and the Holy Grail*, 192.

67 Juliette Wood, 'The Templars, the Grail and Just about Everything Else: Contemporary Legends in the Media', *FLS News*, 45/2; my thanks to Dr Helen Nicholson of Cardiff University for advice on the background and translation of the 'code'.

68 Shugborough Academy website (accessed 30 April 2007) notes the marriage of a Thomas Ansin to Anne Ridell in 1728.

69 James Stuart, *The Antiquities of Athens*, vol. 1 (London, 1762).

70 Baker, 'The Shepherdess's Secret'; Harris, 'Cracking the Poussin Code: The Key to the Shepherd's Monument at Shugborough'. See Shugborough Academy, 'Hermit Poem on an Emblematical Basso Relievo after a famous picture of Nicolas Poussin', which mentions Arcadia and contains the line, 'life's fleeting moments gently steal away'.

71 James Stuart, *The Antiquities of Athens*, vol. 1.

72 Thomas Pennant, *Journey from Chester to London* (Chester, 1782).

73 Baigent, Leigh and Lincoln, *The Holy Blood and the Holy Grail*, 39; Putnam and Wood, *The Treasure of Rennes-Le-Château*, 98–9.

74 Baigent, Leigh and Lincoln, *The Holy Blood and the Holy Grail*, 191.

75 Andrews and Shellenberger, *The Tomb of God*, 88.

76 'Can You Crack the Code', www.amazing-shows.co.uk/codebreakers/moncode.htm (accessed 30 August 2005).

77 Jonathan Riley-Smith, interviewed in *The Da Vinci Code – The Greatest Story Ever Sold* ('Time Shift' series, BBC Four (BBC Bristol), 2006 quoted Priory-of-Sion.com.

78 John Senior, *The Way Down and Out* (Cornell University Press, 1959), 186–7.

79 Bill Ellis, *Aliens Ghosts and Cults: Legends We Live* (Jackson: University of Mississippi, 2001) xiii–ix, 60.

80 Burstein, *Secret of the Code*.

81 Knight, *Conspiracy Culture*, 3–4, 58, 103, 116.

Conclusion – The Grail Legend Today: Conspiracy and Beyond

1 W. J. Keith, *A Glastonbury Romance Readers Guide*, 700 (772). See the Powys Society, www.powys-society.org.

2 *A Glastonbury Romance*, 756–7; John B. Marino, *The Grail Legend in Modern Literature*, Arthurian studies (Cambridge: D. S. Brewer, 2004),

50–4; Jeremy Hooker, *John Cowper Powys* (Cardiff: University of Wales Press, 1973).

3 Oliver Marlow Wilkinson and Christopher Wilkinson, *Jack and Frances, the Love Letters of John Cowper Powys to Frances Gregg* (London: Cecil Woolf, 1994), 80.

4 Juliette Wood, 'The Holy Grail: From Romance Motif to Modern Genre', *Folklore* 111 (2000), 169–90.

5 The present discussion does not attempt to provide a comprehensive analysis of this literature. See Cindy Mediavilla, *Arthurian Fiction: An Annotated Bibliography* (London: Scarecrow Press, 1999).

6 Marino, *The Grail Legend in Modern Literature*, 36, 121.

7 C. B. Cox and Arnold P. Hinchliffe, eds, *T. S. Eliot, the Waste Land: A Casebook* (London: Macmillan, 1968); Charles Moorman, *Arthurian Triptych: Mythic Materials in Charles Williams, C. S. Lewis, and T. S. Eliot* (Berkeley: University of California Press, 1960).

8 Mary Butts, *Armed with Madness* (London: Wishart & Co., 1928).

9 T. S. Eliot, *Collected Poems 1909–1962* (London: Faber and Faber, 1963), 'The Waste Land', 61–79, notes 80–1; Leon Surette, *A Light from Eleusis: A Study of Ezra Pound's 'Cantos'* (Oxford : Clarendon Press, 1979), 36, 60–3.

10 Tom Gibbons, 'The Wasteland Tarot Identified', *Journal of Modern Literature* 2 (1972), 560–4.

11 Charles Williams, *War in Heaven* (London: Victor Gollanz, 1930); Gunnar Urang, *Shadows of Heaven: Religion and Fantasy in the Writing of C. S. Lewis, Charles Williams and J. R. R. Tolkien* (London: SCM Press, 1971), 51–92; Marino, *The Grail Legend in Modern Literature*, 128–31.

12 Charles Williams, *The Greater Trumps* (London: Victor Gollanz, 1932); Urang, *Shadows of Heaven*, 92.

13 Charles Williams and C. S. Lewis, *Arthurian Torso* (London and New York: Oxford University Press, 1948; repr. 1952); Marino, *The Grail Legend in Modern Literature*, 67.

14 C. S. Lewis, *That Hideous Strength: A Modern Fairy Tale for Grown-Ups* (London: Bodley Head, 1945).

15 Marino, *The Grail Legend in Modern Literature*, 134–6; Moorman, *Arthurian Triptych*, 115.

16 Dorothy James Roberts, *Kinsmen of the Grail* (Boston: Little, 1963), 357–68; Marino, *The Grail Legend in Modern Literature*, 58–9.

17 Martin B. Schictman, 'Hollywood's New Weston: The Grail Myth in Francis Ford Coppola's *Apocalypse Now* and John Boorman's *Excalibur*', in Dhira B. Mahony, *The Grail: A Casebook* (New York: Garland, 2000), 566–74.

18 A. A. Attanasio, *Kingdom of the Grail* (New York: Harper, 1992).

19 Dan Nastali, 'Arthur without Fantasy: Dark Age Britain in Recent Historical Fiction', *Arthuriana* 9/1 (1999), 5–22.

20 Wouter J. Hanegraaff, *New Age Religion and Western Culture* (New

York: State University of New York Press, 1998), 302–31.

21 Rosemary Sutcliff, *The Light Beyond the Forest: The Quest for the Holy Grail* (London: Bodley Head, 1979).

22 Marion Zimmer Bradley, *The Mists of Avalon* (New York: Knopf, 1982).

23 Marino, *The Grail Legend in Modern Literature*, 61–4; Raymond H. Thompson, 'The Grail in Modern European Fiction: Sacred Symbol in a Secular Age', in Mahony, *The Grail: A Casebook*; N. J. Higham, *King Arthur: Myth-Making and History* (London: Routledge, 2002).

24 Charles Butler, *Four British Fantasists: Place and Culture in the Children's Fantasies of Penelope Lively, Alan Garner, Diana Wynne Jones and Susan Cooper* (London: Scarecrow, 2006), 44.

25 Susan Cooper, *Over Sea under Stone* (New York: Harcourt, 1965); eadem, *Greenwitch* (New York: Athenaeum, 1975).

26 James P. Blalock, *The Paper Grail* (New York: Ace, 1991).

27 http://www.lib.rochester.edu/camelot/intrvws/cooper.htm; Butler, *Four British Fantasists*, 47–54.

28 Penelope Lively, *Astercote* (London: Pan, 1973); Butler, *Four British Fantasists*, 48–9, 51.

29 Michael Clynes, *The Grail Murders: Being the Third Journal of Sir Roger Shallot Concerning Certain Wicked Conspiracies and Horrible Murders Perpetrated in the Reign of King Henry VIII* (London: Headline, 1993).

30 Jonathan Gash, *The Grail Tree* (London: Collins, 1976).

31 See Chapter 1.

32 Victor Canning, *The Crimson Chalice* (London: Heinemann, 1976). See Chapter 3.

33 Bernard Cornwell, *The Warlord Chronicles*, *The Winter King*, *Enemy of God*, *Excalibur* (London: Penguin, 1995–8).

34 Bernard Cornwell, *The Grail Quest*, *Harlequin*, *Vagabond*, *Heretic* (London: HarperCollins, 2000–03).

35 Dan Brown, *The Da Vinci Code* (2003). See http://www.adultcatholiced.org/downloads/DaVinci_Code.pdf for a Catholic assessment of the novel.

36 Sharan Newman gives a good summary of the background in *The Real History Behind the Da Vinci Code* (New York: Berkley Books, 2005), 54–60, 132–3, 150–9, 258–63.

37 Umberto Eco, *Il pendolo di Foucault* (Milan: Gruppo Editorale Fabbri Bompiani, 1988); tr. by William Weaver as *Foucault's Pendulum* (New York: Harcourt Brace Jovanovich, 1989; paperback edn, New York: Ballantine Books, 1990). Eco revisits the theme in *Baudolino* (Milan: Bompiano, 2000).

38 Mark Twain, *A Connecticut Yankee in King Arthur's Court* (London: Chatto & Windus, 1908), 92–4.

39 Naomi Mitchison, *To the Chapel Perilous* (London: Allen, 1955); Marino, *The Grail Legend in Modern Literature*, 54–7;

http://www.lib.rochester.edu/Camelot/intrvws/mitchisn.htm interview with Naomi Mitchison.

40 Lionel and Patricia Fanthorpe, *Rennes-Le-Château, Its Mysteries and Secrets* (Middlesex: Bellevue Books, 1991), 204–05.

41 Kate Mosse, *Labyrinth* (London: Orion, 2005).

42 Jane Jensen, *Gabriel Knight 3: Blood of the Sacred, Blood of the Damned* (Sierra On-Line Games 1996).

43 Marcus L. Rowland, *Queen Victoria and the Holy Grail* (Games Workshop Ltd.1985), 3.

44 Lawrence Schick, *Heroic Worlds: A History and Guide to Role-playing Games* (New York: Prometheus Press, 1991), 76–80.

45 Surette, *A Light from Eleusis*, 35–41.

46 Hanegraaff, *New Age Religion and Western Culture*, 421–2; Surette, *A Light from Eleusis*, 34–9; 60–3.

47 Hanegraaff, *New Age Religion and Western Culture*, 418–21.

48 Ibid., 113–18.

49 *The Messianic Legacy* (cover).

50 Peter Campbell, 'Conspiracy and Political Practice from the Ancien Regime to the French Revolution', in Coward and Swann, *Conspiracies and Conspiracy Theory*, 197–213.

51 Coward and Swann, *Conspiracies and Conspiracy Theory*, 9.

52 Ibid., 1–12, 13–35.

Further Reading

PRIMARY TEXTS AND TRANSLATIONS

Bliocadran: A Prologue to the Perceval of Chrétien de Troyes, ed. Lenora Wolfgang (Tubingen: Niemeyer, 1976).

Chrétien de Troyes, *Perceval the Story of the Grail*, tr. Nigel Bryant (Cambridge and Totowa: Brewer, 1982).

The Continuations of the Old French Perceval of Chrétien de Troyes, ed. William Roach (Philadelphia: University of Pennsylvania Press, 1949–83).

The Didot Perceval, ed. William Roach (Philadelphia: University of Pennsylvania Press, 1971); tr. D. Skeeles (Seattle: University of Washington Press, 1966).

The Elucidation: A Prologue to the Conte del Graal, ed. Albert Wilder Thompson (Geneve: Slatkine, 1982).

Fouke le Fitz Waryn, ed. E. J. Hathaway *et al.* (Oxford: Blackwell, 1975).

The Golden Legend of Jacobus de Voragine, tr. Granger Ryan and Helmut T. Ripperger (New York: Arno Press, 1969).

The Grail Quest, ed. and tr. P. M. Matarasso (Harmondsworth: Penguin, 1969).

Guest, Charlotte, *The Mabinogion from the Llyfr Coch o Hergest and other Ancient Welsh Mss*, 3 vols (London and Llandovery: Longmans, Rees, 1838–49).

Hardyng, John, *The Chronicle of Iohn Hardyng . . .*, ed. Henry Ellis (London: F. C. and J. Rivington, 1812).

Heinrich von dem Türlin, *The Crown* (Diu Crône), tr. J. W. Thomas (Lincoln and London: University of Nebraska Press, 1989).

John of Glastonbury, *The Chronicle of Glastonbury Abbey* (*Cronica sive antiquitates Glastoniensis ecclesie*), ed. James P. Carley, tr. David Townsend (Woodbridge: Boydell, 1985).

Lancelot-Grail: The Old French Arthurian Vulgate and Post-Vulgate in Translation, ed. Norris J. Lacy (New York and London, 1993–6).

Lovelich, Henry, *History of the Holy Grail*, ed. F. J. Furnivall, Early English Text Society, Extra Series (London , 1874–1905).

The Mabinogion, tr. Sioned Davies (Oxford: Oxford University Press, 2007).

Malory, Thomas, *Works*, ed. Eugene Vinaver, rev. P. J. C. Field (Oxford: Oxford University Press, 1990).

Merlin and the Grail: Joseph of Arimathea, Merlin and Perceval: the trilogy of prose romances attributed to Robert de Boron, tr. Nigel Bryant (Cambridge and Rochester: D. S. Brewer, 2001).

The Nag Hammadi Library in English, Coptic Gnostic Library Project (Leiden: Brill, 1977).

Perlesvaus or The High Book of the Grail, tr. Nigel Bryant (Cambridge: University Press, 1978).

Varagine, Iacopo de, *Chronica civitatis Ianuensis*, ed. Giovalli Monleone (Rome, 1941).

The Vulgate Version of the Arthurian Romance, ed. H. O. Sommer *et al.*, 8 vols (repr. New York: The Carnegie Institution, 1979).

Walter Map, De Nugis Curialiam: Courtiers Trifles, ed. and tr. M. R. James, rev. C. N. L. Brooke and R. A. B. Mynors (Oxford: Oxford University Press, 1983).

William of Malmesbury's *De antiquitate Glastonie Ecclesie* (*The Early History of Glastonbury*), ed. John Scott (Woodbridge: Boydell & Brewer, 1981).

Wolfram von Eschenbach, *Parzival*, tr. Cyril Edwards (Oxford: University Press, 2006).

Ystoryaeu seint greal, ed. Thomas Jones, J. E. Caerwyn Williams, Ceridwen Lloyd-Morgan and Daniel Huws (Cardiff: University of Wales Press, 1992).

RESOURCES FOR MODERN GRAIL STUDIES

Andrews, Richard and Paul Shellenberger, *The Tomb of God, the Body of Jesus and the Solution to a 2000 Year Old Mystery* (London: Little, Brown, 1996).

Amery, Ethelwyn M., *Sought and Found* (n.p. 1905; repr. 1910).

Aroux, Eugene, *Les mystères de la chevalerie et l'amour platonique en moyen âge* (Paris: V. J. Renouard, 1858).

Baigent, Michael, Richard Leigh and Henry Lincoln, *The Holy Blood and the Holy Grail* (London: Jonathan Cape, 1982; reissued Corgi 1982, 1996; new edn, London: Century, 2005). [American edn, *Holy Blood Holy Grail*.]

_____, *The Messianic Legacy* (London: Corgi Books, 1987).

Baigent, Michael and Richard Leigh, *The Temple and the Lodge* (c.1989; repr. London: Arrow, 1998).

Bayley, Howard, *The Lost Language of Symbolism*, 2 vols (London: Williams and Norgate, 1851).

Bennett, Janice, *St Laurence and the Holy Grail* (Denver: Ignatius Press, 2004).

Bligh Bond, Frederick, *The Gate of Remembrance* (Oxford: B. H. Blackwell, 1918).

———, *The Hill of Vision: Forecast of the Great War ... through the Hand of John Alleyne* (London: Constable & Co, 1919).

———, *The Glastonbury Scripts: Tales of Glastonbury Abbey Purporting to be Automatic Writings* (Glastonbury: Central Somerset Gazette, 1921).

———, *The Company of Avalon: A Study of the Script [i.e. automatic writing], on the Subject of Glastonbury Abbey* (Oxford: Basil Blackwell, 1924).

———, 'The Story of King Arthur and How He Saw the Sangreal, of His Institution of the Quest of the Holy Grail, and of the Promise of the Fulfilment of that Quest in the Latter Days' (Glastonbury: Central Somerset Gazette, 1925).

Brydon, Robert, *Rosslyn: A History of the Guilds, the Masons and the Rosy Cross* (Rosslyn: Rosslyn Chapel Trust, 1994).

Burstein, Dan, *Secret of the Code the Unauthorized Guide to the Mysteries behind the Da Vinci code*, rev. and expanded (CDS books, 2006).

Collins, Andrew, *Twenty-First century Grail the Quest for a Legend* (London: Virgin Books, 2004).

Currer-Briggs, Noel, *The Shroud and the Grail: A Modern Quest for the True Grail* (London: Weidenfeld & Nicolson, 1987).

Eisen, Gustavus, *The Great Chalice of Antioch*, 2 vols (New York: Konchakji Freres, 1923).

Evans, Sebastian, *The High History of the Holy Graal* (London: J. M. Dent & Co., 1898).

Fortune, Dion, *Glastonbury: Avalon of the Heart* (Boston, MA: Weiser Books, 2000).

Graves, Robert and Joshua Podro, *The Nazarene Gospel Restored* (London: Cassell & Co., 1953).

Griffin, Justin, *The Holy Grail: The Legend, the History, the Evidence* (Jefferson, NC: McFarland, 2001).

Goodchild, John Arthur, *The Light of the West: An Account of the Dannite Settlement in Ireland* (London: Kegan Paul & Co., 1898).

Lange, Hans-Jürgen, *Otto Rahn und die Suche nach dem Gral* (Engerda: Arun, 1999).

————, *Kreuzzug gegen den Gral: Luzifers Hofgesind*, in *Otto Rahn: Leben & Werk* (Engerda: Arun, 1995).

Lehmann, Rosamund, *My Dear Alexias, Letters from Wellesley Tudor Pole to Rosamund Lehmann* (Sudbury: Neville Spearman, 1979).

Lewis, Lionel Smithett, *St. Joseph of Arimathea at Glastonbury* (London: James Clark, 1955; repr. 1964).

Machen, Arthur, *The Secret of the Sangraal: A Collection of Writings* (East Sussex: Tartarus Press, 1994).

————, *Things Near and Far* (London: Richards Press, 1951).

Magre, Maurice, *Le sang de Toulouse. Histoire albigeoise du XIIIe siècle* (Paris: Fasquelle, 1931; rev. edn 1972).

————, *The Return of the Magi*, tr. Reginald Merton (London: Philip Allan, 1931); repr., Dennis Wheatley Library of the Occult; vol. 36 (London: Sphere Books, 1975).

————, *La clef des choses cachées* (Paris: Fasquelle, 1935).

Maltwood, Katherine, *King Arthur's Round Table of the Zodiac* (Victoria, BC: Victoria Printing & Publishing Co., 1946).

————, *A Guide to Glastonbury's Temple of the Stars* (London: John Clarke, 1964).

Matthews, John and Caitlin Mathews, *Hallowquest: Tarot Magic and the Arthurian Mysteries* (Wellingborough: Aquarian Press, 1990).

Morgan, Owen (Morien), *The Light of Britannia: The Mysteries of Ancient British Druidism Unveiled* (Cardiff: Daniel Owen, 1894).

————, *The Royal Winged Son of Stonehenge and Avebury* (Pontypridd: Glamorgan Free Press Office, 1911).

————, *A History of Wales from the Earliest Period, including Hitherto Unrecorded Antiquarian Lore* (Liverpool: Edward Howell, 1911).

Péladan, Joséphin, *La philosophie de Léonard de Vinci d'après ses manuscrits* (Paris: F. Alcan, 1910).

————, *Constitutions de la Rose-Croix, le Temple et le Graal: Ordre de la Rose-Croix du Temple et du Graal* (Paris: Secrétariat, 1893).

————, *Le Secret des Troubadours de Parsifal à Don Quichott* (Paris, 1906).

Phillips, Graham, *The Search for the Grail* (London: Century, 1995).

————, *The Marian Conspiracy* (London: Sidgewick and Jackson, 2000).

Picknett, Lynn, *Mary Magdalene: Christianity's Hidden Goddess* (London: Robinson, 2003).

————, and Clive Prince, *Turin Shroud: In Whose Image? The Shocking Truth Unveiled* (London: BCA, by arrangement with Bloomsbury, 1994).

————, *The Templar Revelation: Secret Guardians of the True Identity of Christ* (Reading: Corgi, 1998).

Rahn, Otto, *La croisade contre le Graal,* tr. Christiane Roy (1934, new edn, Paris, 1974).

Ralls, Karen, *The Templars and the Grail* (Wheaton, IL: Quest Books, 2003).

Ravenscroft, Trevor, *The Spear of Destiny: The Occult Power behind the Spear which Pierced the Side of Christ* (London: Spearman, 1973; repr. London: Sphere 1990).

Roché, Déodat, *Le catharisme: son développement dans le Midi de la France et les croisades contre les albigeois* (Carcassonne: Les Imprimeries Gabelle, 1937; 3rd edn, Narbonne: Editions des Cahiers d'études cathares, 1973).

————, *Contes et légendes du catharisme,* 4th edn (Arques: Editions des Cahiers d'études cathares, 1971).

————, *L'Église romaine et les cathares albigeois* (Arques: Editions des Cahiers d'études cathares, 1957).

Sinclair, Andrew, *The Sword and the Grail: The Story of the Grail the Templars and the True Discovery of America* (New York: Crown Publishers, 1992).

————, *The Discovery of the Grail* (London: Century, 1998).

————, *The Secret Scroll* (London: Christopher Sinclair-Stevenson, 2001).

————, *Rosslyn – the Story of Rosslyn Chapel and the True Story behind the Da Vinci Code* (Edinburgh: Birlinn, 2005).

Spence, Lewis, 'The Secret Tradition in Britain: Its Sources and Affinities', *Occult Review* (April 1940), 99–103.

————, 'The Arcane Cult of Arthur', *Occult Review* (July 1940), 145–9.

————, 'Occult Centres of Scotland', *Occult Review* (October 1940).

————, *The Occult Causes of the Present War* (London: Rider, 1940).

————, *The Occult Sciences in Atlantis* (London: Rider, 1943).

————, *The Magic Arts in Celtic Britain* (London: Rider, 1945).

————, *Myth and Ritual in Dance, Game and Rhyme* (London: Watts, 1947).

————, 'Mystical Roslin', *Scottish Motor Traction Magazine* (1952).

Starbird, Margaret, *The Woman with the Alabaster Jar: Mary Magdelene and the Holy Grail* (Santa Fe: Bear and Co., 1993).

Stein, Walter Johannes, *Weltgeschichte im Lichte des heiligen Gral. Das neunte Jahrhundert,* 1928, *The Ninth Century and the Holy Grail* (Loughborough: Temple Lodge Publishing, 2001).

Steiner, Rudolf, *Christ and the Spiritual World and the Search for the Holy Grail* (Sussex: Rudolf Steiner Press, 1963).

Ussher, James, *Britannicarum ecclesiarum antiquitates: quibus inserta est ecclesiam inductae haereseos historia* (Dublinii: Ex officina typographica Societatis Bibliopolarum, 1639).

————, *Strange and Remarkable Prophecies and Predictions: To which is Prefaced a Short Sketch of his Life* (Dublin, 1840).

Waite, A. E., *The Mysteries of Magic: A Digest of the Writings of Eliphas Lev.* tr. Alphonse Louis Constant (Eliphas Levi) (London: Temple Chambers, 1894).

————, *The Hidden Church of the Holy Grail* (London: Rider, 1909).

————, *The Secret Tradition of Freemasonry*, 2 vols (London: Rebman, 1911).

————, *The Holy Grail: Its Legends and Symbolism* (London: Rider, 1933).

————, *The Pictorial Key to the Tarot: Being Fragments of a Secret Tradition under the Veil of Divination* (London: Rider, 1911; repr. New Hyde Park, NY: 1951).

————, tr., *Transcendental Magic: Its Doctrine and Ritual* (London: Redway, 1896).

————, tr., *The History of Magic* (London: Rider, 1913).

Wallace-Murphy, Tim and Marilyn Hopkins, *Rosslyn: Guardian of the Secrets of the Holy Grail* (London: Element, 1999).

Williams, Mary, ed., *Glastonbury: A Study in Patterns* (London: Research into Lost Knowledge, 1969).

Wright, Thomas, ed., *Fouke le Fitz Waryn & Early English Miscellanies in Prose and Verse*, ed. J. O. Halliwell (London: Warton Club, 1855).

————, *Narratives of Sorcery and Magic, from the most authentic sources*, 2 vols (London: R. Bentley, 1851).

————, ed., *A Discourse of the Worship of Priapus by Richard Payne Knight. Essay on the Generative Powers during the Middle Ages* (London: printed privately, 1865).

MODERN GRAIL LITERATURE AND FILM

Attanasio, A. A., *Kingdom of the Grail* (New York: Harper, 1992).

Blalock, James P., *The Paper Grail* (New York: Ace, 1991).

Bradley, Marion Zimmer, *The Mists of Avalon* (New York: Knopf, 1982).

Brown, Dan, *The Da Vinci Code* (New York: Bantam, 2003).

Butts, Mary, *Armed with Madness* (London: Wishart & Co., 1928).

Canning, Victor, *The Crimson Chalice* (London: Heinemann, 1976).

Clynes, Michael, *The Grail Murders* (London: Headline, 1993).

Cooper, Susan, *Over Sea under Stone* (New York: Harcourt, 1965).

————, *Greenwitch* (New York: Athenaeum, 1975).

Cornwell, Bernard, *The Warlord Chronicles: The Winter King, Enemy of God, Excalibur* (London: Penguin, 1995–8).

————, *The Grail Quest: Harlequin, Vagabond, Heretic* (London: HarperCollins, 2000–03).

Costain, Thomas, *The Silver Chalice* (New York: Doubleday, 1952).

Davies, Edward Tegla, *Y Greal Sanctaidd* (Wrecsam: Hughes, 1922).

Eco, Umberto, *Foucault's Pendulum*, tr. William Weaver (New York: Harcourt Brace Jovanovich, 1989). [*Il pendolo di Foucault* (Milan: Gruppo Editoriale Fabbri Bompiani, 1988).]

————, *Baudolino* (Milan: Bompiano, 2000).

Eliot, T. S., *Collected Poems 1909–1962* (London: Faber and Faber, 1963).

Gash, Jonathan, *The Grail Tree* (London: Collins, 1976).

Graves, Robert, *King Jesus* (London: Cassell, 1946).

Jensen, Jane, *Gabriel Knight 3: Blood of the Sacred, Blood of the Damned* (Sierra On-Line Games 1996).

Jones, David, *The Anathemata* (London: Faber, 1952).

————, *In Parenthesis* (London: Faber, 1937).

————, *The Sleeping Lord and Other Fragments* (London: Faber, 1974).

Kazantzakis, Nikos, *The Last Temptation: A Novel*, tr. Peter Bien (New York: Simon & Schuster, 1960).

Kyle, Duncan, *Black Camelot* (London: Collins, 1978).

Lewis, C. S., *That Hideous Strength: A Modern Fairy Tale for Grown-Ups* (London: Bodley Head, 1945).

Lively, Penelope, *Astercote* (London: Pan, 1973).

Machen, Arthur, *The Secret Glory* (East Sussex: Tartarus Press, 1998).

————, 'The Great Return', in *Holy Terrors: Collected Short Stories* (London: Penguin, 1946).

Magre, Maurice, *Lucifer: roman moderne* (Paris: A. Michel, 1929).

————, *Le trésor des Albigeois: roman du XVIe siècle à Toulouse* (Paris: Fasquelle 1938),

Mitchison, Naomi, *To the Chapel Perilous* (London: Allen, 1955).

Monro, Hector Hugh (Saki), *The Chronicles of Clovis* (London and New York: John Lane Co., 1912).

Mosse, Kate, *Labyrinth* (London: Orion, 2005).

Owen, John Dyfnallt, *Y Greal a cherddi eraill* (Aberystwyth: Gwasg Aberystwyth, 1946).

Parry, Tom, *Saint Greal y chwedl wedi ei hailadrodd* (Llandysul: Gwasg Gomer, 1933).

Roberts, Dorothy James, *Kinsmen of the Grail* (Boston: Little, 1963).

Rowland, Marcus L, *Queen Victoria and the Holy Grail* (Games Workshop Group, 1985).

Sutcliff, Rosemary, *The Light Beyond the Forest: The Quest for the Holy Grail* (London: Bodley Head, 1979).

Twain, Mark, *A Connecticut Yankee in King Arthur's Court* (London: Chatto & Windus, 1908).

Waite, A. E., *The Hidden Church of the Holy Grail* (London: Redway, 1909).

Wheatley, Dennis, *They Used Dark Forces* (London: Hutchinson, 1964).

Williams, Charles, *War in Heaven* (London: Victor Gollanz, 1930).

———, *The Greater Trumps* (London: Victor Gollanz, 1932).

SECONDARY SOURCES AND COMMENTARY

Adolf, Helen, *Visio Pacis, Holy City and Grail* (Harrisburg: Pennsylvania State University Press, 1960).

Barber, Malcolm, *The New Knighthood: History of the Order of the Temple* (Cambridge: Cambridge University Press, 1994).

———, and Keith Bate, tr., *The Templars: Selected Sources* (Manchester: Manchester University Press, 2002).

Barber, Richard, *The Holy Grail: Imagination and Belief* (London: Allen Lane, 2004).

Baring-Gould, Sabine, *Curious Myths of the Middle Ages* (1st edn 1866 and 1868; new enlarged edn 1901; Dover edn 1976).

Benham, Patrick, *The Avalonians* (Glastonbury: Gothic Image Press, 1993).

Birchall, Clare, *Knowledge Goes Pop: From Conspiracy Theory to Gossip* (Oxford: Berg, 2006).

Birch-Hirshfeld, A., *Die saga von Gral* (Liepsig: Vogel, 1877).

Bollard, John K., 'Theme and meaning in *Peredur*', *Arthuriana* 10 (2000), 73–5.

———, 'Peredur: The Four Early Manuscripts', *Bulletin of the Board of Celtic Studies* 28 (1979), 365–72.

Bromwich, Rachel, ed., *Trioedd Ynys Prydein: The Triads of the Island of Britain*, 3rd edn (Cardiff: University of Wales Press, 2006).

———, A. O. H. Jarman and Brynley F. Roberts, eds, *The Arthur of the Welsh: The Arthurian Legend in Medieval Welsh Literature* (Cardiff: University of Wales Press, 1991).

Brown, Arthur C. L., *The Origin of the Grail Legend* (Cambridge, MA: Harvard University Press, 1943).

Bruce, James Douglas, *The Evolution of Arthurian Romance from the Beginnings Down to the Year 1300*, 2nd edn, 2 vols (Baltimore: The Johns Hopkins University Press, 1928).

Bruford, Alan, *Gaelic Folktale and Medieval Romance* (Dublin: Folklore of Ireland Society, 1969).

Butler, Charles, *Four British Fantasists: Place and Culture in the Children's Fantasies of Penelope Lively, Alan Garner, Diana Wynne Jones and Susan Cooper* (Lanham, MD: Scarecrow, 2006).

Calcagno, Domenico, *Il mistero del sacro catino* (ECIG Colla Nuov Atlantide, 2000).

Carley, James P., ed., *Glastonbury Abbey and Arthurian Tradition* (Cambridge: D. S. Brewer, 2001).

———, 'Melkin the Bard and Esoteric Tradition at Glastonbury Abbey', *The Downside Review* 99 (1981), 1–17.

Conway, Martin, 'The Sacro catino at Genoa', *Antiquaries Journal* 4 (1924), 11–18.

Cooper, Robert L. D., *The Rosslyn Hoax? Viewing Rosslyn Chapel from a New Perspective* (Surrey: Lewis, 2006).

Cormier, Raymond J., 'Tradition and Sources: the Jackson/Loomis Controversy Re-examined', *Folklore* 83 (1972),101–21.

Coward, Barry and Julian Swann, eds, *Conspiracies and Conspiracy Theory in Early Modern Europe: From the Waldensians to the French Revolution* (Aldershot: Ashgate, 2004).

Cox, C. B., and Arnold P. Hinchliffe, eds., *T.S. Eliot, the Waste Land: A Casebook* (London: Macmillan, 1968).

Cutting, Tracy, *Beneath the Silent Tor: The Life and Work of Alice Buckton* (Great Britain: Appleseed Press, 2004).

Davies, Sioned, and Peter Wynn Thomas, eds, *Canhwyll marchogyon: cyd-destunoli Peredur* (Cardiff: University of Wales Press, 2000).

Dobson, Roger, Godfrey Brangham and R. A. Gilbert, eds, *Arthur Machen: Selected Letters* (Wellingborough: Aquarian Press, 1988).

Dummett, Michael, *The Game of Tarot* (London: Duckworth, 1980).

Ellis, Bill, *Aliens Ghosts and Cults: Legends We Live* (Jackson: University of Mississippi, 2001).

Fielding, Charles, and T. Carr, *The Story of Dion Fortune* (Loughborough: Bible Land Mission Society, 1998).

Fisher, Lisette Andrews, *The Mystic Vision in the Grail legend and in the Divine Comedy* (1917; repr. New York: AMS, 1966).

Fraser, Robert, *The Making of the Golden Bough: The Origins and Growth of an Argument* (London: Macmillan, 1990; reissued Palgrave, 2001).

———, *The Golden Bough*, 3rd edn, 13 vols (London: Macmillan, 1906–15; 1st edn, 1890; abridged and ed. Robert Fraser, Oxford: Oxford University Press, 1994).

Gentle-Cackett, S. W., *The Antioch Cup* (London, 1935).

Gibbons, Tom, 'The Wasteland Tarot Identified', *Journal of Modern Literature* 2 (1972), 560–4.

Gilbert, R. A., 'Arthur Machen and A. E. Waite: A Forgotten Collaboration', *Antiquarian Book Monthly Review* 11/4 (April 1976), 7–8.

——, *A. E. Waite: A Magician of Many Parts* (Wellingborough: Crucible, 1987).

——, ed., *The Hermetic Papers of A. E. Waite* (Wellingborough: Aquarian Press, 1987).

Goetinck, Glenys, *Peredur: A Study of Welsh Tradition in the Grail Legends* (Cardiff: University of Wales Press, 1975).

Gogan, Liam S., *Ireland's Holy Grail* (Dublin: Browne & Nolan, 1932).

Goodrick Clarke, Nicholas, *The Occult Roots of Nazism: Secret Aryan Cults and Their Influence on Nazi Ideology* (London: I.B.Tauris, 1992).

——, *Black Sun: Aryan Cults, Esoteric Nazism, and the Politics of Identity* (New York: New York University Press, 2002).

Grayson, Janet, 'In Quest of Jessie Weston', *Arthurian Literature* 11, ed. Richard Barber (Cambridge: Boydell and Brewer, 1992), 1–80.

Hanegraaff, Wouter J., *The New Age Religion and Western Culture* (New York: State University Press, 1998).

Haskins, Susan, *Mary Magdelen Myth and Metaphor* (London: HarperCollins, 1993).

Holmes, Urban T. and M. Amelia Klenke, *Chrétien Troyes and the Grail* (Chapel Hill: University of North Carolina Press, 1959).

Hooker, Jeremy, *John Cowper Powys* (Cardiff: University of Wales Press, 1973).

——, 'David Jones and the Matter of Wales', in David Blamires, *David Jones: Artist and Writer*, 2nd edn (Manchester: Manchester University Press, 1978).

Horgan, A. D., 'The Grail in Wolfram's Parzifal', *Medieval Studies* 36 (1964), 354–81.

Ivakhiv, Adrian J., *Claiming Sacred Ground Pilgrims and Politics at Glastonbury and Sedona* (Bloomington: Indiana University Press, 2001).

Jones, David, 'The Arthurian Legend', in *Epoch and Artist: Selected Writings by David Jones*, ed. Harman Grisewood (London: Faber, 1959).

Jung, Emma and von Franz, Marie-Louise, *The Grail Legend*, tr. Andrea Dykes, 2nd edn (1960; Princeton: Princeton University Press, 1998).

Keller, Joseph, 'Paradigm Shifts in the Grail Scholarship of Jessie Weston and R.S. Loomis: A View from Linguistics', *Arthurian Interpretations* 1 (1987), 10–22.

Further Reading

Kenawell, William, *The Quest at Glastonbury: A Biographical Study of Frederick Bligh Bond* (New York: Helix Press, 1965).

Knight, Peter, *Conspiracy Culture: From the Kennedy Assassination to the X-files* (London and New York: Routledge, 2000).

Lacey, Norris J., *The New Arthurian Encyclopaedia* (Chicago and London: St James Press, 1991).

Lloyd-Morgan, Ceridwen, 'A Study of "Y Seint Greal" and "Percevel" in Wales: Late Medieval Welsh Grail Tradition', in *The Changing Face of Arthurian Romance*, ed. Alison Adams, Armel H. Diverres, Karen Stern and Kenneth Varty (Cambridge 1986), 78–91.

Lofmark, Carl, 'Wolfram's Source References in Parzifal', *Modern Language Review* 67 (1972), 820–44.

Loomis, R. S., *Celtic Myth and Arthurian Romance* (New York: Columbia Press, 1927), rev. edn 1935.

———, *Arthurian Tradition and Chrétien de Troyes* (New York: Columbia University Press, 1949).

———, *Wales and the Arthurian Legend* (Cardiff: University of Wales Press, 1956).

———, ed., *Arthurian Literature in the Middle Ages* (Oxford: Clarendon Press, 1959).

———, *The Grail: From Celtic Myth to Christian Symbol* (Cardiff: University of Wales Press, 1963).

Lovécy, Ian, 'The Celtic Sovereignty Theme and the Structure of Peredur', *Studia Celtica* 12/13 (1978), 133–46.

Mahony, Dhira B., *The Grail: A Casebook* (New York: Garland, 2000).

Marino, John B., *The Grail Legend in Modern Literature*, Arthurian Studies 59 (Cambridge: Boydell & Brewer, 2004).

Martinez, Antonio Beltran, *Estudio sobre el Santo Caliz de la catedral de Valencia* 4th edn (Zaragoza octavio y Feles, 1984).

Marx, Jean, 'Le cortège du château des merveilles dans le roman gallois de Peredur', *Etudes celtiques* 9 (1961), 92–108.

———, 'Observations sur la structure du roman gallois de Peredur', *Etudes Celtiques* 10 (1963), 88–108.

Matthews, J. F., 'Olympiodorus of Thebes and the History of the West', *Journal of Roman Studies* (1970), 79–80, 91–3.

Moffett, Joe, 'Anglo-Saxon and Welsh Origins in David Jones's *The Anathemata*', *North American Journal of Welsh Studies* 6/1 (Winter 2006), 1–6.

Moorman, Charles, *Arthurian Triptych: Mythic Materials in Charles Williams, C. S. Lewis, and T. S. Eliot* (Berkeley: University of California Press, 1960).

Morán, Asunción Alejor, *Presencia del Santo Cáliz en al arte* (Valencia: Ajuntament de Valencia, 2000).

Newman, Sharan, *The Real History Behind the Da Vinci Code* (New York: Berkley Books, 2005).

Nicholson, Helen, *Love, War and the Grail: Templars, Hospitallers, and Teutonic Knights in Medieval Epic and Romance, 1150–1500* (Leiden: Brill, 2001).

——, *Templars, Hospitallers and Teutonic Knights: Images of the Military Orders, 1128–1291* (Leicester: University Press, 1993).

——, *The Knights Templar: A New History* (Stroud: Sutton, 2001).

Nitze, William A, 'The Fisher King in the Grail Romance,' *Publications of the Modern Language Association* (1909), 411–13.

——, *Perceval and the Holy Grail* (Berkeley, CA: University of California Press, 1949).

Nutt, Alfred, *Studies in the Legend of the Holy Grail: With Especial Reference to the Hypothesis of Its Celtic Origin* (London: David Nutt, 1888).

——, *Legends of the Holy Grail* (London: David Nutt, 1902).

——, *The Mabinogion*, tr. Charlotte Guest, notes by Alfred Nutt (London: David Nutt, 1902).

Owen, Alex, *The Place of Enchantment: British Occultism and the Culture of the Modern* (Chicago and London: The University of Chicago Press, 2004).

Pagels, Elaine, *The Gnostic Gospels* (London: Wiedenfeld & Nicolson, 1980).

Partner, Peter, *The Knights Templar & Their Myth* (Rochester: Destiny Books, 1990).

Peebles, Rose Jeffries, *The Legend of Longinus in Ecclesiastical Tradition and English Literature and Its Connections with the Holy Grail* (Baltimore: J. H. Furst Company, 1911).

Putnam, Bill and John Edwin Wood, *The Treasure of Rennes-le-Château: A Mystery Solved* (Stroud: Sutton, 2003, rev. 2005).

Raine, Kathleen, *Yeats: The Tarot and the Golden Dawn* (Dublin: Dolmen Press, 1972).

Rhŷs, John, *Studies in the Arthurian Legend* (Oxford: Clarendon Press, 1891).

Roberts, Brynley F., 'A Text in Transition', *Arthuriana* 10/3 (2000), 59–61.

Robinson, J. Armitage, *Two Glastonbury Legends: King Arthur and St. Joseph of Arimathea* (Cambridge: University of Cambridge Press, 1926)

Runciman, Steven, *The Medieval Manichee* (Cambridge: University of Cambridge Press, 1947).

Simpson, Jacqueline, 'Rationalising Motifs and contemporary Legends', *Folklore* 92 (1981), 203–07.

Sumption, Jonathan, *The Albigensian Crusade* (London: Faber and Faber, 1999).

Sweetser, Wesley D., *Arthur Machen* (New York: Twayne, 1964).

Treharne, R. F., *The Glastonbury Legends: Joseph of Arimathea, the Holy Grail and King Arthur* (London: Cresset Press, 1967).

Urang, Gunnar, *Shadows of Heaven: Religion and Fantasy in the Writing of C. S. Lewis Charles Williams and J. R. R. Tolkien* (London: SCM Press, 1971).

Valentine, Mark, *Arthur Machen* (Bridgend: Wales Poetry Press, 1995).

Vickery, John B., *The Literary Impact of the Golden Bough* (Princeton: Princeton University Press, 1973).

Villiers, Oliver G., *Wellesley Tudor Pole: Appreciation and Valuation* (Canterbury, 1977).

Weston, Jessie Laidley, *The Legend of Sir Perceval: Studies upon Its Origin, Development, and Position in the Arthurian Cycle*, 2 vols Grimm Library 17, 19 (London: David Nutt, 1906–09).

———, 'The Grail and the Rites of Adonis', *Folklore* 18 (1907), 283–305.

———, *From Ritual to Romance* (1925; repr. Princeton: Princeton University Press, 1993).

Westwood, Jennifer and Jacqueline Simpson, *The Lore of the Land: A Guide to England's Legends* (London: Penguin, 2005).

Whitaker, Muriel, 'The Arthurian Art of David Jones', *Arthuriana* 7/3 (Autumn 1997), 137–56.

Williams, Charles and C. S. Lewis, *Arthurian Torso* (London and New York: Oxford University Press, 1948; repr. 1952).

Williams, Mary, 'The Story of Peredur: Its Sources', *Journal of the Welsh Bibliographical Society* 3 (1927), 73–81.

———, 'Arthuriana: Chrétien's Perceval', in *Mélanges Bretons et Celtiques Offerts a M. J. Loth* (Rennes: Plihon et Hommay; Paris: Champion, 1927), 418–21

———, 'The Dying God in Welsh Literature', *Revue Celtique* 46 (1929), 167–214.

———, 'The Keepers of the Threshold in the Romance of Perlesvaus', in *A Miscellany of Studies in Romance Languages & Literatures Presented to Leon E. Kastner*, ed. Mary Williams and James A. de Rothschild (Cambridge: W. Haffer, 1932), 560–67.

———, 'Apropos of an Episode in *Perlesvaus*', *Folklore* 43 (1937), 263–6.

———, 'Some Aspects of the Grail Problem,' *Folklore* 71 (1960), 85–103.

————, 'The Episode of the Copper Tower in the *Perlesvaus*,' 150-62 in *Mélanges offertes à Rita Lejeaune* (Gembloux: Editions J. Duculot, 1969).

Wood, Juliette, 'Maelgwn Gwynedd: A Forgotten Welsh Hero,' *Trivium* 19 (1984), 103–17.

————, 'The Creation of the Celtic Tarot', *Folklore* 109 (1998), 15–24.

————, 'Folklore Studies at the Celtic Dawn: Alfred Nutt: Publisher and Folklorist', *Folklore* 110 (1999), 3–12.

————, 'Nibbling Pilgrims and the Nanteos Cup: A Cardiganshire Legend', in *Nanteos: A Welsh House and Its Families*, ed. Gerald Morgan (Llandysul: Gomer, 2001), 137–50.

————, 'The Holy Grail: From Romance Motif to Modern Genre', *Folklore* 111 (2000), 169–90.

————, 'A Welsh Triad: Charlotte Guest, Marie Trevelyan, Mary Williams', in *Women and Tradition: A Neglected Group of Folklorists*, ed. Carmen Blacker and Hilda Davidson (Durham, NC: Carolina Academic Press, 2000), 259–76.

————, 'Folk Narrative Research in Wales at the Beginning of the Twentieth Century: The Influence of John Rhŷs (1840–1916)', *Folklore* 116 (2005), 324–43.

Zahlten, Johann, 'Der "sacro catino" in Genua Auflärung über eine mittelalterliche Gralsrelique', in Reinhold Baumstark and Michael Koch, *Der Gral artusromantik in der Kunst des 19 Jahrhunderts* (Köln, Bayerisches Nationalmuseum 1995), 121–31.

INTERNET SOURCES

www.priory-of-sion.com/

www.shugborough.org.uk/AcademyShepherdsMon-169

www.shugborough.org.uk/AcademyHome-156

www.bbc.co.uk/wales/mid/sites/weird/pages/nanteos.shtml

www.grahamphillips.net/Books/Grail.htm

www.aragonesasi.com/libros/santocaliz.php

www.geocities.com/Athens/Rhodes/3946/santocaliz/

www.arch.den.org/dcr/archive/20020911/20029112n.htm

www.rosslyntemplars.org.uk

www.powys-society.org.

www.lib.rochester.edu/camelot/intrvws/cooper.htm.

FILM AND TELEVISION

Monty Python and the Holy Grail, dir. Terry Gilliam and Terry Jones (1975).

Excalibur, dir. John Boorman, script Rospo Pallenberg and John Boorman (1981).

Indiana Jones and the Last Crusade, dir. Steven Speilberg, script Jeffrey Boam (1989).

The Fisher King, dir. Terry Gilliam, script Richard LaGravenese (1991).

BBC *Chronicle: The Lost Treasure of Jerusalem?* (1972); *The Priest, the Painter and the Devil* (1974); *The Shadow of the Templars* (1979).

Timewatch: The History of a Mystery, BBC2, 17 September 1996.

The Nanteos Cup, Fortean TV, Channel 4, March 1997.

The Search for the Holy Grail, BBC2, 12 February 1998.

In Search of the Grail, The Learning Channel/Bluebook Films, 2003.

The Da Vinci Code – The Greatest Story Ever Sold, 'Time Shift' series, BBC Four (BBC Bristol), 2006.

The Real Da Vinci Code, Channel 4 (Wildfire Television) February 2006.

Index

Index